THE WORLD,
THE WEST
AND PRETORIA

THE WORLD,
THE WEST
AND PRETORIA

Alexander Steward

David McKay Company, Inc.
NEW YORK

From Mom and me to
ALEXANDRA,
for her inspiration

Library of Congress Catalog Card Number: 77-72689
ISBN: 0-679-50767-1

MANUFACTURED IN THE UNITED STATES OF AMERICA

Contents

The Pretoria Theme: Co-Existence

Acknowledgements

My thanks are due (in alphabetical order) to the academics, broadcasting systems, communists, cosmopolitans, demonstrators, egalitarians, foundations, "freedom fighters", governments, humanists, ideologues, newspapers (and particularly the *Rand Daily Mail,* the *Guardian* and the *New York Times),* the Organisation of African Unity, politicians, protesters, pseudo-liberals, radicals, rationalists, revolutionaries, sportsbusters, students, television networks, the United Nations and all those others who in their opposition and challenge to this nation have fortified its power of purpose. I exclude from this list of opponents only those Churches and churchmen who have given Christian sanction to violence in Africa. To acknowledge them, even in good humour, would be a blasphemy.

INTRODUCTION /
The Kit, Instructions, etc.

A World in Miniature

As with a do-it-yourself kit, this book begins with a description of its contents, directions and the over-all method of construction. The object is to build an answer to some of the most puzzling of contemporary questions concerning human and international relations, as indicated by the experience of the Republic of South Africa.

The characteristic of a do-it-yourself job is that it demands ingenuity and originality: what it lacks in professionalism, it makes good in freedom, freshness and audacity. We shall not depend on the professionals–the academics, the technologists, the sociologists or the politicians. We shall refer to them at times with due respect, but we shall not allow ourselves to be dictated to or dominated by them. I speak of "we"–of you and me–and this is in fact a do-it-ourselves job. The task I am setting myself is to select the relevant pieces of the answer which I personally have encountered in the past 30 years or so–in Central Africa, North America, Europe and here in South Africa–and to endeavour to set them out in orderly fashion. But if there is to be success we must put them together, together.

The pieces are of great variety and complexity. They concern the great issues of this and all times–liberty, democracy, self-determination, social justice, material and cultural progress, civilisation and the relationship of men with one another and with God. Since I am writing more particularly about South Africa and its place in the world, about the motives and aspirations of its people and the forces which have formed them, the variety and complexity of our subject matter are inevitable.

South Africa, though it accounts for only some 1 per cent of the earth's surface and some ½ per cent of the earth's population, has in recent decades been a major international concern. And not only now but through the centuries it has been a touchstone of world events and world movements. Contributing to this are its geographical position and the complex composition of its population.

It stands between East and West. Nature has endowed it with an abundance of mineral wealth: with the gold and diamonds which men have sought through the ages for their aggrandisement; with a limitless range of base minerals which industrialised man must now have for his survival. Some believe that South Africa was the first home of *homo sapiens:* certainly, as the result of the migrations of more recent times, it is the home today of a most remarkable and rich assortment of the human species. There are assembled here two kinds of men who came originally from Europe, eight kinds who came from the hinterland of Africa, Bushmen and Hottentots who preceded them, men from Asia, men of mixed blood whom we call Coloureds. They are a most disparate gathering: white, black, brown and yellow; Christians, Muslims, Hindus and heathens. The languages of the black people are unintelligible even to other black people; and levels of civilisation range from stone-age men, who live by bows and poisoned arrows, to men who enrich uranium.

South Africa is the classic example of a country which, in current terminology, is neither developed nor underdeveloped–or which, more accurately, is both. The former United States Secretary of State Henry Kissinger spoke of the conflict between East and West being replaced by the conflict between North and South–between the industrialised world and the Third World. South Africa has both conflicts.

This country is in truth, and like no other, a world in miniature.

A noted South African lawyer, Professor D. V. Cowen, observed some dozen years ago that if the white man in South Africa passed from the stage of history, the reason would be his fear of being great. But an intimation of greatness runs through South Africa's record. Hers all along has been the setting for great events. By no means today only but through the past half-millennium currents of world affairs and human emotions have, like the Atlantic and the Indian Oceans, met about her. On occasion she has guided and shaped them. Modern South Africa was born out of the voyages of discovery and the encroachment of Europe into the world at large. South Africa participated in the penetration of Western civilisation into unknown continents. She felt closely that major modern development in human relations–the abolition of slavery. She of all places was the field for the missionary zeal of the 19th century. At the same time her gold and diamonds in unprecedented quantity concentrated upon her the attention of men seeking riches.

South Africa knows colonialism and imperialism. She experienced its advantages and its disadvantages, its triumphs and its tragedies, and the pain and the deprivation it brought in the Anglo-Boer War at the turn of the century. Thereafter in the age before the Second World War–so distant now, it seems–South Africa contributed largely to the concept and the development of that admirable experiment in international relations– the British Commonwealth of Nations. General Smuts was one of its great inspirators; General Hertzog, in the late 1920s together with MacKenzie King of Canada, one of its main formulators. After World War II South Africa was a focal point of the Commonwealth collapse. South Africa was thus central to the growth of the world's greatest empire, to its transformation and its fall. It was from her, even, that the man–Mahatma Gandhi–came who set India free. At yet wider interna- tional affairs South Africa was also present. Through General Smuts she assisted in the creation of the League of Nations and the Mandates System (which foreshadowed the end of colonialism) and, a generation later, the United Nations.

That is something of the record of the distant and the near past. Today again it is South Africa's lot to stand, in a world of transition and tribulation, where the waves of history are breaking.

History

It was, I think, on first looking into van Loon's *Story of Mankind* that I came to regard History as a master jigsaw maker. Each piece of history fitted in somewhere, some time–in quite unexpected places and times– with some other to build this ever-growing picture of unending fascination. Let me give you an example:

The Roman emperor Constantine (who ruled from 323 to 337), looking for an alternative and safer capital, chose Byzantium. When he died, one of his sons ruled the West from Rome, while the other in Constantinople was master of the East. In 475 the last of the Western emperors, called Romulus Augustulus, was ousted by the commander of a German mercenary regiment. The Eastern empire lasted for close on a thousand years after that until, in 1453, Constantinople was taken by the Turks and Emperor Constantine Paleologus was killed on the steps of the Church of the Holy Sophia. A few years before he died, his niece–Zoë– had married Ivan III of Russia . . . and so did the grand dukes of Moscow inherit the traditions of Constantinople. They also inherited its emblem: the double eagle of Byzantium–symbolic of the division of Rome those many centuries before. The legacy which the dying Byzantine empire bequeathed prospered for some five centuries more amid the vast plains of Russia. It was only yesterday, as it were, that the last wearer of the double-eagled crown was murdered by the communist rabble and thrown with the bodies of his family into a well.

(If you don't find that chain-story fascinating, return this book forthwith to the store and get your money back. But if you're interested, read on and I shall give you two other examples of the jigsaw maker at work, nearer home):

(1) Somewhere about 10,000 years ago the forebears of today's black people of Southern Africa entered the continent from the Fertile Crescent to the north. Gradually–century after century after century– they moved southward and ever further from civilisation. They had the Nile Valley far behind them before Egypt's civilisation burgeoned there. Egypt rose and fell. Athens rose and fell. Rome rose and fell. They knew nothing of it–not a single thing. Then, and on through the dark ages that followed the fall of Romulus Augustulus (when, in Kenneth Clark's term, Western civilisation hung on by the skin of its teeth), their life-style continued as it always had been–adequate for survival but static. At the time of the Renaissance they were approaching the great rugged valley of the Zambesi River. The reborn Western civilisation, as none other before it, exhibited a lust for life, an ebullience, a curiosity concerning all things, a dynamic impulsion to extend the limits of its experience, to explore and expand.

Among its most remarkable sons was Prince Henry the Navigator who in the mid-15th century sent out from Sagres in Portugal the first caravels in search of the unknown. Following the tradition he established came Bartholomew Diaz, Vasco da Gama, the discovery of the sea route round the Cape, and the establishing in 1652 by the Dutch East India Company of a half-way house to the East at the Cape of Good Hope. Soon it was to develop into a settlement and then into the home of a Western nation.

Consider this extraordinary conjunction of events! The black people had had 10,000 years to make all of Africa south of the Sahara theirs. But they had dallied too long: with a hundred centuries at their disposal, they were one or two too late: when the white men began to establish their national home at the Cape the nearest black settlements were some 500 miles to the north (the distance between London and Hamburg) and some 1,000 miles to the east (the distance between London and Rome). And while the white men went on building their national home in South Africa, European nations were taking possession of the homes of black people elsewhere through the length and breadth of the continent. The first of these colonising powers, Portugal, was the last. After half a millennium it finally relinquished its African dependencies. In January of 1975 it signed an agreement for independence with the one that remained, Angola. Members of the revolutionary Portuguese government met with representatives of the black liberation movements of Angola for the purpose. They met in the Algarve whence, 530 years before, Henry the Navigator had directed his operations.

(2) In the Transvaal, a thousand miles from Cape Town and on the highway that sweeps north to Rhodesia, there is a sleepy town called Nylstroom. It was given that name by those white men who opened South Africa's hinterland. Having travelled through arduous months across great mountain ranges and plateaux they believed they had reached the source of the Nile. There were no men of learning or geographers among them. Their guide was the Bible–to heaven and earth: they identified with the Israelites of the Old Testament seeking their promised land flowing with milk and honey. It was with a firm belief in God's guidance that these two people–one in the Middle East and the other in the south of Africa–went forth in confident search of a home of their own. Millennia separated their experience ... but it was in the same month of the same year that they arrived. In May, 1948 the British mandate in Palestine ended and the state of Israel was established. In May, 1948 the long dominance of British influence in South Africa ended, and an all-Afrikaner government under Daniel Malan was formed. As though in celebration of the historic coincidence, Dr. Malan was the first foreign head of government to visit Israel, and his name stands inscribed in Israel's Golden Book.

Through the ages, and for a reason which defies just explanation, the Jews were scorned by the world, and the world's inhumanity towards them reached its culmination in Hitler's Germany. Then, for a period after the War, sympathy for the Jews swept the heart of mankind. In those same years, and again for a reason which defies just explanation, the men who gave the town in the Transvaal the name of Nylstroom–the Afrikaners–were scorned by the world: and as the Jews were seen as the victims of race oppression, so were the Afrikaners presented as the perpetrators of race oppression. But soon the experience of Israelis and Afrikaners was again to coincide.

These were the only two peoples to have established Western nations in predominantly non-white parts of the globe. They were situated moreover at points of crucial strategic significance: and for a power bent upon global domination, such as the Soviet Union, they were marked targets. Accordingly the Kremlin backed the militant Arabs who wanted the elimination of the state of Israel, and they backed the militant Africans who wanted the elimination of white rule in Southern Africa. The United Nations was the main scene of the action, and the Afrikaners were its first scapegoats. But Israel's turn was to come. In 1974 Israel like South Africa was gagged in the General Assembly: in 1975 the resolution was passed equating Zionism with racism: in 1976 Israeli Prime Minister Rabin and South African Prime Minister Vorster met in Jerusalem to

5

sign a pact and set perhaps a new pattern–an association of middle-power states–in international relations.

It was for this sort of reason that I first came to regard History as a master jigsaw maker. Then later, on looking into Robert Hartman's Hegel, I learnt something of the real part it plays: History is the unfolding in time of the pattern of the divine purpose: and I noted Walt Whitman's exhortation that "in the future of these states must arise poets ... luxurious in the epic talent of Homer ... but consistent with the Hegelian formulas."

Dare a political journalist even contemplate such heights–Hegelian formulas? I believe that he may and that he can, provided he eschews the temptation to create himself and confines his endeavour to unravelling patterns already created by History. Creativity in any case is ill at ease in politics. Indeed, those politicians who believe it is given to them to innovate notions for the regulation of human relations are a menace to society. The only guideline here is what has gone before. "We are afraid", declared Edmund Burke, "to put men to live and trade each on his own stock of private reason, because we suspect that this stock in each man is small and that the individuals would do better to avail themselves of the general bank and capital of nations and ages." If we abide within our limitations, I believe we may nevertheless see emerge in the pages that follow that most basic of Hegelian formulas which concerns the progress of History through ever-ascending series of thesis, antithesis and synthesis.

Personal Vantage Point

It has been my good fortune to have been well stationed in space and time to observe recent major movements of History. I was in Central Africa for several years to witness the beginning of perhaps the most momentous of them all–decolonisation. In North America I encountered the post-war era of humanitarianism and idealism unrestrained. In Europe later–from South Africa House in Trafalgar Square in London, the heart of Empire–I observed the Empire's disintegration. And all the time I was intimately concerned with the affairs of South Africa where, as I have pointed out, the waves of History were again breaking.

Apart from being able to witness these general movements at close quarters, there were innumerable incidents in which I was involved which pinpointed them. The office of the South African Commissioner in Nairobi where I worked in the 1940s was in a building which accommodated also the Memorial Hall; and it was in the Memorial Hall that the Kenya Legislative Council met. When I arrived, the blacks of Kenya had one representative in Legco–a white man named the Rev. Beecher. Before I left, he had been replaced by a black man, Eliud Mathu. One day in the gents alongside the Legco chamber, I found myself exchanging pleasantries while pumping ship (that was my father's expression) alongside him. It was a notable occasion. Mathu was (I believe) the first black political representative of all the millions of black people in the British dependencies south of the equator . . . and he was the first black man alongside whom I had pumped ship since those distant days in Zululand when as a child I went bird-shooting with Babu (the son of our Indian handyman) and Bambata (the son of our Zulu *induna)*, and we would challenge one another about how far we could reach.

(Bambata, next to Babu, was my best friend. He taught me how to make clay animals. I taught him how to shoot with my .22–at plump green pigeons with ruby eyes mainly, but sometimes also at mambas, in the thick wild-fig trees. Once when there was a death in our family Bambata brought me a special block of wood which his father had given him, to put under my pillow for comfort. We are bound to meet Bambata later in this book, because the fate which met him and many young black men like him made a substantial impact on my thinking concerning integration, urbanisation, ethnicity and so on.)

I recall my first official meeting with General Smuts. It was in his office in Cape Town opposite the Parliament Buildings; and he had called me from Nairobi to give him a first-hand account of how the newly-devised East African community–of Kenya, Uganda and Tanganyika, as it then was–was working. It was soon before his defeat in the general election of 1948; and he still believed then, I think, in the possibility of a British hegemony, with the Union of South Africa its chief agent, reaching from the Cape to Kenya. It was as an information man with the assignment to help cement the ties which the War was forging between the Union and East Africa that I had been sent to Nairobi in 1943.

General Smuts was far and away the most impressive, awe-inspiring man I had met. He must then have been over 70. He was beautifully dressed in a light grey suit and waistcoat. There was a gold chain across the waistcoat; and he paced about the room, noble white head erect, firing questions at me and from time to time, above his narrow spectacles, scrutinising me with his uncannily penetrating blue eyes. One of South Africa's best-known newspaper cartoonists, Ocshe Honnibal, told me just the other day that General Smuts was for him the most difficult to portray of all the famous South Africans who had been his victims. His eyes had steel in them and yet an unfathomable softness that could not be drawn. Jan Smuts was one of those rare mortals through whom the movement of History could be sensed.

7

I recall the hour–the minute almost (about 7:37 on the morning of March 16, 1961)–that I was called to the suite in the Dorchester Hotel, London, of Dr. Verwoerd. Mrs. Verwoerd was having coffee and toast at a small table in the middle of the room. Dr. Verwoerd was standing at the window. He turned as I entered. Without having known what I would do, I reached out my hand. He clasped it. I said: "I am sure you did the right thing, Sir." "Yes", he said. "Thank you. I am sure I did." Dr. Verwoerd never doubted the rightness of his course: this was the explanation of his strength–of the granite in him. We were referring to his decision the previous evening to withdraw South Africa's application to remain, as a Republic, a member of the British Commonwealth. It was the moment of the disintegration of this greatest empire the world has known. It was the event here that was supreme–not the man; but later I shall be writing about this most remarkable personality himself.

The Diary

It has been my good fortune, as I say, to have been involved time and again in the past 30 years with historic people and historic events. I never kept a diary of them in the ordinary sense of the term; but I have recorded them in countless articles, pamphlets, radio scripts and three books—some 10-million printed words, I would reckon, plus others written in letters to my wife. These are my diary, and I shall be quoting from it as the occasion arises in the pages that follow. Several reasons have decided me to do so. First of all, an impersonal, detached and objective treatment can go only part of the way towards an understanding of South Africa's condition. Her problems and motives and hopes cannot be understood by thinking about them alone: they must also be felt. Much of my diary has been written in response to immediate feeling, in the heat of the moment before perspective has had time to trap emotion. Some of it has been written in novel form which gives freer play to the imagination . . . so I believe these quotes from my diary will be a useful addition to our kit.

There is another consideration. Many in the outside world believe that South Africa's basic philosophy of human relations can be changed by pressure from abroad, and that it has in fact been so changed. This is a dangerous fallacy, but how can it be shown to be a fallacy? With the benefit of hindsight most past positions can be rationalised to conform to present requirements. In short, the books can be cooked. However a diary cannot be cooked–not when it has been printed and published and is there to be examined in its original form. My diary constitutes a continuous record since the 1940s of official thinking on South Africa's problems: and I can say official thinking because during most of that time I was employed as a government information officer. In 1956, for instance, I wrote a reply to the blistering attack on South Africa contained in Father Trevor Huddleston's *Naught for Your Comfort.* My answer, *You Are Wrong Father Huddleston,* was the first book ever to be published on the meaning and intentions of apartheid. Twenty years later there is no statement in that book which needs to be changed and none that has been overtaken, out-dated or proved inconsistent with subsequent events. This is no tribute to myself but to the consistency of Pretoria's policies.

I propose to indicate diary extracts by indenting them and preceding them with place and date. At the back of the book is a list showing from what part of the diary they come. Here is an example:

> *United Nations, Paris, 1948:* I heard Ernest Bevin a day or two ago address the General Assembly. He was magnificent. It was a ray of truth scorching through all this hypocrisy. It was England speaking, and it made me proud of the little association I have with England. I realised then–as once or twice the assembly broke into applause–what a great force in world affairs England still is. As he came from the rostrum, this ugly, fat old man, and waddled along the aisle to his seat halfway down the hall, everyone clapped on and on–except the boys from the Soviets. It's an impression you can't escape here–the isolation of the Soviet people. There is something terrifying about being alone–a man or a nation, no matter how strong. (1)

Terminology

Inappropriate terminology for describing this country and its people is a main cause of misunderstanding of its affairs abroad and at home. Take, to start with, *South Africa.* It is the vaguest of geographical descriptions. *South Africa* is bordered east, south and west by the Indian and Atlantic Oceans. But what are its northern limits: in the east is it the Limpopo or the Zambesi River, in the west the Orange or the Kunene? Is South West Africa geographically a part of *South Africa,* is Rhodesia, is all of Mocambique or only a section of it or none of it? Atlases provide no clear answer. Ancient maps have inscribed across the southern reaches of the continent *Hic Sunt Leones.* Since then the lions, most of them, have departed and *homo sapiens* has moved in. But who of this species are *South Africans,* and what is the extent of their domain? Modern maps do not

9

help us: and a book published several years ago now was entitled *There Are No South Africans.*

The political cartographers drew out their own arbitrary definitions. At the turn of the century *British South Africa* reached from the Cape to Northern Rhodesia (now Zambia) far away across the Zambesi (and on the same latitude as Angola and Mocambique), and the police in that territory were known as the British *South African* Police. In 1910 the Union of *South Africa* was established; and, particularly after Rhodesia declined to join it in the early 1920s, the Union and *South Africa* came to be used as interchangeable terms to denote the area south of the Limpopo. The Union included the Cape, Natal, Orange Free State and Transvaal; incorporation within it was seen in 1910 as the natural destiny of the three British Protectorates of Bechuanaland, Basutoland and Swaziland; and in 1920 the League of Nations decreed that South West Africa, conquered in the recent hostilities by South African forces from Germany, should be ruled as an integral part of the Union. Politically, *South Africa* appeared to be taking shape: it would ultimately consist of the Union plus the territories mentioned above. They would form a unitary state, and all their people together would be its citizens–*South Africans.*

That was the outlook until the Second World War. Since then a combination of internal and external forces (including the charter of the United Nations itself which enshrines the right of self-determination of *peoples,* not states) has smashed the idea of a single state of *South Africa.* Today the Protectorate peoples–the Batswana, the Basuto and the Swazi– are self-determining nations with their own governments and sovereignty. The other black peoples of *South Africa*–the Xhosa, the Zulu, the Tswana, the Sotho, the Shangaan, the Ndebele and the Venda–have governments and homelands of their own. One of them, the Xhosa of the Transkei, became sovereign in 1976: others may become sovereign if they so wish, and the Tswana have announced their intention to do so. That is the position: a variety of nations inhabit this part of the sub-continent. There are the black nations, each of them with its own name. And there is the white nation. It has no name of its own. Its members are merely *South Africans*–no more definitive than if the only name for a Frenchman was a European, or for a Canadian, a North American.

From this elementary inadequacy of terminology has sprung a host of misunderstandings and complications, among our own people and others. Confusion will continue until it is generally recognised that the white people here constitute a distinctive nation of their own. However for general recognition of the existence of this distinctive white nation, a

10

name which distinctively identifies it is fundamentally necessary. But the problem does not end there. The white nation consists of two groups: those who speak Afrikaans (mainly of Dutch, French and German origin) account for some 60 per cent of its numbers; and those who speak English (mainly of British origin) account for the bulk of the rest. The means for describing the first group is simple enough: they are Afrikaners. But no satisfactory description of the members of the second group has been devised. They are called English-speaking South Africans. This is hopelessly inappropriate: the term is unwieldy; there are many people in *South Africa,* not of the white nation, who speak English; and the term results in such illogicalities and absurdities as *an English-speaking* pianist, or an *English-speaking* institution for the deaf and dumb.

If there is to be clarity in the pages that follow, it is essential to cut through this terminological tangle. I propose, therefore, to refer to English-speaking members of the white nation as Anglo South Africans (or Anglosans for short); of the white nation as a whole, as the Anglo-Afrikaner nation, or simply "this nation" or "our people". The state by which the nation is embraced, I shall refer to as Pretoria. This should cause no difficulty: to identify a state with its capital is common practice: we say today, there are signs of increasing tension between Moscow and Peking. The city of Pretoria I shall call Pretoria City. There are precedents for this: Mexico City and Panama City. The homeland, the territory, of the Anglo-Afrikaner nation, I shall refer to as the Republic Proper (until it gets a proper name of its own)–that is, the present Republic of South Africa, excluding the black homelands. "South Africa" will be used as a general description: e.g., it was during the same period of history that whites and blacks were moving into South Africa.

Critics on the Couch

This book will necessarily deal with broad international affairs because, as I have said, our country is so much a part of them. There is also a more specific reason: it is that the attitude of other nations towards us springs at least as much from their own condition as ours. Beauty, it is said, is in the eye of the beholder. So is ugliness. It is commonly said also, in criticism of the psychiatrist, that in the final resort he is looking into his own thoughts and not his patient's: it is altogether impossible for him to dissociate his analysis from what goes on in his own mind. Well, for a quarter of a century and more nations abroad have been analysing Pretoria's condition. To judge the validity of their finding, is it not high time that they

11

took a turn on the couch themselves? Or, more accurately, that external and objective evidence about their own state of mind should be brought to bear on the subject?

I think so, as you will observe from subsequent chapters. Meantime, to appreciate the impact upon us of the foreign diagnosis, it should be pointed out that it took the form, and was given the weight, of a worldwide *public opinion.* Now it is true that the eminent British lawyer, Dicey, noted that *public opinion* "is itself, after all, a mere abstraction. It is not a power that has any independent existence. It is simply a general term for the beliefs held by a number of human beings." Nonetheless, *public opinion* was invested in the post-war era with something like sovereign moral authority. Energetic efforts having been made to sweep effective power (together with the ashes of Hiroshima) under the carpet of places like the United Nations, moral suasion as represented by world opinion was henceforth to regulate mankind's affairs. Not least, it was to prescribe the future of the Anglo-Afrikaner nation: and the nation's struggle for independence (and thus for survival) cannot be understood unless those wishing to understand are constantly reminded of the persistent, unrelenting and remorseless pressure of world opinion that has been brought to bear against it. Day after day for some 30 years without interruption, a flood of indignation, anger, abhorrence and condemnation of its policies has poured from the presses of the world, as also incessant predictions of doom and disaster.

So that you may be aware of this, I propose to reproduce at odd intervals in pages that will follow typical comment by foreign newspapers dating back to the 1940s. You may not read them all: you may find them irritating and distracting. So have we: day after day through all these years they have nagged at us and added their own acute dimension to the problems we shall be discussing. I describe the newspaper quotations that will be reproduced as typical–and typical they are. However there has on occasion been newspaper comment from abroad, sympathetic, compassionate and constructive–but it is exceptional.

Credentials

I am not a member of the governing National Party or of any other party. I was appointed to my post in the foreign service by General Smuts (of the United Party): and a few weeks after the United Party was defeated at the general election in May, 1948 I was chosen by the new National Government–by Mr. Eric Louw–as a member of its first delegation to the United Nations. I have no party affiliations or loyalties.

My loyalty is to the concept of separatism to which I was committed through personal experience many years before *apartheid* entered the political vocabulary.

Context and Theme

That is an outline of the kit we have at our disposal for assembling the jigsaw. As with all such puzzles the pieces may seem at first glance not to fit at all. Is that not the fascination of the thing? The way (as you will know well) to tackle the task is to sort out first the pieces that are apparently of a kind: the ones with straight edges, for example: the blue ones for the sky; the green ones for the grass, and so. As my contribution I am going to gather related pieces into groups of this sort. First, they will be grouped in three periods: 1945 to 1960 ... 1960 to 1970–... and Now. Within each of these periods there will be pieces concerning the world outside this country. For the outside world the periods will be entitled respectively: Idealism ... Disillusion ... Balance. Together they will constitute *The World Context*. For this country the three periods will be entitled respectively: Separatism ... Engagement ... Co-existence. Together they will constitute *The Pretoria Theme*. The arrangement in table form is like this:

	1945 to 1960	*1960 to 1970–*	*NOW*
WORLD CONTEXT	Idealism	Disillusion	Balance
PRETORIA THEME	Separatism	Engagement	Co-existence

The *NOW* above the right-hand column does not necessarily refer to 1976 or to any specific date at all: it is the present time which carries the past and bears the future, and in which three-in-one arrangement balance and co-existence are intimated.

Now, to get on with the job. I hope you will find the task of putting the pieces together as fascinating as the presenting of them is for me. And the picture having been completed–if you hold it in just the right light and observe it in just the right mood–you may see across it the lustre of History's wondrous symmetry. Anyway, the best of Anglo-Afrikaner luck to you!

Pretoria, May, 1976

13

Part one / Section one
1945 to 1960

THE WORLD CONTEXT:
IDEALISM

CHAPTER ONE / 1945 to 1960
North America

Apartheid in the Prairies

Western Canada, 1952: The trip through the prairies was fascinating. The snow had recently melted away, and as the new crop has not come up yet everything is either the golden brown of last year's crop or the dark brown of ploughed soil. There was quite a bit of water lying around in pools, and it was a thrill for me to see numerous wild duck swimming about and circling high over the wheatfields. They tell me that the coming of the duck to these pools generally ends in domestic tragedy. Of course the setting is ideal for them: shallow, clear water with grain to be had on all sides. And so they begin to nest. But often by the time the ducklings are out the water has dried away. I don't think ducks can move their young, so they must be left to die.

What an incomprehensible contrast all this is! The seemingly endless train journey through prairie and mountain . . . and the editor's office in town after town, with the explanations, the arguments, the discussions about apartheid going on and on each day like a gramophone repeating itself.

Then standing beside Lake Louise or feeding sweets to the deer, I wonder what in heaven's name it is all about. Are these far-away people in the prairies and the mountains really interested in whether the Coloured people in South Africa are on a separate or a common voters' roll? They must be. At a restaurant in Banff the other evening Jack and I got into conversation with the proprietor. When he learnt where we were from he said: "I've got a bottle of South African brandy: when you've finished your dinner you must have one with me–and tell me all about this apartheid." Even the Greek proprietor of a restaurant in the heart of the Rockies wanted to know. (2)

It was only four years since the National Party had come to power in Pretoria: and yet accounts of its race policy had already permeated through to the most remote and tranquil regions of the Western world and to the deep recesses of men's minds. In the five years I spent in North America (between 1949 and 1954 at the South African High Commissioner's Office in Ottawa) I learnt why. At every important point apartheid contradicted and challenged the hopes and ideals of the post-war Western world. The mood of the post-war Western world was, of course, shaped by its war experience: by the trauma of Belsen and the horror of Hiroshima. The inhumanity of the aggressor had been met by the mercilessness of the avenger, and people everywhere recoiled from the consequences. The evils were traced in the first place to nationalism, totalitarianism and *herrenvolkism:* and the pattern of post-war thinking was delineated by a determination that these forces should be wiped from the face of the earth forever. In particular, race superiority was to be countered by the theory that for social and political purposes all men could be regarded as essentially the same. Totalitarianism was to be countered by the universal application of democracy and recognition of individual liberty; and nationalism was to be countered by a new international order founded upon a logically-established morality.

Many believed that scientific and technological advances had made this possible: that man had at last gained control of blind evolutionary forces and that he could henceforth channel them towards harmonious and constructive ends. The assumed new unity and closeness of the world, achieved through modern communications, featured large in this thinking. Historian Arnold Toynbee referred to it as "the technological reduction of distance". He argued that, as a result, the continuing existence of groups of people based on kith and kin could no longer be justified. In days gone by, protection of the isolated group had been natural enough, but modern communications had radically altered the relationships between men. All human beings across the face of the earth had been brought closer together. There was a coalescing of humanity, and the distinction between kith and alien had become obsolete. In these circumstances the persistence of the group mentality was not only illogical but immoral and odious.

Ideas of this kind took complete possession of post-war thinking. They were most clearly and enthusiastically articulated in North America; and I was there during the years that they were taking form and rising, to break subsequently in a flood across the world.

The United States had come out of the recent conflagration as incomparably the greatest power on earth. It was confronted with broad choices. One was to accept as they were the nations and peoples of the world, and to limit its "imperial" role to safeguarding and balancing their interests and to maintaining peace–as Rome and Britain had done. The second was to endeavour to secure, in addition to peace and order, a general progress and happiness by reforming the conditions under which humanity lived; by inviting, and if need be coercing, all kinds of men to participate in a new international arrangement that would secure these goals.

The United States chose the second alternative–of world reformer and missionary. I think it was inevitable. In the first place, Americans really believed that they had learnt the secret of progress, and that there was an obligation upon them to make it available to others. No-one can doubt that there was substantial evidence in their own experience for this confidence. They had built within their own society a measure of advancement, of personal freedom and of over-all comfort and prosperity unmatched by any other nation in any other place or at any other time. There was scarcely a branch of human activity in which they were not as good as the best elsewhere–or better; and having been so successful among their own people, it was their duty now as world leader to share their success. Was it right that theirs alone should be God's Own Country?

My work as an information man in North America brought me into constant touch with all kinds of people–students, rotarians, church organisations, academics, politicians, newsmen and countless ordinary citizens–and everywhere I encountered this optimism and faith in the American mission. In some quarters there was a degree of arrogance, but generally what I sensed was an uncomplicated spirit of generosity and of a wish to help others. In those post-war years, as the American compared his good fortune with the ill-fortune of so many others, I think his attitude to world affairs was not unreasonable or even (as it is represented so often these days in retrospect) naive.

However, it was less contemporary conditions than the history of America that made her choice for reformer inevitable.

The war of independence in the final quarter of the 18th century represented for the founders of the United States something immeasurably more significant than a cutting of constitutional ties with Great Britain. It was a complete break with Europe–with what the founding fathers regarded as Europe's reactionary, obsolete and corrupt institutions which through the centuries had brought such misery upon the people.

19

Europe, during these centuries, had had more to offer humanity than any other part of the world, but because of its self-seeking and false standards it had failed to do so. Now America was free from these perverse influences: it was free to institute that kind of society which enlightened European minds advocated but which reactionary European governments rejected.

Was not England the home in the 17th century of John Locke and Isaac Newton? Was not France the home of the philosophers of the Enlightenment? Yes, indeed, it was at the heart of old Europe that the idea was conceived and fostered of the attainment of happiness through the guidance of reason. It was there that reason was placed philosophically in sharp opposition to custom, tradition and prescription, and where the expansion of knowledge and science was held out as the golden hope for the future. But in old Europe, custom, tradition and prescription continued to hold sway. The ideas of the enlightenment had first to cross the Atlantic before they could be incorporated in society–as they were in the words of the Declaration of Independence: *We hold these truths to be self-evident: that all men are created equal; that they are endowed by their creator with certain inalienable rights; that among these are life, liberty and the pursuit of happiness.*

That passage, as all the world knows, was written by Thomas Jefferson, He was stating the terms not only for the New World in America but for a New World to come for all men. He described the United States as "a universal nation pursuing universally valid ideas". And it was the conviction of his great contemporary, John Adams, that "our pure, virtuous, public-spirited, federative Republic will govern the globe and introduce the perfection of man."

When these brave declarations were made, the United States was yet a minor power on the international stage. However her strength grew steadily, astonishingly. By the 1820s she was able, through the Monroe Doctrine, to assert her authority in the Western Hemisphere. A hundred years later, after World War I, she was ready to assert it in the world at large. Her spokesman at Versailles was President Woodrow Wilson, and he spoke in the language and inspiration of Jefferson and Adams. In 1919, when the Treaty of Versailles came up for ratification in the Senate, he declared that "ordered freedom should lend itself to a new purpose and utterly destroy the old order of international politics. Statesmen might see difficulties, but the people can see none and can brook no denial. The world must be kept clean of every power that could renew the terror. The League of Nations is the only hope for mankind." In his second inaugural address, the President stated: "The greatest things that remain to be done must be done with the whole world for stage and in co-operation with the wide and universal forces of mankind. The American principles are not the principles of a province or of a single continent. We have known, and boasted all along, that they were the principles of a liberated mankind."

The United States graduated from World War I as a Great Power: from World War II as a Super Power. The spokesman now was Franklin Roosevelt. The terms again were the same–only, in proportion to America's increased might, more ambitious. Where Wilson had envisaged freedom for all people based on self-determination within nations of their own, Roosevelt envisaged a universal company of nations working in amity, concord and common purpose, inspired by the United States. He returned from Yalta in 1945 convinced that what had been agreed upon there would spell the end of unilateral action, of exclusive alliances, of spheres of influence, of balances of power–in short, of all those expedients which for centuries a Europe trapped in its own history had applied with disastrous consequences. General de Gaulle gave his impression of the Roosevelt vision in his *Memoirs de Guerre* in the following words: "According to Roosevelt's ideological conviction, international democracy was a kind of universal remedy. He believed that the nations, brought together, would examine their complaints and would take in each case the necessary measures for avoiding wars. They would also co-operate towards the progress of the human race. American isolationism would come to an end and Russia, shunned for so long, could be associated with the Western nations."

Roosevelt shared Woodrow Wilson's faith in a co-operative Russia. Speaking in Congress in 1917, Wilson had declared, concerning the Russian Revolution: "Does not every American feel that assurance has been added to our hope for the future peace of the world by the wonderful and heartening things that have been happening within the last few weeks in Russia? Russia was known by those who knew her best to have been always in fact democratic at heart, in the vital habits of her thought, in all the intimate relationships of her people that spoke their natural instinct, their habitual attitude towards life. The autocracy that crowned the summit of her political structure, long as it has stood and terrible as was the reality of its power, was not in fact Russian in origin, character or purpose: and now it has been shaken off, and the great, generous Russian people have been added in all their naive majesty and might to the forces that are fighting for freedom in the world, for justice and for peace."

Despite all that happened in the ensuing years, Roosevelt shared the hope that, accepted within the family of Western nations, Russia would contribute to the achievement of Western aims: that, associated with America's benevolent influence, it would be converted into a potent force for liberty and democracy. *Our pure, virtuous, public-spirited, federative Republic will govern the globe and introduce the perfection of mankind.* It runs, an unbroken thread: from Jefferson and Adams, through Woodrow

Wilson and Roosevelt and–the almost immediate collapse of the dream of a co-operative Russia notwithstanding–on to John Kennedy. Kennedy spoke in his inaugural address of "taking up the torch of the first revolution, the American revolution for liberty and human rights."

The Hope for One World

This line of thought was being projected long after I left North America; but during the late 1940s and early 1950s when I was there the confidence and optimism were at their height. The aspirations embedded in the history of the United States combined with the evidences of success so apparent on all sides to give North Americans a sense of certitude in the rightness of their mission. What hope was there in the circumstances of a fair hearing for Pretoria's case? At every critical point it defied the new world philosophy. It questioned, from its own experience of 300 years of non-Western people, the validity of a universal democracy. (While I was in Ottawa our High Commissioner in London, Dr. Geyer, declared on the subject of universal democracy as Cromwell had on some other: "I beseech you in the bowels of Christ to consider that you might be wrong.") Pretoria championed the virtues of nationalism and patriotism. It contended that there could be no stability unless the rights of the individual were balanced against the rights of society. While the rest of the world was proclaiming the essential sameness of men, it was implementing a policy based four-square on the recognition of the essential differences between them. And while others were declaring the primacy of reason and the attainability of virtue in human institutions, it was announcing their inevitable fallibility and the primacy of God in the affairs of nations. The contradiction was complete: and in the indignant rejection of Pretoria's precepts, the one-worlders believed they had at hand a ready means for justifying themselves and advancing their cause.

Ottawa, 1953: The hope for One World was fastened on science. It was fastened on modern means of transportation. Motor cars, trains, liners, aeroplanes had eliminated distance, and the whole world had been made neighbours. But Hope had confused the earth with the world, which is the earth and everything on it. The earth's distances are measurable in miles, but all distances are not. The distances between the hearts and minds of men are not. They cannot be bridged by steel and gasoline. The Hope was fastened on modern means of communication. It was fastened on synthetic seeing: the photograph, the moving film, television. But the camera tells only part of the truth. It abstracts and selects and works with lights and angles. The Hope was fastened on universal literacy and the written word,

22

but its mass distribution has been abused. The truth is there but the competition is too heavy. It is unconfident, it can't get its lines pat, it falls short on glamour, it lacks audience appeal. The show goes on with the sure things kept in the cast–sensation, suspicion, prejudice, mistrust, scandal and smear. People cry out for One World. They hope for One. They also fear Two. The same science that gave them Hope has given them Fear. They look for something else to fasten Hope upon. We cannot win with better arms, they say: we must win with better Ideas. The pursuit of Ideas is on. They have been captured, processed, made marketable and put into mass circulation. The audience accepts the Ideas their columnists, commentators, newscasters and analysts give them and get from one another. The amateur thinker has been submerged. Millions allow professionals to do their thinking for them. The audience is arming itself with weapons that are stronger than guns. Without checking measurements, multitudes step into ready-made patterns of thought. They wear their Ideas proudly as though they were their own, like bow-ties that fasten at the back.

International and race affairs are ideal stuff for prefabricated thinking. They are not Trivial. They are Significant. Ideas about them is what the world needs. They also offer sensation, emotion, self-righteous indignation and therefore a profitable field for the professional. In addition he has a great advantage in this field. His audience has little opportunity, even if it has the inclination, to judge things for itself. Saying bus fares are too low is risky: some of the listeners may be paying them. But what about the vote in Ruanda-Urundi? (3)

The Pseudo-liberal

Pretoria's case could not get a fair hearing even when its affairs were left altogether on one side and the accumulated experience of the ages was cited. You could quote Cicero: that the people is not every group of men associated in any manner, but is the coming together of a considerable number of men who are united by a common agreement about law and rights and by the desire to participate in mutual advantages. You could quote Grotius: that among the traits characteristic of man is an impelling desire for society organised according to the measure of his intelligence and with those who are of his own kind. You could quote Jean Jacques Rousseau: that society is no aggregation of individuals but an association of people who have common possessions, such as a common language, and a common interest and well-being–"the reciprocal sensibility and internal correspondence of all parts", analogous to the vital principles of a living organism. You could quote Tocqueville: that man has been created by God in such a way that the larger the object of his

23

love the less directly attached he is to it. His heart needs particular passions: he needs limited objects for his affections to keep them firm and enduring: "I am convinced that the interests of the human race are better served by giving every man a particular fatherland than by trying to inflame his passions for the whole of humanity."

Nothing of this was of any avail: for I am afraid that the fact is that the mind of our modern pseudo-liberal, as of those he has indoctrinated, is closed to any wisdom, ancient or modern, which does not conform to his own. I call him a pseudo-liberal for three main reasons. The first is that the objective conditions in which genuine liberalism flourished in the 19th century–notably, mobility of population and free trade–no longer obtain. The second reason is that the genuine liberal set his face against the extension of state interference in the life of his own and other societies: the man who claims to be his heir today advocates far-reaching intervention in political as well as economic affairs and in international as well as national affairs. The third reason is that the genuine liberal was characterised by, of all things, an openness of mind and a readiness to consider points of view other than his own. The men who claim today his honourable name have no patience whatever with opinions that oppose theirs: indeed many of them, whether publicists, politicians, professors or priests, are prepared to have them crushed by force and, if need be, violence. The pernicious influence of the pseudo-liberal was everywhere apparent in my days in America: the pusillanimous intellectual who fooled himself that the narrowness of his mind was extended by the breadth of his illusion.

But at a much deeper level it was apparent to the observer in America in those days that recent movements of history were building a critical contradiction at the heart of the nation's life. On the one hand there were the brave ideals expressed in 1776 when America was in the wings of the world stage; on the other the disenchanting responsibilities of power as it dominated centre stage. For instance, while America crusaded in the name of liberty for decolonisation, she was well aware of the opportunity this afforded her of extending her influence through wide areas of the world at the expense of the colonial powers. General de Gaulle remarked on the point that Roosevelt was counting on the host of smaller nations to weaken the position of the colonial powers and to provide the United States with a vast political and economic clientele. As early as 1949 André Siegfried expressed the view in an article in *Figaro* that the United States, by fermenting revolts, was as dangerous a revolutionary force as the Soviet Union. Commenting in 1963 Vernon McKay, Professor of African Studies at Johns Hopkins University, wrote: "while this may overstate the case somewhat, the decolonisation process has resulted in the retreat of European predominance and an obvious increase of American– and Russian–influence in Africa."

It is altogether justifiable that a power with worldwide responsibilities should seek to extend its spheres of influence. The fact nonetheless is that a head-on collision developed in the handling of America's international affairs between high principle and hard expedience: and a spin-off of this was a coarsening of national politics. At both levels American politics had two faces. The eye-ball to eye-ball confrontation between them that was later to occur–stage-managed by the pseudo-liberals–was a traumatic experience. It happened at Watergate.

U.S. Attitudes to Africa

Meanwhile, we are going to take a look at America's attitude during this period towards Africa in particular. In the case of Pretoria there is now available a secret document (it was declassified in 1975) which sets out Washington's appraisal of the situation following the coming to power of Dr. Malan and the National Party in 1948. The first point to note about it is the importance it attached to securing the goodwill of the new government. In fact, it set as its first goal "the maintenance and development of friendly relations". It acknowledged South Africa's strategic significance; and fearing that sentiment in the National Party might lead to an isolationist spirit, it proposed to persuade Pretoria to maintain "bonds of sympathy" with the Western powers. Towards this end Washington would encourage South Africa's economic development and the growth of its foreign trade. The policy paper observed that what was regarded as the Malan Government's anti-British orientation "may simplify our relations with South Africa in some respects." More than that, the document reveals that the American Administration discussed the possibility of exploiting the departure of General Smuts for its own purposes. But the temptation was resisted: "our interests would not be served by a South African withdrawal for all practical purposes from the British Commonwealth." On South West Africa (already in 1948 a highly-charged international issue), the policy paper expressed the view that Pretoria had a moral, though not a legal, obligation to place the Territory under the trusteeship system of the United Nations. However, as a matter of tactics, the issue required careful handling: it was necessary to avoid action which could cause Pretoria to annex the Territory, as it might do if severely criticised.

This declassified document attests to Washington's resolve to deal with Pretoria with the utmost circumspection. At the same time it discloses a distaste for the new government's race policies and a condescending view of the government itself. On the first point it said (in reference to the proposed incorporation of the three British Protectorates): "In view of the unenlightened Nationalist approach to race problems and the danger which this attitude presents to the future of South Africa itself, we should be particularly alert to any manifestation of an expansionist policy by the present South African Government." And, on the second: "Our policy should recognize the immaturity and lack of experience in international affairs of many of the leaders and supporters of the present government, and should endeavor by the exertion of patience to encourage South Africa to continue her cooperation with other countries, and particularly her participation in the United Nations."

Washington had a high regard neither for the policies of the Malan Government nor for the Government itself. Nevertheless, Pretoria should be handled with kid gloves in America's interest and the West's. That was Washington's view in 1948, and it was not much changed during the rest of the Truman and the Eisenhower era. Throughout this period, official American interest in Africa at large was limited. This was traditionally the sphere of influence of the European colonial powers; and though America might profit.from their departure (and was working towards this end behind the scenes) the colonial powers had not yet left. They were America's partners in the North Atlantic Treaty Organisation and in other areas; and while they remained in charge in Africa, active Washington concern in the continent's business would not be appropriate.

Nevertheless, unofficial American interest was rapidly increasing, and its nature is comprehensively documented in a collection of essays published in book form in the early 1960s under the title, *The United States and Africa*. The publisher was an organisation called The American Assembly (of which General Eisenhower was, at the time, Chairman) and the contributors were among the most eminent of America's academic authorities on Africa. Their views are pointers as reliable as any available to the American attitude as it developed in the 1950s; and they indicate a highly idealised view of Africa. For instance, Africa's people should be free to set their own course while at the same time being rallied to the Western world's standards; and this represented no difficulty since Africa and America shared the same aspirations: democracy, equality, freedom, an open society and the protection of civil liberties and minority rights. America's principal interest in Africa's political systems was that they should be democratic and stable: no other goals would be compatible with the declared aims of the African peoples or with the expressed ideals and national interest of America. The minimum elements in democracy were freedom from alien rule, the existence of effective and regularised restraints on the exercise of political power, and a political climate in which dissent and opposition were not only tolerated but were provided a legitimate functional role in the political process. The prospects for African stability were good. There had been no popular support for at-

26

tempted coups in any state nor any threatened mass revolts, nor in the next few years were there likely to be crises of the kind that periodically shook the Middle East, Asia and parts of Latin America. There had been enough visible evidence of progress to offset moods of disillusionment and doubt about the value of independence.

Such were the views of America experts on Africa as the 1960s began. Professor St. Clair Drake, Director of African Studies at Roosevelt University, described how America's people could help in strengthening bonds with Africa. It was vital, he wrote, that Americans in all walks of life should engage in dialogue through cultural exchanges with the African intellectuals–novelists, essayists, poets, journalists, artists, scholars and religious leaders. The arranging of hospitality during vacations, the provision of part-time employment and perhaps most importantly the development of warm personal relations between visiting African students and American families were direct means by which individuals could further African ambitions. It was at this grass-roots level that the American impact on Africa could have maximum effect. Americans naturally and quite legitimately were concerned with the preservation of the inalienable right of all peoples to life, liberty and the pursuit of happiness. African leaders shared these aspirations and most of them recognised that the United States was trying to realise such a society, though slowly, painfully and not without conflict. They recognised too that traditional African societies also occasionally failed to fulfil these demands.

The Pursuit of Happiness

America struggling to reach a just society . . . traditional African societies occasionally failing to do so: that was the assessment then: the pursuit of happiness–in America, in Africa, in the world at large–the guidestar of American idealism in this period. But the question which overrode all others in my mind as I left North America in 1954 (and still today) centred on the meaning of the pursuit of happiness in the circumstances of the contemporary world.

Life, liberty and the pursuit of happiness . . . there are those who say that Jefferson suffused this declaration with an ethical philosophy–not merely a political and legal one–that permanently nourished the American spirit. Erwin Griswold, Dean of Harvard Law School, said so when he spoke at Natal University in 1967. The truths stated by Jefferson were (he said) self-evident: they were not demonstrated, they were not authoritatively commanded by some supernatural power, their capacity to persuade came from within themselves and from their impact on the minds of individual men: they were goals to be reached, ends to be attained, objectives to be striven for.

But life, liberty, the pursuit of happiness . . . what sort of goals, ends, objectives are these, and what directive do they contain within themselves to their attainment? What responsibilities does the right to life impose on people and governors? No doubt, adequate provision of food and shelter, protection against violence, medical attention. But would this right be consummated in a society which issued to each citizen at birth a certificate guaranteeing an existence on this earth of 100, 200, 1,000 years? It may be possible one day in a deep-freeze to prolong life indefinitely. Liberty . . . what is this? People will reply: freedom of movement, freedom of association, freedom of thought, freedom of expression, freedom of conscience, freedom of choice. These are the quick and common answers: but within itself and outside any framework of reference is the concept of liberty self-evident or even comprehensible? The difficulty is to comprehend the existence of liberty without restraint. Without restraint there is no distinction between liberty and licence: restraint, discipline, authority are the womb of freedom and freedom cannot be conceived without them. The pursuit of happiness . . . It was in Jefferson's America that a black man remarked as the civil rights movement triumphed that he was tired of pursuing happiness. He wanted to catch it. How to catch happiness–is that the preoccupation today of the Western world and its peril? With a high standard of living, a suburban home, a motor car or two, a television set, a swimming pool? With the welfare state? There are more psychiatric cases per thousand of the population, more suicides, more delinquency in the welfare states of this world than most other places on earth. The young people in America and Europe grasp, gasp, for happiness with hemp seed.

Life, liberty, the pursuit of happiness . . . When Dean Griswold was in Natal a Roman Catholic priest in Rotterdam solemnised a marriage between two homosexuals. Mr. Benno Prensala, Chairman of the Dutch Association of Homosexuals, commented that anyone had the right to do things which made them happy. They have the liberty so to pursue happiness, but no life will issue from this union.

Jefferson's truths are like the mists in the morning mountains. There is a certain seduction in their frailty and diffusion. Also they conceal the heights to be climbed and the hard peaks that stand behind. Jefferson's statement is vague and sentimental, ordinary, a cliché, frail and diffuse like the mists. It has no power to define or direct: and from it have been woven the thin and tenuous patterns of modern Western society. All men are not created equal: the inestimable endowment of their Creator is their variety. Life, in itself, is meaningless–and without variety and intensity of experience is less worth living the longer it lasts. Except in obedience to authority there is no liberty; and the pursuit of happiness is,

28

in itself, the chase of the wild goose. Jefferson's self-evident truths are, in themselves, the guideposts to cloud-cuckoo land: on their own, dissociated, their persuasion of individual minds leads to conduct and purpose in confusion.

Jefferson's truths have persuaded individual minds (like Dean Griswold's) in the modern age that the time for prescription is past. "Primitive societies", he said, "use rigid rules and prohibitions. Such a mode of arrangement is not available to us now. There are too many choices, too many opportunities to make it feasible to have everything prescribed in advance. In (modern) society, the makers of the plan–the government–must yield much to those who implement it, the people. Political freedom–democracy–is in fact an expression of faith that the people will succeed as their own masters."

The dominant trend of thought in this country is different. Precisely because of the complexities of modern society, and because democracy has spread and attenuated the source of government authority, the need for prescription is seen today as greater. There is a high regard for democracy among Anglo-Afrikaners, but it must nourish and not undermine the other values and ideals they have inherited. In advanced as in backward societies the present task is not to do away with the prescriptions of tradition, experience and faith but to find the solution that will make them stick. It was the prescription that existed in 1776–of tradition and Christian faith–that circumscribed the ideas of liberty and happiness and gave them meaning. Dean Griswold commented that self-evident truths were not authoritatively commanded: their capacity to persuade came from their self-contained impact on individual minds–and that perhaps is their final and fatal flaw. Private reason is an inadequate guide: and there can be no place for liberty and happiness amid the turbulence of individual wills. Edmund Burke wrote in Jefferson's generation: "Either order in the cosmos is real or chaos exists. If chaos reigns then the fragile equalitarian doctrines and emancipating programmes of the revolutionary reformers have no significance: for in the vortex of chaos only force and appetite satisfy."

The hydrogen bombs and LSD.

CHAPTER TWO / 1945 to 1960
Britain

Bandwagon to Utopia

Britain looked in good shape when I arrived there in 1955 to take up my duties–it was to be for six years–as Director of Information at South Africa House. It was a very different place from what it had been during my previous visit in 1948 when there were queues along the pavement waiting to get into the Strand Palace for breakfast–of synthetic scrambled eggs or, if you were lucky, kipper. Half a dozen years later there was plenty of everything it seemed except accommodation. Key-money to get into normal-sized houses or flats was £1,000 (and that was before inflation). Pretoria treats its foreign service people excellently–but not to the extent of paying key-money. However, large multi-roomed flats were not popular: they could be had without key-money provided the tenant saw to renovations, interior decorating, etc. himself. We took one in an elaborate building in Baker Street. In addition to a dining-room, it had a drawing room, a lounge and ten other rooms. In the drive-in courtyard, Rolls Royces and Jaguars regularly drove in, the chauffeurs opening doors for elegantly dressed ladies. There was a special parking bay for perambulators, waiting to be pushed along the paths and past the ponds of nearby Regents Park. Many of them were quite magnificent vehicles, one or two with monograms. But it was not only our immediate neighbours–everyone seemed to be prospering and enjoying themselves. Woolworths like Harrods was packed with good things and with people eager and able to pay for them. Fans in their scores of thousands streamed on Saturdays to the soccer stadiums, and millions more played the soccer pools. Twickenham and Lords were the arenas for great international encounters at rugby and cricket, making heavy inroads into newspaper space and television time. The Aussies were on one famous occasion, according to an inspired poster, *Licked, Locked and Lakered* (Locke and Laker being

30

two famous English bowlers). Geoff Griffin, South Africa's fast bowler, bowled a hat-trick at Lords, but was subsequently sent home for throwing. It was a national controversy in both countries. The theatre was flourising: there was no standing-room even in the Albert Hall for Malcolm Sargent's prom. concerts; and at Covent Garden the Bolshoi dancers were greeted with wild applause. The workers were being well paid, and the State looked well after those who had no work. Jack, the wife of our char, Eileen, seemed to be as much out of work as in, but Eileen explained that this made little difference to the family income. The national health scheme was in full swing, and people came from abroad on holiday to have their appendices taken out or false teeth put in at the expense of the British taxpayer. The taxpayer didn't mind: was it not true, as a Conservative election slogan was to claim before the decade was out, that he had never had it so good?

Yes. Britain it seemed was climbing aboard the utilitarian bandwagon to utopia. What was the nature of this vehicle? That is a question of immense importance to Britain and all of us today. Well, perhaps we could say that the designer of the vehicle was one Jeremy Bentham. Towards the end of the 18th century he had claimed that: "Nature has placed mankind under the governance of two sovereign masters, pain and pleasure. It is for them alone to point out what we ought to do as well as to determine what we shall do. On the one hand the standard of right and wrong, on the other the chain of causes and effects, are fastened to their throne." From this came the doctrine of the greatest happiness of the greatest number. That was to be the new criterion: the only rational guide both to private morals and public policy–the standard of value and the formula for successful government. Gradually through the 19th century the concept of liberalism, designed in the first place for the advantage of the industrial and commercial middle class, was extended to embrace the well-being of the whole community, and to provide for all a substantial measure of social and economic security. Together with this was a growing scepticism concerning the possibility of achieving social justice under a system of private enterprise and a corresponding demand for legislation to correct and humanise that system.

By the last quarter of the 19th century the way had been opened for the implementation in earnest of "the greatest happiness" principle–and a body of brilliant young people took the opening. Among them were George Bernard Shaw, Graham Wallas and Sidney and Beatrice Webb. In 1884 they founded the Fabian Society. The Fabians had comprehensive plans for transforming society, but perhaps their most notable characteristic was their patience. It was close on a hundred years since Bentham had first expounded his theories, and the Fabians were prepared for a further long delay before they were implemented. Their very name was taken from a Roman general called Fabius the Delayer because of the long-term strategy he employed. Their goal was the establishment of a society in which equality of opportunity would be assured and in which the economic power and privileges of individuals and classes would be abolished through the collective ownership of the economic resources of the community. In particular, they emphasised the equitable distribution of the national wealth. But in contradistinction to the Marxists they were committed to evolution as against revolution and to securing and maintaining their ends through parliamentary democracy.

The importance of the Fabians can scarcely be overstated. They set in train a movement which today, some maintain, has a greater impact on world affairs than the American Revolution, the French Revolution or the Russian Revolution. If this is as yet not more generally understood, it is not least because of the quiet and painstakingly gradual way they went about their task. In innumerable well-informed tracts they set out their beliefs and the practical means for attaining them. They addressed themselves to any person, any institution or any political party that was prepared to listen. But when their efforts to permeate the Conservative and Liberal Parties met with only limited success they helped to organise what, in 1906, became the Labour Party. Some sixty years after the establishment of the Fabian Society, Clement Attlee's Labour Party came to power and Britain was converted, without fuss, into a full-fledged welfare state. The construction of the utilitarian bandwagon was complete. The Conservative Party climbed aboard, and in the years I was in Britain everyone else was doing likewise. If not utopia then at least security from cradle to grave for the British people appeared to have been achieved.

Moral Leadership

Britons were also well satisfied with their international role. Were they not the beneficiaries again of one of those remarkable windfalls of history which so often in the past had dropped their way? At the very moment in history when, as a military power they had been overshadowed, military power was no longer decisive: it had been hamstrung by its own spectacular success, the atom bomb. Military power had become too powerful, potentially too destructive, to be used. In these circumstances, leadership in the world could be assumed by those with dominant moral strength: thus a nobler role even than before now awaited Britain.

She had at her disposal a worldwide stage for its performance. It was the British Commonwealth of Nations. The name of this remarkable association was first suggested by Lord Roseberry in Australia in 1884 (the year the Fabian Society was founded). In 1917 it was revived by

32

General Smuts; and for the next 30 years "the Commonwealth" described Britain and the Dominions–Canada, Australia, New Zealand and South Africa. India and the other dependencies constituted the Empire. Midway between the two world wars, the overseas Dominions won equal sovereignty with Britain under the Crown. With Britain as *primus inter pares*, this was a unique international grouping. Held together by a similar understanding of life, the same kind of political and social institutions, complementary economies and shared defence needs, it was a most potent and beneficent influence in the world. Britain was leader of the world, and the Commonwealth both strengthened and tempered her authority.

That was the first phase of the Commonwealth. The second began with the era of decolonisation following World War II. Churchill had declared that he had not become Prime Minister to preside over the liquidation of the Empire. Nevertheless, with the pressures coming from the Fabian-minded (the Fabian Society had established its Colonial Bureau in 1940) and the United States, the Empire was liquidated. The process could not be checked. But Churchill's successors welcomed it: they were confident that it could be turned to Britain's advantage by expanding the pre-war Commonwealth to include as sovereign members each and all of the emancipated territories. As Washington regarded the United Nations as an instrument for promoting its influence in the world, so did London regard the Commonwealth. It would secure for Britain the kind of place she had previously enjoyed in mankind's affairs. Her political position would be strengthened, and at the same time this great association of liberated wards–a vast congregation of men of different colour, culture and creed–would demonstrate the general validity and virtue of British institutions.

While the Americans hoped that the new African leadership would be attracted into their orbit, the Britons were confident it would remain in theirs. The Americans counted on reaction against the former overlord; the Britons, in continuing confidence and reliance on him. The British had a lot going for them: political institutions in the colonies based on theirs, and administrations staffed by their own men, the services of many of whom would still be required after independence; financial and trade ties; a positive response to Britain's readiness to withdraw, and the general advantages which membership in the Commonwealth would offer. These were seen as substantial factors in Britain's favour–and there was another, the ace of trumps:

Through the years a procession of young men and women had come from all quarters of the Empire to study in Britain. The Fabians, with their eye always on the future, understood the key part which this élite had to play in the fulfilment of their long-term plans, and they spared no effort to convert them to their philosophy. The London School of

Economics (a Fabian stronghold), it has been said, was regarded in Asia and Africa as the most important institution of higher learning. And in her autobiography, Beatrice Webb wrote that she and her husband "felt assured that, with the LSE as the teaching body, the Fabian Society as the propagandist organisation, the London City Council as object lesson in electoral success, our books as the only elaborate original work in economic fact and theory, no young man or woman who is anxious to study or to work in public affairs can fail to come under our influence." The confidence of the Webbs was well-founded; and the British socialism embraced by Gandhi and then by Nehru and the Congress Party at the time of India's independence in 1947 was seen as setting the pattern for the rest of the colonial empire.

However in 1947 it was not supposed by the Fabians (or anyone else in Britain) that independence for Africa was at hand. Committed as always to a steady, evolutionary and carefully-planned approach, they measured the distance from that goal in decades not years. The view held in those days was later described by Miss Margery Perham, who was closely acquainted with colonial administrators and had many friends and former students among the new black élites. "I recall the days", she said in a BBC talk in 1963, "when the desire of most of those Africans who suddenly saw African life with our eyes was to grow out of it and into ours as quickly as possible. I believe that at one time all, or nearly all, of us had hoped that the African majorities in settled areas would grow gradually, peacefully, into partnership with the ruling European as they gained the European level of education and prosperity. They would climb, perhaps, rung by rung the ladder of a qualified franchise."

That was the expectation: a step by step advance, in partnership with white settlers, towards independence in new non-racial nation-states, guided and moulded by British precepts–and those of the Fabians in particular. Amid much enthusiasm it was put to its first test in 1953 when the Central African Federation of Southern Rhodesia, Northern Rhodesia and Nyasaland was founded. The Federation was to be the model (and Pretoria especially should take note) of the proper management of race relations and constitutional development in Africa and elsewhere in the Commonwealth.

As for Britain herself, she would be the open, non-racial heart of this multi-racial community of nations. She would show that in an environment of tolerance and opportunity, all men could belong harmoniously and undifferentiated in a common society. Were not Britons tolerant people? Through all the generations of Empire, most of them quite honestly believed they were. Just and humane administration of dependencies thousands of miles away persuaded them that Britons had the knack of getting on with the natives; and those they encountered at home–the Africans at universities and the West Indians and the pukka

34

Indians at Lords and the Oval–were unquestionably capital chaps. But Eileen (our char) wasn't so sure in the second half of the 1950s. It wasn't that she disliked the blackies, it was just that they went about doing things in odd ways. For example there was the family in the flat next to hers, and they seemed to have parties with loud music till all hours of the morning every morning of the week. So my wife should please understand if sometimes she was a bit late for work.

On one occasion I visited the residential area of Birmingham that Jamaicans and Asians had moved into. There was the evidence I knew so well from our own experience of Indian penetration in Durban: falling property values, disgruntlement among established residents and a general latent tension. The local official who was showing me round conceded that it was the same in Birmingham but that the political parties, none of them, would tackle the issue. It was too hot a potato. He was quite right. The ideal of a non-racial society was shared and eagerly advocated by Socialists, Conservatives and Liberals alike; and during the 1950s when scores of thousands of people of colour were flooding into Britain, the three parties vied with one another in denying that the problems they brought with them had anything to do with race. They satisfied themselves and tried to persuade the people that the issue of race was, at most, incidental; that the real cause of whatever trouble there was, was confined to difficulties the newcomers experienced in obtaining housing, education, employment, credit facilities and other such non-racial matters.

All this being as it was, I met in opinion-making quarters in Britain an antagonism to apartheid as intense as in America, and much more substantial. The antagonism in America was largely emotional, but in Britain very real issues were at stake. Unlike Washington, London was directly responsible for millions of people in Africa. The three British Protectorates of Bechuanaland, Basutoland and Swaziland were either within or upon Pretoria's borders, as was the Central African Federation. In these adjoining regions of the sub-continent, Pretoria and London were applying diametrically opposed policies; and if British Governments were to persuade their electorate that theirs was right, it was necessary to show that Pretoria's was wrong. In addition, there was the abrasive effect of Pretoria's presence in the Commonwealth and the irritation it caused in Britain's relations with the non-white members. But as in the case of Washington–though much more so–there were factors which tempered London's official attitude. This country was one of Britain's most important markets and trading partners; it was an uncommonly rich and rewarding field of investment; its soldiers had fought in two world wars alongside Britain, and strategically it continued to be an important ally, especially in defending the Cape sea route.

However the very fact of a government attitude moderated until the 1960s by expedience, incited the agitators against apartheid. There was a host of them in London. Fabians and pseudo-liberals apart (they abounded also in Britain), London was the headquarters of the worldwide anti-apartheid campaign; and in the 1950s apartheid competed with the Campaign for Nuclear Disarmament as the focus of the new cult of protest and demonstration.

In the post-war years, the character of protest and demonstration–of dissent–underwent radical change. At South Africa House we had what might be called intimate experience of this, but soon learnt to regard it for what it was. For instance, on one occasion Dr. Verwoerd was speaking informally to a group of leading Fleet Street men in his suite in the Dorchester Hotel. The Prime Minister was in a relaxed mood, sitting in an easy chair with his back to an open window. The briefing lasted about an hour and all the time a throng in the street below was chanting "Fascist go home, fascist go home!" At the end of the meeting the newsmen shook hands with Dr. Verwoerd as they left. One of them (I think it was Tom Stacey, then of the *Sunday Times*) remarked: "I noticed, Mr. Prime Minister, you didn't pay any attention to all that noise outside. Didn't you hear it?" Dr. Verwoerd replied immediately: "Oh yes, I heard it but I took no notice, I know that isn't the voice of Britain." On another occasion, a group of demonstrating students held a cross above the entrance to South Africa House. We had to walk under it each time we entered or left the building–all of us, from the High Commissioner down to the messengers ... Protest marches, placards, slogans, abusive language, cursewords, spit, tomatoes, eggs, tacks (for sports fields), flour bombs, the cross–they showed much virtuosity, these modern dissenters. Extravagantly they were exploiting the reputation which dissent in an earlier age had accumulated.

Then, it had contributed substantially to social reform. The activity of the British suffragettes at the turn of the century is text-book stuff, and so is the protest made against unemployment and poverty in Britain in the 1930s. The success of operations of this kind enhanced respect for dissent; and as the 20th century advanced, dissent was increasingly regarded as something of a hallmark of democratic society and of a free and enlightened citizenry. But the motivation of post-war dissent was different, and perceptive observers have more recently explained why. John Lehmann, for one, pointed out a dozen years ago that the causes for which his and earlier generations protested were real. The suffragettes chained themselves to the rails of the House of Commons because of the demonstrable fact that those Britons who were female were not represented there. In the decade before World War II, many bright young men in Britain crusaded against the demonstrable fact that unemployed families were living ten to a room without bath or lavatory. John Lehmann was among them; and according to him there was, post-war, an inadequacy of such public events to excite the genuine response of the radical. Consequently, where dissent had previously been expressed for the sake of bettering clearly-distinguishable social conditions, it was now expressed for its own sake. Where causes had previously produced dissenters, dissenters now produced causes.

With everyone aboard that bandwagon to utopia, dissent had to find other targets–and it found them. Among them were the old loyalties and traditional values. It became the sign of the emancipated soul to scorn patriotism, the motherland and the means for its protection; to debunk God, the family and fidelity; to protest the suppression of licence and promiscuity; to crusade for the liberation of Humanity (not Humanity at Home, because that had already been taken care of, but Humanity Everywhere). Class distinction at home having been challenged by the State, new concepts for the elimination of all distinctions between men everywhere were formulated, and angry opposition was organised against those who upheld them and saw good in them. The dissenter was no longer moved by objective injustice in the conditions of society around him, but by subjective notions concerning mankind and the world at large. Characteristic in this department was the assumption that all men are the same, with the same inalienable right to go undifferentiated to the dogs.

Allied to protest and demonstration against apartheid, and organised by the same small groups of men, were moves to isolate, ostracise and boycott this country. Late in 1959 you could have found one such group busy at work in the basement of 200 Gower Street in London, below a doctor's surgery. Untidy, muddled and murky, it was the headquarters of the Boycott South Africa Movement. Working there were ex-patriates from South Africa–members of the African National Congress, the Indian Congress and the South African Liberal Party–and British sympathisers. They were engaged in the first of many efforts to break Pretoria's policies by external economic pressure: and in the process they were preparing the distribution of (literally) millions of pamphlets, arranging meetings around the country, lining up speakers, and organising protest marches and the picketing of South Africa House. The object of the exercise was to persuade British shoppers not to buy South African goods; and already the Gower Street group had enlisted powerful support–including the Trade Union Council, the Labour Party and newspapers like the *Guardian*.

In the event it all proved an excellent advertisement, not for the Boycott Movement but for South Africa's exporters. Shopkeepers

37

displayed the origin of South African goods more prominently than before. "Many people ask specifically for the stuff", one of them said in a newspaper interview, "so we make a point of advertising what it is." In the season that followed, sales soared. It was an augury of the counter-productivity of such campaigns. In our next period, 1960 to 1970–, protest and boycott were extended from pineapples and sherry to ostracism in sport, embargoes on arms supplies and proposals for a naval blockade and, if need be, an invasion.

CHAPTER THREE / 1945 to 1960
World Movements

(1) THE UNITED NATIONS

San Francisco

On April 30, 1945 Anthony Eden sent from San Francisco the following telegram to Churchill: "On the whole we are a pretty good Empire party here. Smuts has been most helpful at every point and we are giving him the chairmanship of the most important commission (on the General Assembly). Mackenzie King (of Canada) has intermittent colds in head and feet, brought on by the imminence of his general election, but on the whole he is in good heart and very helpful. Evatt (of Australia) and Fraser (of New Zealand) are making clear to the Americans and all concerned that we do not control their votes."

It is a fascinating passage. Britain might not control the votes of Australia and New Zealand, but for Eden and Churchill this was no "Commonwealth" but still an "Empire party" . . . some 15 years after the passage of the Statute of Westminster which declared Canada, Australia, New Zealand and the Union of South Africa to be Dominions no less sovereign than Britain. And it is clear from the telegram that South Africa, under General Smuts, was a most valued and respected member of the party. It stood as a symbol of reconciliation between Britain and Boer, of a thriving partnership between victor and vanquished based on fairplay and mutual confidence. In the war just ended, the Union's armed forces had made their full contribution; and generally it was a country highly regarded by Britain and the comity of nations. Then there was General Smuts himself, his wisdom so esteemed that during the war he had been consulted not only on Allied planning but on changes in the British Government. With Churchill he had a remarkable relationship.

He was one of the few men in no way awed by him: he would admonish him at one meeting for his strategic exuberance and, at the next, for over-taxing his physical strength. "The friendship of Churchill and Smuts always fascinated me", Eden wrote on another occasion. "They were such contrasting personalities; the one with his neat philosophic mind, the other a man 'so rammed with life'. I remember one evening, in particular, alone with them at Chequers. The horizon was beginning to clear and the talk was of future military plans. Mr. Churchill paced up and down the room, cigar in hand, his thoughts ranging widely. Smuts sat quietly in his chair, commenting occasionally and, almost literally, pouring water into the Churchillian wine. Yet the partnership was incomparable."

And at San Francisco, General Smuts was accorded an honour greater even than the chairmanship of the commission on the General Assembly: he was invited to draft the preamble to the Charter of the United Nations: and he drafted it as follows:

We, the peoples of the United Nations determine

To save succeeding generations from the scourge of war, which twice in our lifetime has brought untold sorrow to mankind, and

To reaffirm faith in fundamental human rights, in the dignity and worth of the human person, in the equal rights of men and women and of nations large and small, and

To establish conditions under which justice and respect for the obligations arising from treaties and other sources of international law can be maintained, and

To promote social progress and better standards of life in larger freedom,

And for these ends

To practise tolerance and live together in peace with one another as good neighbours, and

To unite our strength to maintain international peace and security, and

To ensure by the acceptance of principles and the institution of methods that armed force shall not be used, save in the common interest, and

To employ international machinery for the promotion of the economic and social advancement of all peoples.

Paris

In the year the National Party came to power, I was instructed to proceed from my foreign service post in Nairobi to Paris, and to join there the South African delegation–led by Mr. Eric Louw–to the Third General Assembly of the United Nations.

40

Paris, September, 1948: Gerhard Jooste (later Secretary for Foreign Affairs) and I were among the first of our delegation to arrive in Paris. The atmosphere was electric. The Berlin blockade was on; and on the first evening as we strolled along the sidewalks of the Champs Elysée, newspaper vendors were announcing the assassination of Count Bernadotte the Palestine mediator. But the cafes were gay for all that and we whiled away the time there. As we returned to our hotel, midnight struck. Two girls appeared from nowhere and stood immediately in front of us, barring our way. They spoke in French. I asked Gerhard what they were saying, and he explained they were saying it wasn't customary after midnight in Paris for men to return home alone. Then all at once they turned on their heels and walked sharply away. Why? I asked. Gerhard said he didn't know, but that in reply to a question he had just told them we were South Africans. We commented that our reputation must be pretty bad if to be South African was enough to put off a pair of Paris prostitutes. But we decided they probably supposed we were mocking them, as they would have had no doubt that all Africans–south, north, east and west–were black . . .

What a confusion of impression! On Thursday evening we attended a rendering of sacred music in honour of the UN Assembly in Notre Dame. It is a magnificent place, and the pomp and ceremony with all the flags of members of the United Nations flying from the walls was overwhelming. There were people of every nationality crowded into the great Cathedral listening breathlessly to the majestic music. There were two choirs–one in front of us and one way back behind us, high up somewhere. At the end there was a sevenfold amen: the amens came alternately from in front and from behind, meeting there above us . . .

The Assembly sits in the Palais de Chaillot. It is a vast place built recently, I understand, to house an exhibition. It looks out on to great expanses of lawn and, across the river, to the Eiffel Tower. The hall in which the Assembly gathers is actually a theatre: the delegates sit in the stalls and the public in the gallery. It is all done in red. In the "boxes" round the theatre and pushing and crowding along the aisles as the session is about to open are a host of photographers, cameramen, cartoonists, artists. I watch them working with their cameras and pencils. When the movie-men get going from high above, lamps are beamed on the various delegations they are interested in. When you are in the limelight, you can feel the heat on your face; and I believe we shall often be in the limelight, not so much because of our controversial policies as the alphabet.

The seating is alphabetically arranged, and so the Union of South Africa is in the immediate company of the United States of America, the Union of Soviet Socialist Republics, the United Kingdom and the Ukraine. That means that sitting within a few feet of me this morning were Manuilsky (of the Ukraine who is said to be a key man from behind the iron curtain),

41

Vishinsky of the Soviet Union, Ernest Bevin of England and George Marshall and Foster Dulles of the United States. There seems to be a casual–almost friendly–relationship between these men. I watched Hartley Shawcross (Britain) walk over to Vishinsky and take his hand as though he was greeting an old pal. Yet with no end to the Berlin blockade in sight, their two countries are on the brink of war. (4)

It was only three years before that the Great Powers in San Francisco had solemnly dedicated themselves to peace: but already they were in critical confrontation . . . and one of the small powers, the Union of South Africa, was already considering withdrawing from the world body. Why was it that so soon the United Nations was in such disarray? The terms of its association, the Charter, had been drafted with meticulous care and with the experience of the League of Nations to draw on. It had been understood at San Francisco that the essential requirement for an effective and lasting world organisation was that the sovereignty of its members should be entrenched and respected. To secure the sovereignty of the Great Powers, the formula arrived at was the veto: any one of the five permanent members of the Security Council–Britain, China, France, the Soviet Union and the United States–would be entitled to vote down any Council resolution. Roosevelt's dream of recruiting Russia to the cause of Western democracy was broken even before San Francisco, and without the veto neither country would have signed the Charter. With the veto, it was hoped that they would co-operate at least in areas where their immediate interests were not threatened. However the differences between them were too deep to be bridged by any kind of voting formula; and from the beginning, and while American influence in the world body was dominant, the Kremlin used the veto persistently to block all manner of effective action.

However it was not only the sovereignty of the Great Powers that was at issue: the small powers were no less insistent that theirs also should be safeguarded. For their part they, and General Smuts in particular, would not have signed had it not been for Article 2(vii) of the Charter. This Article states: "Nothing contained in the present Charter shall authorise the United Nations to intervene in matters which are essentially within the domestic jurisdiction of any State, or shall require members to submit such matters to settlement under the present Charter." There is no equivocation about 2(vii): there is no ambiguity about the word "nothing", nor could the language of the clause be clearer. In addition to that, there is the evidence of the intention of those who drafted it. One of them, Mr. Foster Dulles, speaking for the United States at San Francisco, said: "We have general principles which tell members that they must refrain from doing certain things, and also we have a principle which says to the world organisation: 'You too must refrain from doing certain

42

things. You must refrain from interfering in the domestic affairs of any member state.' "

Nevertheless, interference in South Africa's internal affairs began immediately. At the first General Assembly in 1946, *The Treatment of Indians in South Africa* was placed on the agenda and discussed. At that time General Smuts was leader of the South African delegation; and he reported back to Parliament in Cape Town: "I say we will stand behind the United Nations if it honours the Charter we drafted at San Francisco. If it does not do that it will fail. But it will not fail because of us: it will fail because it has not been true to its principles."

Pros and Cons of Membership

The warning was not heeded. At the Paris Assembly the Indian question was again on the agenda, as was South West Africa. South West Africa was a German colony which South African forces had conquered in World War I and which Pretoria was required to administer as an integral part of its own territory under a League of Nations mandate. From the beginning, the United Nations tried to bring South West Africa under its trusteeship system, but Pretoria maintained that it was not legally obliged to enter into a trusteeship agreement. As a result of increasing agitation on these two issues, the new Government in Pretoria was already in 1948 considering the termination of its United Nations membership. One of my first tasks as the delegation's public relations officer in Paris was to draft and distribute a series of answers to questions which were being asked in the committee rooms and corridors of the Chaillot about our policies; and one of them was: *Is South Africa's threat to leave the United Nations a bluff?* It was not: but then, and for the next 27 years, the advantages of membership were considered to outweigh the disadvantages. It was a delicate balance, the arguments for and against being as follows:

PRO: Since she became an independent country in 1910, Pretoria has made her full contribution to international affairs. At Versailles after World War I, her spokesmen were active in deliberations which preceded the setting up of the League of Nations and the related Mandates System. One of her representatives, Mr. Charles te Water, was subsequently a distinguished President of the League. Again at San Francisco in 1945 when the United Nations was conceived, Pretoria played a prominent part. Five years later she was one of only 16 countries to respond to the call of the Security Council to resist aggression in Korea. This is the broad background to the simple contention that Pretoria has every right to membership of the world body, that that right should be defended in all circumstances and that it should in no circumstances be yielded at the behest of a bunch of immature members whose positive contribution to international affairs has been negligible. Apart from principle, it is said moreover that it is expedient for Pretoria to stay. With much of the world condemning her policies and intent upon isolating her, the United Nations provides an important forum for stating her case and for maintaining contact with other nations. To resign would therefore be to play into the hands of her opponents. It could also threaten her position in important specialised agencies of the United Nations (such as the International Civil Aviation Organisation and the International Monetary Fund). Other *pro* points are these: friendly Western nations cannot be expected to speak up for Pretoria in the General Assembly (or the Security Council) unless she is prepared to do so herself: the patience, forebearance and civilised manner in which she has reacted throughout to extreme provocation has won wide respect among responsible members; and there is the danger that the vacating of her seat in the General Assembly might invite its occupation by some government-in-exile.

CON: The United Nations soon ceased to be an effective organisation: numerically dominated by underdeveloped states without real power, it degenerated into a talking-shop for which the substantial powers have little regard. Regularly Pretoria has stated her case in the General Assembly and its various committees: but the impact on hostile governments has been less than nil: it has been counter-productive: and there are many ways more effective than the turbulent channels of Turtle Bay by which Pretoria can speak to friendly governments. Membership has been used to distort and magnify Pretoria's international problems. For nine months of the year the embers smoulder beneath them: then, as the General Assembly meets in September each year, they take flame and blaze into the Republic's headlines. The enemies get, year after year for free, publicity which they could not buy for millions of dollars . . . and the copy-making factor is the presence in the Assembly and its Committees of Pretoria's delegates. Here is the prey offering itself to the predators to be demonstrated against, walked out upon, tormented, insulted and abused. More than anything else (so this argument goes), it is Pretoria's presence at the United Nations that keeps the agitation against her boiling, subjects her delegates to humiliations which ill become a self-respecting nation, and grossly exaggerates in the mind of the Republic's people the extent and quality of world hostility.

Such are the *pros* and the *cons:* but between the two courses which they suggest is a third. It is that Pretoria should not resign, but withdraw until such time as the world body learns to conduct itself in a civilised manner and in accordance with the provisions of the Charter. While remaining a member and keeping her right to vote in crucial issues, she would maintain only a token representation and take no active part in deliberations. The contention here is that in this way she would safeguard the advantages while diminishing the disadvantages of membership: denied the prey to bait, the annual anti-Pretoria circus at Turtle Bay would lose its main attraction.

Those are the three options debated through the years–but was there not perhaps, in the beginning at any rate, a fourth?

Paris, December, 1948: It was the last night of the Third General Assembly of the United Nations. We were sitting in the Press bar of the Chaillot, and Harold King, one of Europe's top political correspondents, was talking. "I can put your problem in a nutshell", he said to me. "You haven't learnt the first lesson in international politics. You are always sticking your necks out. You're too honest." There was a general discussion: and the consensus was that if we had to have discrimination then have it, but don't write it so blatantly in our laws. Instead, write into them a high-sounding objective about the equality and brotherhood of man. That was all that was needed to disarm the critics. India did it, and she got away with her caste system all the time. (5)

I was to hear that argument many times in the years that followed, and so were all of us who were involved in South African affairs abroad. The Government in Pretoria treated it with contempt. Whatever else may be said about the laws which they passed at home and the statements they made on the subject abroad, it cannot be said that they practised evasion. The wise boys with all their experience of international diplomacy were wrong on this one. The world line-up being what it was in 1948 and is today (or was until yesterday), this kind of subtlety would not have prospered long; and in the result a psychological advantage accumulated to Pretoria which with the passage of time has counted increasingly in its favour. It was in 1962 that the Nigerian Prime Minister observed–it seemed in exasperation–that Dr. Verwoerd and his Government and people spoke about apartheid "with so much honesty and sincerity".

Nevertheless, following 1948, the agitation against Pretoria and interference in its affairs increased year by year. In the early 1950s a three-man "apartheid" committee was set up to inquire into Pretoria's policies, and it produced a 513-page report dealing among others with the following subjects: land tenure, the public service, transport, the suppression of communism, the armed forces, nationality, the franchise, population movement, immigration, the professions, social services, health, criminal law, taxation, housing, the liquor trade, food subsidies, local government, labour conditions and pensions. There was, indeed, scarcely an aspect of the country's internal affairs that was not dealt with.

As well as reporting, the commission made recommendations and came to conclusions. Its general conclusion–in October, 1953–was that the situation in South Africa was becoming daily more explosive and that "soon the only way out will be through violence with its inevitable and incalculable dangers." Gerhard Jooste, Pretoria's representative, replied that the report was unwarranted, irresponsible and little short of an incitement to revolt–with the added implication that a revolt would have the sympathy of the United Nations. Two years later, the life of the Apartheid Committee was extended: Mr. Louw declared that this was a transgression of Article 2 (vii) more flagrant even than the one in respect of Algeria which had recently caused France to withdraw her delegation; and he instructed his delegation likewise to have no further part in the proceedings of the remainder of the session.

The next year, considering still that the *pros* of membership outweighed the *cons*, Pretoria returned to the General Assembly: and each year for the following two decades submitted itself to the Assembly's annual hammering. It was not until 1975 that it again followed the course taken by Mr. Louw 20 years before.

(2) The Church

Evangelism and Politics

There have been three broad phases in the work of the Church among the black peoples of Southern Africa, represented respectively by the pioneer missionary, the political missionary and the social gospeller.

To the pioneer missionaries as much as to anyone else must go the honour of making the sub-continent known to the outside world. It was they who often established the bridgeheads of civilisation. Their primary motive was to bring Christianity to the black people, but together with their religion they brought also tools and ploughs and crops which Africa had not known before. In order that the natives might learn Christianity they had to be taught to read and write, and thus the missionaries became also the first educators. The Bible has been translated into some 300 African languages and this likewise was the work of the missionaries. It enabled the black people not only to go to the source of Christianity themselves but, through their language now in written form, to commit to paper their tribal traditions and folklores and to produce a literature of their own. In this way the pioneer missionaries established the bridgeheads of civilisation, but they would not have been able to hold them and extend them alone. White settlers–farmers, traders, professional men–were also necessary, and they were forthcoming. Mission

46

outposts were transformed into villages, villages into towns, and civilisation became rooted in this strange environment. Thus the first missionaries and the settlers were partners in a common undertaking, and there is much evidence of comradeship and mutual trust between them. These men of the Church were respected by the settlers because they had also given themselves hand, heart and soul to Africa.

The Belgian Congo, 1942: I shared a compartment after leaving Elizabethville with a dying man. He was already there, lying on one of the bunks, when I boarded the train, a heavy bandage with a dark yellow stain bound round his head. From the clothes he wore it was obvious he was a missionary. As I stood in the doorway he raised his hand as though to say he was sorry to be a nuisance, and then it fell limply back. His companion in the corridor told me he had a tumor on the brain and that a series of operations in Cape Town had been unsuccessful. He came originally from France: he had not seen his family for many years; and when it became known that there was no hope for him, arrangements were made to send him home. But he would have none of it: he insisted on returning to his station in the Congo to die. He was on his way there now. Two or three hours out of Elizabethville the train stopped at a small halt in the sultry heat of mid-afternoon. The platform was thronged with black children, dancing about with their hands above their heads, waiting to catch whatever might be thrown to them from the train. Suddenly the centre of interest changed. A truck backed in across the platform, and in a second or two the children congregated about it. There was much gesticulating, and then the children saw who it was being carried on a stretcher from the train. There was complete silence. The merriment was removed from their faces as though it were a mask. Some of them said softly, "Ow!", some of them clasped their hands and others raised them. They said quietly what meant: "Father, Father!". The truck moved off. It moved slowly through the leaden atmosphere along a dry, treeless track until it disappeared from view in the dust. (6)

I do not know the name of that man, and the world certainly does not know it: he did not seek publicity and he was given none. There were these two types of missionary in Southern Africa. Most of them were like this one who in the end went back to his station. But there were also the political missionaries. They too worked for the advancement of the black people; but in their effort to achieve it, treated with contempt the beliefs and rights of others whose home is equally Africa, and set themselves up as the arbiters of a sub-continent's destiny. Among the first of the political missionaries in the early 19th century were van der Kemp and Read of the London Missionary Society. They took upon themselves the role of prosecutors-in-chief of the Cape settlers, supporting whatever charge however unsubstantial of maltreatment of non-white people that was brought against them. In 1819 John Philip stepped on to the scene to co-ordinate the anti-settler campaign. Superintendent of the London Society's stations in South Africa, he was a man of influence in Britain, and in the late 1820s travelled home to whip up feeling against the white men in the Cape. Towards this end he published a book entitled *Researches in South Africa*, and enlisted the backing of the powerful philanthropic societies. In his day he was regarded abroad as a great Christian: but later, historian G. McCall Theal was to declare that in championing the cause of the coloured people he acted as a general might who was determined to win a victory but was indifferent as to the weapons he used: to secure support and confidence, he said and wrote and did much "that all who are regardful of truth must pronounce decidedly wrong." I. Agar-Hamilton wrote of Philip as a provoker of native wars, and expressed the opinion that he was largely responsible for the beginning of the long conflict between Boer and Briton.

The campaign was continued through the 19th century–by, among others, John Mackenzie. In 1882 the spectacle was repeated of a missionary hastening back to England "with a firm determination to educate public opinion on the position in South Africa and to induce people and government to accept their imperial responsibilities." Of Mackenzie, the noted South African author Sarah Gertrude Millin wrote: "He was a virtuous, courageous and determined man. By the time he had finished doing his duty to the Bechuana, a number of people were thoroughly hating and distrusting one another and still more the professed servants of God."

The Campaign Continues

The campaign continued deep into the 20th century and culminated in Father Trevor Huddleston. In 1943 he was sent to take charge of a mission in Sophiatown, a Johannesburg slum inhabited mainly by blacks. The station was run by the Community of the Resurrection, a monastic institution within the Church of England. When the National Party government came to power in 1948 it put into operation a vigorous slum-clearance programme. Sophiatown was one of the slums to be removed, its inhabitants to be settled in a new township called Meadowlands. This sparked Father Huddleston's hatred of the Afrikaner Government, of its policy of separatism and more particularly of its measures for controlling the influx of black people from the rural to the urban areas–the "pass laws". Like Philip some 125 years before, he had published in England–in 1956–a book to acquaint the British public with his feelings. It was called

48

Naught for Your Comfort. Passionately and poetically written, few books have ever received greater publicity in the British press; and, ranking with Alan Paton's *Cry the Beloved Country,* it was a major influence in turning world opinion against Pretoria. In his writing, broadcasting and television appearances in Britain, Father Huddleston was supremely confident that it had been given to him to interpret Christian principle in the context of South African race relations, and he felt justified in carrying his campaign into the homes of millions of Britons. The issue as he saw it, he stated with great force and vehemence: Pretoria's policies were evil, they must be smashed, and the way to smash them was through pressure from abroad. It was he, in the mid-1950s, who advocated the boycotting and isolating of Pretoria, economically and in sport, and its expulsion from the Commonwealth.

But persuasive though he was, his arguments were based in emotion, not reason. This is how he described Sophiatown: "Above it all you see the Church of Christ the King, its tower visible, north, south, east and west, riding like a great ship at anchor upon the grey and golden waves of the town beneath . . . Why should we care so much to preserve what, on any showing, is two-thirds a slum area? I know Sophiatown at its worst: in all weather, under all conditions, as a slum living up to its reputation. I still love it and believe it has a unique value . . . The over-crowded rooms of Sophiatown, wherein whole families must sleep and must perform all their human functions as best they may, do not make morality an easy thing . . . So you have to be prepared if you live in the midst of it as a priest, for every conceivable problem at every hour of the day or night. How, then, can you fail to love it? You are home, your children are around you—ten of them, a hundred, a thousand: you belong to them and they will never let you forget it. How then can you fail to love the place where such things happen? Its dusty, dirty streets and its slovenly shops, its sprawled and unplanned stretches of corrugated iron roof: its foetid and insanitary yards.

As I pointed out in my reply, *You Are Wrong Father Huddleston,* an attitude such as this to a slum cannot be explained in ordinary terms: this is the approach of the poet or the mystic. Father Huddleston saw ugliness as beauty (though the slum-dwellers didn't), and the transforming agent *for him* was love. He tells how he won the love of the people there; and their moving to Meadowlands meant he would lose it. It was the flock being taken beyond the reach of the shepherd: the new pastures might be better (as Father Huddleston freely admitted they were) but they were beyond his reach. But it is absurd to contend that because a man experiences love in a slum, the slum is thereby justified. Yet in his encounter with Pretoria, Father Huddleston had the world on his side. It is a stark indictment of the nature of the world's hostility to the Afrikaner and his government.

And condemnation of its policies was no longer confined to churchmen with a special interest in South Africa: in sermons and prayers around the Western world it was a recurring theme. On a Sunday morning in 1952 I attended a suburban service in Ottawa. The service was entitled "Driftwood". People, said the minister, were the driftwood. He mentioned some of the currents that were sweeping them away, and then he came to the current of race prejudice. He described how he had been in an hotel one evening in the Southern states with a distinguished Negro professor. A crowd gathered in the street below, clamouring that the Negro should leave: he wasn't allowed in that part of the town at that time. The people in front of the hotel were blameworthy (said the minister) insofar as they didn't resist the current. But the real evil was the leaders who set the current in motion and gave it direction. One day they would come face to face with their Maker, but today it was the duty of all Christians to raise their voice against them. "Consider for a moment what is happening in South Africa", he said. "The leader of that country professes to be a Christian, a doctor of divinity, a man who holds powers in the name, he says, of God by exploiting the racial differences of his fellow men. I tell you, my friends, that what the leaders in South Africa are doing today is enough to bring tears to the eyes of Christ."

The congregation of Canadians that morning did not have the facts against which to measure the minister's remarks (I doubt whether the minister had them himself): and perhaps they felt some satisfaction in having the blame for race prejudice in North America shifted in this way to the white man in South Africa. But what was exercising my mind more then was the effect of this kind of attack on my own people. Political, economic and military action they could deal with without any trouble to their conscience: but would not this persistent campaign by the Church ultimately cause them to doubt and undermine their morale, or embitter them and warp their judgment? Well, that was in 1952, and in the quarter of a century since then, it has not happened. I think a main reason is that the censure of the Church was soon to be stripped of all Christian and moral authority. Following men like Father Huddleston and the minister in Ottawa came the exponents of the social gospel–of the theology of Christ as a secular revolutionary and of a god who was dead. We shall be taking a look at this theology later: meantime it is enough to say that in betraying the fundamental faith of Christianity it forfeited altogether the respect of the Anglo-Afrikaner. And if the Church's censure was not worthy of respect, whose was? Surely not that of politicians or governments or the United Nations or the Organisation of African Unity? The condemnation of a morally-bankrupt Church had the counter-productive effect of generally strengthening Pretoria's determination.

CHAPTER FOUR / 1945 to 1960
Black Africa

Africa–the Pernicious Friend

Of Africa that perceptive observer, Hendrik van Loon, wrote in *Van Loon's Geography:* "Then what is wrong with this continent? I don't know. Everything is there but nothing seems to be where it could possibly be of any use to anyone. The whole arrangement is wrong. With the exception of the Nile, all the rivers and mountains and lakes and deserts serve no purpose. Even the Nile, which at least flows into a sea of great commercial importance, is hampered by too many cataracts. As for the Congo and the Niger, they have no comfortable access to the sea, while the Zambesi starts where the Orange River should end and the Orange River ends where the Zambesi should start. Modern science may eventually make the desert bear fruit and drain the marshes. Modern science may find ways to cure the dysentery and the sleeping sickness which have wiped out entire countrysides in the Sudan and the Congo regions, as modern science has set us free from yellow fever and malaria. Modern science may turn the high central and southern plateaus into replicas of the French Provence and the Italian Riviera. But the jungle is strong and persistent and the jungle has a handicap of millions of years. Let modern science relax but for a moment and the jungle and all its atrocities will be back at the white man's throat and will throttle him and it will breathe its poisonous breath into his nostrils until he dies and is eaten by the hyenas and the ants."

> *Aboard a paddle-steamer on the Lualaba (Congo, Zaire) River, 1943:* As we approach the villages on the river banks, there are always naked native children waiting. They plunge into the water among the crocodiles and swim out to us. They come a hundred feet and more from the banks, shrieking with delight and wiping the water from their shining faces . . .

51

What do they come for? They don't seem to want the money we drop them: they don't seem to want the bread: they seem only to want to get as close as they can to this strange evidence of another world. And as the boat passes on, a host of black balls bob about in the water behind. These are the dark children on their way back, back among the crocodiles, back after their thrilling adventure, to their shacks on the bank of the Lualaba.

It has been intensely hot. All day the sun blazed on the river so that we couldn't look out without shielding our eyes. When dusk came, the harshness suddenly lifted, and the singing of the birds and the other daytime noises stopped. The boat seemed unreal then in the quiet beauty that surrounded it, and it moved on silently and smoothly like a reflection across the ripples. To where the sun was setting, the earth spread out still and uninterrupted. The papyrus stood gaunt along the banks and disappeared into shadows in the distance. Fish eagles made streaks of black across the water on their way home. The sun disappeared, and the searchlight was switched on to cast a beam of yellow across the water. The croaking of the frogs began, from the banks and from the horizon.

It was difficult to sleep that first night, and I lay awake listening to the churning of the paddle. Then I pulled on my gown and went out on the deck. The stars were intensely bright: the milky-way was like a heavy fog driven across the heavens and dividing them in two. I leant over the rails and could see the sparks of burning wood which eddied from the funnel, mingled momentarily with the stars and floated down like flakes of golden snow until they touched the water and oblivion. I fancied that the River chuckled as he snuffed them out and that it was a chorus of derision that came from the nightbirds and from the insects that buzzed around my head and from the frogs. Our boat seemed a trespassing midget, surviving only at the pleasure of the vast power that closed it in. And I thought that if the old River did chuckle, I knew the reason why. He was a symbol of Africa, of the Dark Continent. Through the centuries he had rolled on, unmoved and unchanged by the affairs of men. He had seen men die from the diseases that rose from his waters and he had heard them cry out to be avenged against the works of nature–the droughts and the floods, the animals, the insects and the reptiles. He had watched all this bar their progress, but he had rolled on.

And yet now, holding back the papyrus so that boats could pass freely by were man-made stakes driven into the earth beneath the swamp. Threaded through the forest I had seen during the day telephone wires. At one port where we stopped the quay was heaped high with thousands of ingots of tin. The mine was far away, about 30 miles, I believe. But the forests and swamps and mosquitoes had been overcome and a railway had been put down. Holes had been dug in the earth and the minerals that came from them were being shipped along the rivers to industries and armament factories across the world.

52

Were we just a trespassing midget or, perhaps, the vanguard of a force greater even than Nature in Africa? Sensing the magnitude of the wild power that surrounded me, I was given an inkling of why it was that Africa for so long had withstood the encroachment of civilisation. What would be the outcome of the clash now developing between civilisation and Africa? The outcome, I thought, would depend neither on Africa nor civilisation alone: between the two was a third force that would be the determining factor. It was the black man. If, in his millions, he could be allied to civilisation, civilisation would triumph: if not it was doomed. (7)

In those thousands of years that he moved south through the Dark Continent, the black man brought little light–the light of technological progress–to it. The odds against him were too heavy. His environment provided him with no incentive. Food, not in abundance but enough, came relatively easily from the earth. The climate was kind, so kind that it demanded little enterprise in the making of clothes and homes, but enervating. Deserts, jungles and disease belts and the bowl-like shape of the sub-continent, with mountain ramparts and unnavigable rivers at its rim, cut its peoples off from the outside world, while the vast spaces of Africa isolated them from one another. Through the millennia they fragmented into some 5,000 tribes, each with its own customs and beliefs and with a language unintelligible to others.

In these conditions it was relatively easy for them to continue to live, but difficult to improve their material conditions of life. That is in the nature of Africa: it is a continent of contrast without gradations, and it did not provide the opportunity for gradual development. The obstacles on the way to civilisation could not be overcome step by step: they demanded the type of evolutionary hurdle which men cannot make. Progress had to await the arrival of skills and technique devised through the ages in more helpful surroundings. Nature in other parts of the world was the stimulating opponent of man: in Africa it was his pernicious friend. For these reasons the black people, left to themselves, were destined to survive but not to progress. In the circumstances they adopted the common-sense course of making their survival as pleasant as possible. For the accomplishment of the every-day affairs of life which they could understand and direct they worked out a rare pattern of co-operation among themselves, and to deal with the things they could not understand they relied upon the supernatural powers they believed responsible for them. The tribe was the organisation which encompassed both these functions: it was responsible alike for the natural and supernatural welfare of its individual members. Everything that the tribe possessed–its land, animals, crops and the very lives of its people–were the property of the Chief. He was not only the sovereign but the symbol of the community's common interests: according to H. P. Junod, the noted authority on the

Bantu people of Southern Africa, he was the earth, he was the supreme ruler and judge.

Loyalty to the tribe, embodied in the Chief, was the foundation of Bantu society and the explanation of Bantu behaviour and moral sense. The question was not whether this action was good and that bad but whether it was in the interests of the tribe. Co-operation and harmony depended on the like-mindedness of the individual tribesmen: there was an instinctive suspicion of foreign things and the motives of others: any deviation from the common and normal disturbed the equilibrium and called, moreover, for the corrective attention of the witchdoctor. He was the intermediary: the link between the natural and the supernatural—and the supernatural intruded into every aspect of the Bantu's daily life. The men, the huts, the trees which he saw about him were only part of his experience: the spirits that continually hovered over him and the spells of the sorcerer that ensnared him were the other and more important part. If his crops failed it was because the "medicine" with which he had treated his fields was not strong enough. If he was sick it was because the spirits were displeased with him or because a mortal enemy had bewitched him.

When I was a boy in Zululand, Zaba, our cook, talked to me about some of these things, as he squatted in his white uniform cleaning pots beside the rainwater tank in the back yard. I would tell him about the tall buildings and shops I had seen in Durban; and it was from him that I learnt for the first time about the god of the Zulus, the Unkulunkulu, the great-great one. He was the first man, and he was the cause of all other men. "We do not know his wife", the Zulus say, "and the ancients did not tell us he had a wife. We heard it said that he broke off the nations from uthlanga, the reed. After man had been made, the great-great one sent a chameleon to him to proclaim his immortality. 'Go, Chameleon, and say: Let no man die.' The chameleon set out, but slowly. It loitered on the way and was delayed further by the *ubukwebezane* tree, the fruit of which it found most tasteful. Then the great-great one sent a lizard to proclaim to man his mortality: 'Lizard, when you have arrived, say: Let men die.' The lizard hurried and made his proclamation, and by the time the chameleon was through with his loitering, his happy news was too late. 'Oh, we have already heard the word of the lizard', men said. 'Now we cannot hear your word.' And the lizard having said that death would be, the great-great one gave men the spirits of the dead and doctors and diviners to care for them.

"At first we saw that we were made by the Unkulunkulu", the Zulus say, "but when we were ill we did not worship him nor ask anything of him. We worshipped those whom we had seen with our eyes, their death and their life among us. So then we began to ask all things of the *amadhlozi*, our ancestor spirits, whether for corn or children or cattle or health. By then it began to be evident that Unkulunkulu had no longer a

54

son who could worship him. There was no going back to the beginning, for people increased and were scattered abroad and each house had its own connections. And we are now like children who have no father or mother, who have their own wills about things they would not do if their father and mother were still living. But when anyone finds fault with us, we say to him at once: 'Since you say it is not proper that this thing should be done, why did Unkulunkulu create what is evil?' And the other is silent."

Partners in Civilisation

Are not we white men, most of us, confronted with the same problem? And though the black man built little of stone or steel, he wrought from his own hard environment qualities of spirit that evoke admiration and envy. Where machines and mathematics, technology and organisation are not involved, there is little that we can teach and much that we can learn from him. It is true that his easily-aroused emotions can cause him to act with quick violence, but he is by nature patient, long-suffering and courteous. He is capable of great generosity to his kith and kin. In his traditional upbringing he is taught that a good person is not quarrelsome but peaceful, that he does not use abusive words, that he shares his food with others and is hospitable, that he keeps secrets told to him, that he tries to reconcile families that hate one another, that if he sees a person developing bad habits he stops him and talks to him–though not in front of others. Many black people have an instinctive good taste, a feeling for decorum. Walking through the streets of Johannesburg it often strikes me that they have even a better sense of dress–particularly the mothers and their children–than many white women. They laugh easily (though loud laughter is frowned upon by the well-mannered among them), and they sing beautifully–a false note is unknown to them. Most of their languages are a pleasure to hear, and grammatically are complex and sophisticated. A Zulu in the city who hears a wrong word or a wrong construction will quickly correct his fellow. Oratory comes naturally to them and they revel in debate and discourse. "Africans", according to a leading British expert, Richard Cox, "are indeed innocent in the fields of engineering and economics. But they are born politicians: from birth they have played in the shade while their elders wrangled." Thomas Hodgkin writes in his *Nationalism in Colonial Africa* of the black man's pride in the qualities of pre-European African societies: "their achievements in such fields as the plastic arts, work in gold and bronze and ivory, music and dancing, folk story and folk poetry; the complexity and depth of their religious beliefs and metaphysics; their conception of the community as consisting of the dead, the living and the unborn; their rational attitude to sexual relations and to the place of women in society; their delight in children and reverence for the aged; their view of education as a process continuing through life; their dislike of autocracy, and their delicate political mechanisms for securing the expression and adjustment of different interests and wills."

There is every reason for the black man's pride in these qualities which marked his traditional society: and that brings me back to the question I pondered on the Lualaba River a generation ago: Can the black man in his millions be allied to civilisation? In modes of personal behaviour, I believe he has the capacity not only to ally himself to civilisation but to enrich it. In religion, should it not be possible to take Zaba and his people back to the beginning, to return the authority of the spirits and the diviners to the Unkulunkulu and, with the help of Christian teaching, to persuade them to acknowledge him as the great-great caretaker of all the tribes of men? Those best able to express an opinion say that their traditional religion enables the Bantu to appreciate at once the very centre of Christianity, and that it prepares them excellently for a comprehension of the idea of the paternity of God. And there is another wondrous bridge between the black man and Western culture–or, at any rate, Anglo-Afrikaner culture: we share in like manner that redeeming grace in life–a sense of humour. Although white and black minds are mysteries to each other in so many ways, there is this remarkable fact that we laugh at the same things. A joke which I crack, immediately grasped by my black companion, might be incomprehensible to an Oriental and fall pretty flat with some Europeans.

It is in the areas of technology that the black man is so utterly dependent on Western culture–and in the related areas of efficiency, organisation, administration, planning, conservation, exertion and perseverance. And though these may be among the less attractive of human attributes, the brutal fact is that in the modern world the very survival of the black man–of his culture and all its fine characteristics–rests upon them. According to a United Nations *Review of Economic Conditions in Africa,* published in 1951, black Africa is economically among the least developed regions of the world, with the lowest of levels of production and consumption. It is caught in the throttling grip of a backward subsistence economy. Three-quarters of its people–the highest of any continent–are engaged in a primitive type of agriculture, their productivity being the worst anywhere whether measured per person or per acre. "These are basic conditions of its past and present", writes Professor Rupert Emerson of Harvard. "The tragic cycle of poverty repeats itself endlessly: malnutrition, ill-health, lack of sanitary and medical facilities, inadequate skills and techniques, lack of capital and an economy based either on low-standard subsistence production or on export industries from which Africans derive a meagre living wage." And he observes: "There is on the face of it no reason to assume that, if there had been no European intervention, Africa would have overcome its age-old poverty."

This explains why Nature in Africa has always held the whip hand: but the question on the paddle-steamer concerned the new prospect for the contest between Nature and the black man, now that he had the white man's know-how to help him. I was on my way then to join the staff of the South African Commissioner in Nairobi and, in broad terms, that issue was dominant during the six years I served there. My job was to foster co-operation between Pretoria and East Africa; and this was but part of a larger plan for co-operation for the development of the sub-continent as a whole. In 1945 General Smuts convened a conference in Cape Town of the representatives of eight Southern African Governments to discuss plans for common action. The redemption of Africa, he told the delegates, had already reached an advanced stage: it was a call not to be daunted by Africa's vast problems but, by combined effort, to work for its further development. During Dr. Malan's Premiership, the Commission for Technical Co-operation in Africa South of the Sahara was established: it consisted of European Governments with colonies in Africa, and Pretoria. This was the pattern: co-operation among white governments for the benefit of Africa and the black man, but without his participation. In the enlightened colonialism of those days the black man's interests were given high priority: but he was the ward, not yet able to stand on his own feet in the strenuous circumstances of the modern world (the words of the League of Nations Mandates System), and not yet fit to take part in decision-making and planning. With at least three out of four of his numbers illiterate and with black university graduates in some of the colonies countable on the fingers of two hands, it was not an unreasonable attitude.

In my six years in Nairobi I had no dealings at all with black men in responsible positions because there were none such. When I arrived the only representative of Kenya's black people was one white man, the Rev. Leonard Beecher. Before I left, a black man–Mr. Eliud Mathu–was appointed to the Legislative Council, but this was merely token representation. Legco was run by members of the colonial administration and representatives of the handful of white settlers. All my official contacts were with one or other of these two groups. Discussion on colonial matters centred on how best white men could govern black. Should there be direct rule or indirect rule (the use, that is, of traditional black authorities as agents of the colonial government)? Endless debates and long chapters in a book such as Lord Hailey's monumental *An African Survey* were devoted to that subject. Was not the Belgian Congo (to explode in chaos as the 1960s began) a model of colonial management? Had Tanganyika been worse or better administered by the

57

Germans before than by the British after World War I? . . . and so on. Nowhere, as a matter of practical politics, was attention given to the possibility of the governing of the colonial territories by black men: their effective participation would no doubt come in due course, but not in the foreseeable future–perhaps by the turn of the century. Meantime a seat or two in Legco, an added power to the local jurisdiction of a Chief here and there would meet the situation.

In 1946 I worked with Sir Alfred Vincent, leader of the Kenya settler community, on a speech to support a proposal he was to put before Legco. The speech was duly made and the proposal carried. It was for a Pan-African conference. Nothing could have demonstrated more clearly the radical change that so soon was to come. Sir Alfred's Pan-African conference envisaged a gathering of white governments to promote the sub-continent's interests: the Pan-African movement started by Kwame Nkrumah was designed to overthrow white governments, despite the sub-continent's interests.

Fallacies of the New Politics

The admirable qualities of the black man I have written about had not equipped him in the past to deal with Africa or to participate in the present in a materialistic, competitive, technological, Western-orientated world. And in the new nationalistic role he was about to assume, even his flair for politics, his oratory and rhetoric were to serve him ill: they camouflaged his dearth of actual potential for progress and caused himself and others grossly to over-estimate his real capacity for governing in a technological age. Moreover in the years preceding decolonisation, the authority of the traditional leaders (the custodians of those admirable qualities) was increasingly taken over by what have come to be called "urban élites". According to Professor Walter Goldschmidt of the University of California in 1963: "The new leadership is recruited from among that element of the African population which is most highly acculturated, most thoroughly urbanised, and alienated from their tribal backgrounds. The very fight for independence required such persons who are impatient with old ideas. Nkrumah, Mboya and Nyerere have all expressed in one way or another their distaste for tribal orientations and old customs, and have acted to destroy or diminish the powers of traditional leaders."

The nature of black society and the mode of its politics were drastically altered. The ancient form of political discussion ("the elders sitting under the big tree and talking till they agree", in the words of Nyerere) gave way to the mass meeting: and though the new leaders like Kenyatta

58

might address a crowd of 30,000 and receive tumultuous applause, it was the emotional response of the moment, without firm foundation, fragile and undependable. "When this technique of mass emotion meets Western voting methods (in the view of British Africanist Richard Cox) it gives crushing majorities to the popular leaders. If this gives them strength to act boldly, it also encourages impetuous, conceited behaviour. It reinforces the chance of absolute power: but the real danger arises when this mass majority comes from one tribe and is founded on tribal loyalty. On the surface the new leaders are 20th century men, but underneath they are overwhelmingly subject to the feeling of their tribe."

The arbitrary drawing of the colonial boundaries had taken no account of this overriding issue of tribalism. They included haphazardly within them members of different tribes and separated members of the same tribe. Nevertheless the élitist leaders, as they moved towards and achieved independence, insisted on retaining the colonial borders–believing, with the encouragement of the metropolitan powers, that this difficulty could be solved by introducing the concept of the nation-state. But the concept was totally foreign to Africa, and its importation was an error of a most fundamental and incalculably dangerous order. In spatially-restricted Europe, where the nation-state originated, communities had staked out their claims to territory, settled there and by dint of skill and care brought from the earth–a fixed number of acres of it–their requirements. They stood together in defence of it when it was threatened, and their territory–their "country", their nation-state–was the focus and inspiration of their common interest and loyalty. In spatially-expansive, thinly-populated Africa, it was very different. There, communities carelessly took from the earth what it offered and then, its bounty exhausted, moved on. Similarly, when they were threatened by a stronger community, they did not unite in defence of their land but readily abandoned it–since there was much to be had elsewhere. The unifying factor in their society was not land but tradition and custom, encompassed by the tribe and personified in the Chief. A warrior would readily have understood, would have taken for granted, that he should if need be fight and die for his King: but to fight and die for his country would have been totally incomprehensible to him. In the 1957 edition of his *An African Survey,* Lord Hailey rejected the term "nationalism" to describe the contemporary political movement in Africa: African peoples brought together only by the accidents of history lacked the tradition of a common origin and a common outlook on their political future: "the majority have in the past missed the dynamic influence of the concept of territorial nationalism." Nevertheless the Western world and the élitist leaders regard tribalism as anachronistic, and proceeded with their endeavour to substitute a shared loyalty to a state–a stretch of land–as the means of uniting the disparate individuals within its borders. With tribalism denigrated and discarded,

59

the prospect for a stable and harmonious political structure built on the unsubstantial foundation of the nation-state was poor indeed. The cement of black society is likemindedness among kith and kin: and in the degree that the culture of the black man through the millennia was a culture of movement, that cement has been strengthened: historically, it has nothing to do with attachment to territory.

Meantime, the terms of the conflict as I had seen it that night on the Lualaba River were being tragically transformed: no longer Africa vs. white and black together: but black vs. white, with Africa waiting to reassert her primeval authority.

Part One / Section one
1945 to 1960

The Pretoria Theme:
Separatism

In 1912 my maternal grandfather, Lynn Lyster, had his *Ballads of the Veld-Land* published (by Longmans, Green) to celebrate the establishing of Union two years before. The first piece was about a mother telling her children of the heroic events in South African history; and it ended:

> When they ask her of our heroes
> Will their lineage she trace,
> Naming this one Boer or Briton?
> Will she speak of blood or race?
> Nay! for she will whisper softly
> In those quiet evening hours,
> Looking down the years' dim vista,
> " 'Tis enough to call them ours".

CHAPTER FIVE / 1945 to 1960
The White Nation

The Afrikaner

While Americans were planning the reformation of mankind and Britons were introducing their welfare state at home and their new Commonwealth abroad, Afrikaners were tackling the problem of establishing a *modus vivendi* among what is perhaps the most heterogeneous population on earth. For the first time in close on half a century–since the defeat of the Boer Republics by Britain–an all-Afrikaner Government was in power.

Who were these Afrikaners? The objective facts about them are well enough known. Their first forebears, mainly Dutch but some German, settled in the Cape in the years following the establishing there of a half-way house to the East by the Dutch East India Company in the mid-17th century. Soon they were joined by a group of Huguenots fleeing from religious persecution–and the vitality of this strain is attested to by the column upon column of French names which appear in our telephone directories today. These settlers–the Boers, or farmers–moved year by year further from Cape Town into the interior. When, after some 100 years, they first met the black man migrating southward along the coastal belt, they struck northward into the hinterland, and in the second half of the 19th century set up the Republics of the Orange Free State and the Transvaal. It was these Republics that were conquered by Britain as the 20th century opened.

Such are the objective facts. But *what* were these Afrikaners: *how* were they? That is an altogether different question and one about which there is much ignorance and misrepresentation. Let us take a look first at the way in which men in the outside world depicted the Afrikaners as they assumed responsibility for the destiny of this country and its people. The

' following vignette was provided by the *Guardian,* London, on December 16, 1949:

Today at Pretoria a great concourse . . . will see the Voortrekker Monument unveiled . . .

South Africans will meditate on the heroic qualities of the Voortrekkers. For they were heroic. Whatever their shortcomings, whatever the false lessons that may have been drawn from their experience when applied to today's problems, nothing can detract from the quality of the men themselves. Their journey is comparable with that of the Pilgrim Fathers to New England, of the early Mormons to Utah, perhaps with that of the children of Israel to the Promised Land. They were not, like Cortez's men, adventurers who became colonists almost by chance; or like the early British traders to India, merchants maintaining a barricaded foothold on the coast for a few years till they made their fortunes and went home. Like Abraham leaving Ur, but that there were some 12,000 of them, group by group over a span of years, they took with them their families and all they had, and went out to plant new homes in an unknown, untilled and probably hostile land. They looked forward to no fortunes won in precious metals, like the conquistadors, or in trade, like the East India merchants, but to an arduous living wrung from harsh soil in patriarchal solitude. They were limited, unimaginative, self-centred; they were untempered by the humane and liberal spirit which has always flickered and sometimes burned with a clear flame in British colonial ventures. Their contempt for the Africans has bequeathed to their descendants the most thorny and intractable of the world's racial problems. But their hard, simple virtues lived on in their grandchildren and great-grandchildren, so that fifty years ago (during the Anglo-Boer war) the finest elements in Britain rallied instinctively to their side against the agents of a newer imperialism.

The Voortrekkers were never beaten, only outdated at last. If their kin live on it is as magnificent anachronisms where the climate of things favours their survival, like the bedouin. The monument at Pretoria is at once a memorial and a tomb; even such, and by this token, has their time passed away.

Vignette . . . or subtle caricature to support this newspaper's implacable hostility to the policies of the Afrikaner Government?–because, whatever else it says about the Afrikaner, it represents him as unfit to govern in the modern world. But what is the truth? Evidence will be presented in the chapters which follow on which to judge: meantime, the two master clues to an understanding of the Afrikaner are his total identification with Africa and his determination to protect his identity. The Afrikaners are the only people in all of this vast continent to have incorporated "Africa" in their name: and their one-ness with Africa, the spirit of Africa, they incorporated in their language. Afrikaans is of Africa: Afrikaans is the Afrikaner, and without it he could not be.

Mount Meru, Tanganyika, 1946: Later I met the dominee of this shabby but proud community of Afrikaners. It had been established at the beginning of the century, when Tanganyika was a German dependency, in the foothills of Mount Meru by men and women who were not prepared to live in South Africa under the Union Jack. I asked the dominee why, in what was now an English-speaking country, his people clung so desperately to Afrikaans. He explained that for them their language was something to place over against all their other tribulations. It gave them self-respect: it united them with their people in the South who had brought Christian civilisation to the continent and who alone in the end (the dominee said with defiant conviction) would have the faith to defend it. I could understand this. Not here but elsewhere on the continent the Afrikaner's faith had successfully answered Africa's challenge. It had led the Afrikaners through two lost centuries and, some of them, into the forefront of world affairs. It had protected the embryo nation in the years of its formation: but, I reflected, like the silk of which the cocoon is made, new patterns had now to be woven from it. (8)

By 1948 it had become desperately urgent that the Afrikaner Government should weave new patterns not only for its own people but also for all those others for whom it was responsible, since internal and external forces were wrenching apart the old one. However the first priority was seen as the safeguarding of Afrikanerdom itself–its language, culture and religion–within a completely independent and sovereign state.

A minority of folk speaking a little-known Dutch patois called Afrikaans have established themselves in power and set out to work off their inferiority complex by wreaking vengeance on the rest of the population: Frank Barber in the *News Chronicle,* London, 11.8.59.

The brilliant Afrikaans journalist, Schalk Pienaar, commenting on the challenge of those days, wrote that his was a small nation, but one with as great a right as any to its place in the sun. It had been moulded in the mills of a struggle for survival that lasted for three centuries . . . and now had come the demand that it should submit to a new imperialism, the numbers of Africa. Not unnaturally, the answer was no; and in this the

65

Afrikaner's determination was immovable. Unlike the English in India or the Dutch in Indonesia, he had nowhere else to go. For him there was no central shrine of national existence to survive the death of the outposts: on the soil of Africa he and with him his history stayed or perished.

There was the new imperialism to which Mr. Pienaar referred, and the Afrikaner had no doubt that it would triumph over him unless he freed himself first from the old imperialism of Britain.

Britain had been magnanimous after her victory over the Boers in 1902. Moreover her Empire, inspired by the concept of colonies developing into autonomous British Dominions, was by and large more benevolent than any the world had known. The promise of a *primus inter pares* dispensation–with Britain the *primus* and South Africa one of the *pares*–looked singularly fair and reasonable, and Boer leaders of the calibre of Smuts and Botha settled for it. They carried with them many of their own people and virtually all their countrymen of British descent–that is, our Anglosans. Transvaal, Orange Free State, Cape and Natal united in 1910 to form a self-governing Dominion of the mighty British Commonwealth; and in doing so joined the ranks of Canada, Australia and New Zealand. The Union Jack flew throughout the land. In Cape Town a Parliament for the new State was established on the model of Westminster; and a Governor General, the personal representative of the British monarch, surveyed (from a distinguished residence in Pretoria, designed by Sir Herbert Baker) with pride and sense of accomplishment the achievement. It seemed to him and the world at large that as a partner of Britain, though a junior one, the new nation's fortunes were well set.

> Hans Strydom, Malan's successor as South African Premier, is an ardent member of a sub-Christian sect, the Dutch Reformed Church: the Rev. H. Thornton Trapp in the *St. Marylebone Record*, London, 6.1.55.

But for a steadfast body of Boers (they were beginning generally to be called Afrikaners) there was no comfort to be had from this dispensation. For them, *primus inter pares,* Dominion status, constitutional independence under the Crown, was not enough. Their consuming passion was the preservation of all that was uniquely their own, and no arrangement was acceptable to them unless it made this certain. Thus the stage was set for a new kind of conflict–not about territory or between armies, but for Afrikanerdom against anglicisation. In this encounter there were few physical casualties, few bodies maimed or destroyed, but the wounds inflicted upon the emotions of the people were deep and cruel. The antipathies generated then were cold, calculating and unmitigated by the courage and comradeship of the battlefield.

The Afrikaner is the world's greatest isolationist who seeks racial exclusiveness not for expansion but to be left, as he sees it, alone so that he may grow in his own national garden. He will resist assimilation to the last. The Afrikaner is tough and brave but his character tends to explosive brutality: Charles Janson in the *Guardian,* London, 8.8.60.

And the attitude of Britain at this time to her sovereign independent partner is illuminated in secret Cabinet papers that were declassified in 1968. Among them is comment made by the First Lord of the Admiralty on the visit to London of Mr. Oswald Pirow, the Union's Minister of Defence, in June, 1936. The comment was considered of sufficient weight to circulate among members of the British Government:

Pirow's boyish enthusiasm and willingness to agree to matters of detail may easily result in the greater matters of principle being overlooked. This must not happen with Master Pirow. All questions of detail as regards expenditure on coastal defence and so forth fall into insignificance unless assurance is given beforehand that in the event of the Empire becoming embroiled, South Africa can be depended upon to take its place: That, above all, whatever stance South Africa may be willing to take itself, all ports in the Union, as well as Simonstown, shall at all times be open to H.M. Navy as a matter of right, and that England's right to land troops and move them across the Union shall be unquestioned.

The "great matter of principle" is clear enough: it was South Africa's duty to serve Britain's interests and generally to be at Britain's disposal. When, in September, 1939, the Union Parliament, by a 13-vote majority, declared war on Germany, the committed Afrikaners had no doubt that their country was again being placed at Britain's disposal.

The Anglo South African

So when Dr. Malan assumed office as Prime Minister three years after the War, the first priority was to achieve a sovereign Republic. This was regarded as the essential framework for a solution of the country's other problems ... But before we come to that we are going to take a quick look at the second component of the Anglo-Afrikaner nation: it is at times almost as badly misunderstood and misrepresented as are the Afrikaners.

There are many Nationalists who would like to see

67

It was in 1820, 14 years after Britain finally took possession of the
Cape, that the first group of British settlers–some 3,500 of them–arrived
in the eastern Cape. The coming of these people completed, as it were,
the conception of the nation: it added the final chromosome. Already
contained in the embryo were the other three strains, derived from
Holland, France and Germany. By 1820 these three had long since cut
themselves off from their origins, committed themselves to their new
environment and merged as Afrikaners. Thus the arrival of the British
settlers, though welcomed as a reinforcement of the frontier against the
southward-moving black people, was at the same time an intrusion; and
from the beginning there was a divided sentiment towards the newcomers. It was to persist through the generations: but looking back today
it can be seen that it was these conflicting attitudes no less than co-
operation, tension no less than harmony, that stimulated the development
which through a century-and-a-half has since occurred.

In the early years the Afrikaner and Briton each had his part in
extending and protecting the borders of their country. However the
special contributions that they were to make were different. While the
Afrikaner drew strength from his isolation, the Briton kept open the lines
of communication with the outside world: while the Afrikaner built the
granite framework of nationhood, the Briton improved it with much that
was best in his own traditions of civil administration, justice and
education: while the Afrikaner worked with the soil and civilised the
countryside, the Briton struck deep into the earth for its yield of mineral
riches, and fashioned and turned the wheels of industry on which the
economic security of the nation depends. The political achievement was
the Afrikaner's, but the Anglo South African has stamped his imprint
clearly on the pattern of the nation's life. It can be seen in the country's
financial institutions, in the proceedings of its Parliament and courts of
law, in its newspapers, at a village school where Afrikaner boys in blue
blazers answer the roll call, at a game of rugby at Ellis Park in
Johannesburg or of cricket under the oaks at Newlands in the Cape.

Afrikaner and Anglosan have given much to each other and the nation: but until a dozen years ago each was deeply suspicious of the other–and some still are. For the Afrikaner, the "English-speaking" South African was a man who divided his loyalty between South Africa and Britain. And for the "English-speaking" South African, the Afrikaner's loyalty was one which he gave, not to his country and compatriots, but exclusively to his own people. This was always the essential cause of division. There were other differences between the groups. There still are and they will remain: but group differences occur in all nations and even the most united of them. Uniformity and identity of outlook are not necessary for national unity. What is necessary is a common loyalty; and the dispute about the nature of the loyalty of these two groups was the sharp edge that cut the nation apart. The question to which an answer has now become clearer is whether either side was justified in charging the other with a loyalty to the country less worthy than its own.

The "English-speaking" South African was accused of being more English than South African, and the accusation arose from his desire to maintain a close association with Britain. However his contention is that he believed that this was the best, and perhaps the only, way of safeguarding and promoting South Africa's interests. It was an honest belief and reasonable. In the first years of Union, Britain was militarily and economically the most powerful of all nations. The way the "English-speaking" South African saw it, the Royal Navy was the surest guarantee of the country's protection; British commerce of its prosperity–and the man who would jeopardise such advantages was a knave or a fool.

This contention that the "English-speaking" South African's attitude to Britain was subordinate to concern for his own country is borne out by the conduct of people of British origin in other parts of Africa. Thus, in 1948, the leaders of the white settlers in Kenya (including a cousin of the Queen) sent a message of support to Dr. Malan. They wanted him to know that, for them, their overriding concern was for their adopted country and for the future of Kenya and their children. There is likewise no doubt where the loyalty of the Rhodesians lies; and it is unreasonable to suppose that "English-speaking" South Africans with far longer associations with Africa were, at heart, differently motivated.

So far as the Afrikaner was concerned, he believed that the rebuilding and strengthening of the Afrikaner identity were essential for the preservation of the white nation. This was to be the bulwark against the rest. For him there had to be an inner citadel of strength. He had no faith in the outside world as the protector of his nation–and the man who relied, in particular, on Britain was a knave or a fool.

For 50 years, Britain was the pivot about which the dispute swung. When the pivot fell, the dispute could be seen for what it was. The fault of the "English-speaking" South African is not that he was disloyal. It is

that he was mistaken. The Afrikaner has been proved right. It may be
that his belief had its origin less in wisdom than in a prejudice towards
Britain which events had made inevitable. But he was right for all that:
the citadel of inner strength was indispensable. There is no need for
recrimination. This was not the work of individuals or groups. They
could not have changed it. It was the work of History.

> "Whom the gods would destroy they first make mad." One
> can see only tragedy ahead for the South Africans–the
> ruling Afrikaners, the spiritually distressed white English-
> speaking minority, and the great majority of blacks, colored
> (mixed blood) and Asians: the *New York Times*, 31.5.61

The charge that Anglosans as a group have not pulled their weight for
the country is unfounded; and there are good reasons also for the small
part they have played in guiding its political destiny. The first is a matter
of simple arithmetic: they account for some 40 per cent of the electorate;
and for as long as the Afrikaners (some 60 per cent) remained, and
remain, united in the National Party it is inevitable that theirs should be
an opposition role. Secondly, they had in any case no body of shared
experience to bind them. Their backgrounds were very different: of the
1820 settlers who pioneered in the toughest conditions in the eastern
Cape; of the fortune-hunters who responded to the call of diamonds in
Kimberley and gold in Johannesburg; of the men who first came to know
South Africa through service with the British forces during the Anglo-
Boer War; of the immigrants who were subsequently attracted by the
economic and other opportunities of a settled and now-prospering
country. They spoke English, it is true, but so did hundreds of millions of
others in various parts of the world, and the use of the language did not
create a sense of community among them. Their church had nothing like
the same significance as theirs did for the Afrikaners, and in any case they
were divided among half-a-dozen denominations. In the first half of the
century they shared an attachment to the British Sovereign (who was
constitutionally, and separately, the South African Sovereign), and they
faithfully followed General Smuts–leader of the South African Party
which was to become the United Party–since he personified the
Commonwealth and ardently championed the British connection.
However this single unifying factor crumbled in the post-war years with
Britain's fall from power and the Commonwealth's changed character.

> The United Party was always a mixed pack. Its liberal
> elements were at odds with its conservatives and its
> opportunists. It hung together because it seemed the only
> instrument by which the Nationalists could be dislodged
> before they did the Union irreparable harm. It has failed in

70

that, and one wonders whether it can hang together much
longer: the *Guardian,* London, 17.4.53.

There are reasons enough why political power has not been exercised
by the Anglosans–but this does not mean that they have been politically
ineffective. On the contrary, and despite the frustration of close on 30
years in opposition, their party, the United Party, has rendered the
country important service. It has been an indispensable part of the proper
functioning of the parliamentary system. Commanding, as it always has, a
large section of the electorate, it has throughout kept the Government on
its toes; and while it has not projected a magnetic policy of its own, it has
stuck to its task of exposing the faults of the Government's. It has
performed all along with integrity, and has maintained for the country at
large the best democratic standards. In crucial domestic and foreign issues
affecting the security of the State it has stood by the Government. The
fact is that underlying sharp and real differences, the National Party and
the United Party share a wide area of common ground. They are both
conservative; both believe in an evolutionary solution of the country's
problems; both are committed to safeguarding the position of the Anglo-
Afrikaner nation (though they disagree on the means for doing this), and
they both support private enterprise and orthodox economics.

> Afrikaners assure you that once a Republic was set up
> within the Commonwealth the last obstacle to fraternal co-
> operation with the English-speaking South Africans would
> have been removed. But this is impossible to believe: *The
> Times,* London, 1.3.60.

The United Party, representing the Anglosans, has made an undrama-
tic but invaluable contribution to balance and orderliness in the nation's
life, while providing that tension that is needed for dynamic action in any
society. Moreover, the country has survived this turbulent quarter
century because it has been economically strong. The most steadfast
political determination would not have prevailed against the world
without the reinforcement of material resources. Today this is a country
of account economically, industrially and technologically–and here the
part of the Anglosans has been no less large than that of the Afrikaners in
politics. The combined consequence is that the country has the resolution
and resources to withstand hostility from abroad and to go ahead with its
plans at home.

> The aim of the uninhibited Afrikaner is, bluntly put, to
> keep the Kaffir in his place and the English out of the
> country: *The Times,* London, 7.3.60.

71

The Afrikaners have led the nation politically through the long crisis, but they could not have done so without the economic support–or done so so well without the political opposition–of the Anglosans. Appearances to the contrary, it has been a most effective partnership: I would say it has been as good a disposition of the nation's human resources as there could have been for its safe conduct through these perilous years.

The image of the Anglosan as money-making, uninterested in the country's fate, bored and frustrated is false. Outside of government, there is no branch of the nation's life in which he does not equal or surpass the Afrikaner. His initiative in industry and commerce speaks for itself: he has contributed his full share to the physical building of the country: he is prominent in the professions: he holds his own in the arts: Anglosan names feature together with Afrikaans in the country's sporting achievements. And should it be necessary to defend the nation at war, the Anglosan will be there together with his Afrikaner compatriot.

Why, then, the false image? It is mainly the product of those who claim to speak for the Anglosans but who in fact (as will be shown) do not: editors, academics, churchmen and cliques of students at English-language universities as unrepresentative and fatuous as their counterparts overseas whom they ape. Even sincere Anglosan intellectuals have been taken in by the false image. They must enjoy their periodic bouts of solemn introversion: there is no other reason for it.

CHAPTER SIX / 1945 to 1960
The Cross-roads

Left or Right?

It was the Afrikaners and the National Party who had to make the fateful decision in 1948. The National Party is unlike democratic parties elsewhere which speak for sections of the electorate or are motivated by particular social or economic goals. The National Party is the *volk* in political action. The allegiance of the Afrikaner to his party is thus different from that of the Tory or Socialist or Liberal to his in Britain, or of the Republican or the Democrat to his in the United States. The party is not the instrument of the Government or the parliamentary caucus or the professionals. It belongs to the *volk:* and unity does not come from monolithic regimentation or imperative blueprints, but from individual participation in the common cause of promoting the interests of Afrikanerdom. The party is not judged by its members against success or failure in reaching specific objectives: the touchstone is the well-being of the *volk:* and while that is being served, specific objectives may be revised, altered or abandoned. This affords a National Party Government a freedom and boldness of action not allowed conventional democratic parties.

> Since the Nationalist Party came to power, the Dominion
> of South Africa has been sinking into a political twilight,
> sinister, obscurantist and smelling of decay. Its native policy
> has been the deepest shadow of this night, but it is not the
> only one: the *News Chronicle,* London, 30.11.49.

The Government in 1948 needed that freedom to act boldly because it was confronted with nothing less than the collapse of the traditional structure of South African society. Economic development between the

73

two world wars had shattered the pattern of generations during which, in a mainly agricultural economy, there had been the opportunity for the country's different peoples to live out their lives in their own way in their own parts of the land which they themselves had chosen in their respective migrations. Industrialisation and urbanisation threw white, black and brown together, disrupting the life-style and order they had previously known and unleashing forces over which the individual had no control. This had placed the Union in 1948 at the cross-roads. "Cross-roads" is a tired image, but refresh your mind to what it means: a road to the left, a road to the right, a road ahead. It is a useful image considered in this way, because what Dr. Malan and his National Party had to choose then was not a programme–not a two-year or a ten-year or a 20-year plan–but a direction.

The new signpost to the left was marked *Integration*. A *laissez faire* approach during the pre-war and wartime United Party regime had allowed it to be put there: and now, in revulsion against the disaster recently inflicted on mankind by theories of race superiority and aggressive nationalism, the whole world was turning in this direction. Internal and external pressures on Pretoria to take the road to the left were formidable . . . but there were conditions in this country determining the choice that were different from any others anywhere. To start with, the Afrikaners were the first white people to have established a nation in a predominantly non-white part of the world: and one consequence of this was their understanding of the importance of nationalism and the sentiment of nationality in its pristine, unperverted form.

> Behind them (Dr. Malan and Mr. Havenga) stand the younger and uninhibited doctrinaires of the party, Mr. Swart and Mr. Strydom, ruthless and energetic, whose word to those who are not of "the folk" is likely to be, with Rehoboam's, "my father chastised you with whips, but I will chastise you with scorpions": the *Guardian*, London, 17.4.53.

As the War was ending the noted American author, Lewis Mumford, wrote in *The Condition of Man* that nationalism was often treated as a political phenomenon of the same sort of order as socialism. But in fact its roots went much deeper: the sources that fed it were remote and subtle elements in the soul. The individuality of groups of men was as genuine a fact as personality itself; and "he who uproots nationality kills personality." That was the view of one of America's leading thinkers. In Europe the nation-state had come into being so that the state could serve the nation and safeguard this sentiment of nationality of its people. In the

74

beginning it did: but more and more the concerns of the state became dominant: the sentiment of nationality was overridden and exploited: it was used to power aggression–and this was the kind of nationalism against which the post-war world revolted.

> In practice, therefore, Apartheid is merely a theoretical facade behind which the Nationalists are implementing the doctrine of white supremacy in its purest form: stripped of all political and civil rights, the Africans will be reduced to a vast *lumpenproletariat* to be moved at will according to the demands of the white economy: *The New Statesman,* London, 23.2.57.

But the Afrikaner, from his own experience, knew the sentiment of nationality in its unperverted form; and he also understood the importance to black men of their sentiment of nationality–and how different it was from his. Leopold Senghor, professor, poet and now President of Senegal, has declared that the African genius is essentially different from the European and has produced different sorts of fruits. African culture is the complex of activities, symbols and rhythms through which African man expresses his understanding of the world and society and sense of unity with them. African culture is what it is because Africans are what they are–rational, but in a different way from Europeans, understanding through insight and sympathy rather than through discursive thought. There is this difference, according to Senghor, in the depths of the African psyche.

After generations of contact with black men, Afrikaners were aware of the difference: hence the scepticism in Pretoria in 1948 concerning the possibility–let alone the desirability–of building, sharing and operating together a common society. Moreover among themselves the black nations of South Africa differ as much as do the Belgians, say, and the Italians of Europe. And on top of that there was the experience of the two groups of the white nation. On this point Mr. Pienaar observed in the essay I have already quoted: "If two groups so closely related in every field of civilisation are–after a co-existence of more than a century-and-a-half, after a political union that has lasted for half a century–still struggling to achieve complete partnership, can anyone seriously suggest that a third partner be taken in–one so totally dissimilar in every way as the Bantu? Experience over many years screams into the very face of such an attempt." And wrapping up the all-important argument about the sentiment of nationality, Mr. Pienaar pointed out that the Bantu was neither a backward black Englishman nor a backward black Afrikaner. He was a Zulu, a Xhosa, a Sotho–a member of a nation in its own right. "One should not, as a matter of principle, denationalise a nation: one

75

cannot, as a matter of practice, denationalise a nation. Within living memory an attempt to denationalise the Afrikaner more than failed: it triggered off an Afrikaner national movement of explosive power and engendered long-lived bitterness. There is in South Africa a scorched earth on which the seeds of denationalisation will not grow."

> But how long do South Africans believe they can inhabit an island of reaction in a progressive world? With every day that they deny the black and coloured man his right to walk upright, they will be storing up a more dreadful reckoning. There is only one possible end to the Strydom policy–blood and darkness: the *News Chronicle*, London, 6.12.54.

The Nature of Race Prejudice

The road to the left led inexorably to scorched earth country. But now, immediately–at the very cross-roads–it bristled with hazards. Integration was distorting the generations-old relationship between white and black. The contention of the *Guardian*–in that article on the Voortrekker Monument–that the Afrikaner traditionally held the black man in contempt has no basis in fact. It is true that when the white individual had come into contact with the black, the relationship between them was invariably that of master and servant. Since the white man was educated, resourceful and the employer, and the black man was uneducated, unresourceful and the employee, it could scarcely have been otherwise. But this did not imply contempt: on the contrary there are innumerable Afrikaners today who will tell you that as children on their farms in the *platteland* they were required by their parents to treat the black people with respect and that they were punished if they did not do so. Outside of individual relationships, the leaders of the white communities in the last century were at all times ready and eager to *negotiate* with the leaders of black communities. Meetings between them occurred regularly. For instance, in 1854 J. P. Hoffman, President of the Provisional Government of the Orange Free State, invited for discussions to Bloemfontein Chief Moshesh, of the Basutos, and his three sons, Nehemiah, David and Majara. At a State banquet given in honour of the guests, Chief Moshesh said: "I have noticed that Mr. Hoffman has feeble limbs and must use crutches. But when all persons who are blessed with sound limbs kept running backwards and forwards in times of disturbance, that gentleman stood his ground, stuck to his farm and, honestly adhering to the truth, fearlessly admonished and reproved me, and at other times the British Government."

There is no sign in this occasion of anything other than the best of good humour as expressed between equals–and it was typical. Authentic black leaders were treated with due regard; and for as long as the Afrikaner's institutions, Church and State, were not threatened there was neither contempt nor prejudice.

> It is extremely plain that apartheid must end in disaster, though no-one can see what form the disaster will be bound to take. There is, most important of all, a lack of that outlook and temperament which can lead in the end to harmony: the *British Weekly*, 27.1.55.

The fact here is that it is not any kind but a particular kind of contact between races that causes prejudice. Many kinds are congenial and stimulating: the foreigner visiting France is charmed by the Parisienne; the European visiting Asia finds the strangeness of the people he meets there fascinating; friendship at university between students of different races is common; the Oriental family in the house next door adds a touch of colour to the neighbourhood. It is when Orientals come to occupy the houses on either side of yours and across the street; when you find your children playing with others whose habits or language or accent is different from yours; when you find at your job that an immigrant or an alien is prepared to work for less than you are–it is then that the trouble starts. Prejudice results, in short, from a special set of circumstances: from a kind of contact in which the presence of one group threatens the identity, the institutions, the culture, the life-style or the standard of living of another.

Such were the circumstances that were fast establishing themselves in the Union's industrial areas in the years before and during the War. The white man feared the undercutting of his wages by black labour; the black man found the competition of members of more resourceful groups overwhelming. Politically, the authentic leaders (like Moshesh) of the black communities–the focal points of their sentiment of nationality–were being superseded. Polyglot movements such as the African National Congress, consisting of the so-called "urban élite", were taking their place. With no grass-roots support among their own people, with no respect for their own culture and institutions, they were espousing Western ways and, more particularly, a single system of government for the whole country based on one-man-one-vote. Politically as well as economically the white man was being threatened–and so, too, the survival of the black man's identity and nationhood.

Historically there had been *differentiated* treatment of the country's various communities. In a statement to the United Nations in 1947, General Smuts explained why: "In South Africa these distinctions cannot

77

be abolished without jeopardising the development, if not the survival, of the races concerned–especially of the less-advanced races. The truly fundamental rights (and it was General Smuts who enshrined these in the preamble to the UN Charter) of all races cannot be safeguarded in the union without distinction in regard to non-fundamental rights." In illustration of this proposition, General Smuts pointed out that if all distinctions were abolished: black-owned land would be thrown open to white and Indian penetration; the individual black person would be submerged in an amorphous mass of landless paupers; legislation which enabled the different communities to live and arrange their affairs according to their own native laws and customs would have to be repealed; mother-tongue education would disappear. There are innumerable examples of the advantages that flow from differentiated treatment. But by 1948, for the reasons given, differentiation in a variety of areas had hardened into discrimination against the black man. The Union was at the cross-roads. Which direction would lead to an open and tranquil country? Surely not leftwards: there lay the flames, fanned by race prejudice, of the frustrated sentiment of nationality–the scorched earth.

> A black man recently told the Bishop of Johannesburg: You are one of the greatest friends the Africans have got, but when the day comes we shall kill you like all the rest: the Rev. Chad Varah in *Picture Post,* London, 12.2.55.

The signpost to the right was marked *domination.*

The whole history of the Afrikaner people had been a ceaseless effort to escape from domination–from the domination of the Dutch, then from the domination of Britain, then from the domination of British influence within their country. Already in the 18th century the Afrikaners had sought freedom from the Dutch in the establishment of pocket republics in the Cape. A generation after the occupation of the Cape by Britain, they sought freedom in movement across the mountains. History records with clarity the purpose of this trek. It was to secure their own way of life: it was not to impose it on others. Compared with experience elsewhere in the world, white settlement in South Africa was notable in that it at no time contemplated either the liquidation or the subjugation of the indigenous people, but chose rather to live in peace alongside them. When the Voortrekker leader, Piet Retief, set out for the hinterland in the 1830s, he made the following declaration: "We do not want to take their territory from them (the Bantu). We want to establish our own states and we will respect their states and their rights. We wish to live together as good neighbours, but if they attack us then I will assuredly wreak vengeance." When the whites came into armed conflict with the

78

blacks it was to protect what was their own. The solution applied to the "native" problem in America and Australia was, here, not attempted and not desired. There is no tittle of evidence in the record of a wish among Afrikaners to dominate others. They were determined only to secure their freedom, and believed it could best be done by recognising the right of the black men to their own identity and territory.

> An explosion is not imminent in South Africa, but if things go on as they are it is inevitable. To avoid disaster in South Africa is going to take all the skill, humanity and far-sightedness possible. There is no evidence whatever that the Strydom Government possesses these qualities: Ed. Murrow in *Illustrated News*, London, 18.6.55.

Statutory evidence of this was legislation passed in 1913. The constitutional arrangement three years before–the Act of Union–had set aside from the Union (although their incorporation later was provided for) the black territories of Bechuanaland, Basutoland and Swaziland. But other territories which were the traditional home of black peoples–such as the Transkei and Zululand–but which had been closely associated administratively with one or other of the constituent Provinces of the Union, were included within its borders. The 1913 legislation guaranteed these territories against penetration or alienation. And this was at a time when the paramountcy of the white man in all those parts of Africa which he had colonised was nowhere questioned.

The new Government did not choose the way marked *domination:* to have done so would have been against the Afrikaner's history and against his own interest, since it was discerned that that way lay the threat also to his own freedom.

CHAPTER SEVEN / 1945 to 1960
Apartheid

No Sudden Choice

When the National Party Government came to power in 1948, it turned neither left nor right. It went straight ahead; and though it put up a new signpost, *apartheid,* that was merely to indicate more accurately the course that had traditionally been followed. Apartheid was not a policy–as the world supposes it to be–suddenly chosen in 1948. It was not the choice of one man, or of one group of men, or of one party, or of one race. It was the prescription of the accumulated experience of all kinds of South Africans.

The early missionaries from overseas, and more particularly John Philip, the vehement critic of the afrikaners, were among its champions in the first half of the 19th century. Historian W. M. Macmillan says of Philip that he alone came near evolving a hopeful, practical policy both for the Coloured people within and the Bantu people who were then beyond the borders of the Cape Colony. "His policy", says the historian, "was that these backward people should be firmly fixed in homes and on lands of their own. With a secure home base, they might well have provided all that was needed in the way of a reserve of labour, without being wholly and utterly dependent on their chances of wage-earning alone; and South Africa might have escaped the clogging of its prosperity and the complication of its social life by the dispersal through its farms, towns and dorps alike, of a great mass of landless and homeless, poorly-equipped and helpless unskilled workers. His (Philip's) practical policy at every stage of his career was a passionate struggle to secure, first for the Hottentots, later for Griquas and Kaffirs, lands and homes of their own, with the opportunity to live and develop their own separate existence."

Perhaps one may hope in the long run that the segregation

80

policy will be the rope that hangs the Nationalists or brings them to their senses: the *Guardian,* London, 29.5.48.

It was not Philip alone among the missionaries who favoured separation: Adams and Lindley were associated with Shepstone, the British administrator, in applying it in Natal. Their policy was to allocate the Zulus some ten separate areas: they laid emphasis on the improvement in these areas of economic conditions, on the introduction of schools and churches and on the retention of the tribal system and of Bantu customary law. In Griqualand, also on the advice of missionaries, a system of separation was applied. Macmillan comments that it was here for the first time that it was recognised that black and white must share the land between them, that their different standards made it desirable to keep the races apart as far as possible, that in unrestricted competition the backward race was at a hopeless disadvantage and that "the highly desirable separation can be maintained only by the demarcation of a minimum of native land as inalienable *Reserve.*"

> The African (in South Africa) is discovering almost by accident a new and tremendous power coming into his hands. And who will blame him if he learns to use it more and more effectively in the days ahead? The ultimate consolation is that a regime built on terror cannot survive: the *Christian World,* London, 24.2.55.

Cecil Rhodes, Prime Minister of the Cape Colony, was the first man to legislate for separatism, and did so in the Glen Grey Act of 1894. General Smuts, champion of the British Commonwealth, leader of the South African Party and lifelong opponent of the National Party, defined separatism in the clearest terms 30 years before *apartheid* was coined. Addressing a gathering in London in 1917, he said:

> There is now shaping in South Africa a policy which is being expressed in our institutions and which may have very far-reaching effects in the future civilisation of the African continent. A practice has grown up in South Africa of giving the natives their own separate institutions on parallel lines. On these parallel lines we may yet be able to solve a problem which otherwise may be insoluble. We have felt more and more that it is useless to try to govern black and white in the same system. Their political institutions should be different while always proceeding on the basis of self-government. In land ownership, settlement and forms of government our policy is to keep them apart.

81

Twelve years later, in 1929, General Smuts enunciated the same principles when he delivered the Rhodes Memorial Lectures at Oxford University:

It is clear that a race so unique, and so different in its mentality and its cultures from those of Europe, requires a policy very unlike that which would suit Europeans. Nothing could be worse for Africa than the application of a policy the object or tendency of which would be to destroy the basis of this African type–to de-Africanise the African. If Africa is to take her rightful place among the continents, we shall have to proceed on different lines and evolve a policy which will not force her institutions into an alien European mould, but which will preserve her unity with her own past, conserve what is precious in her past, and build her future progress and civilisation on specifically African foundations.

The basic error of Apartheid is that it is a policy designed to safeguard Western civilisation by methods which are a flat denial of the principles of that civilisation–methods which in Nazi Germany and Fascist Italy had to be extirpated from the Western way of life if it was to survive: Sir Stephen King-Hall in the *National and English Review*, May, 1957.

Here is the crux of the proposition as stated by one of the great statesmen of this century. Equally illuminating in the context of the 1948 choice are the views of Professor Alfred Hoernlé, a man well-known in Britain for his philosophical writing before he settled in the Union to make the study of race relations his life's work, and to become a major force in the liberal South African Institute of Race Relations. During the course of a Phelps-Stokes lecture in 1939, he drew a distinction between *segregation* and *separation*. He described segregation as an instrument of domination "which retains the segregated in the same social and political structure with the dominant white group, but subjects them to the denial of important rights and keeps them at a social distance, implying inferiority." On the other hand, he saw separation as the creation of separate, self-contained, self-governing societies, co-operating on a basis of mutual recognition of one another's independence. In their own territory the Bantu would escape from domination, they would develop along their own lines, but would have unhindered access to European culture which they could gradually absorb insofar as they were able and chose to. Segregation, in other words, is a horizontal division of society with one group imposed above another: separation is a vertical division with one group alongside the other. Professor Hoernlé saw in separation the only solution that went to the fundamentals of society, but he believed that the integration of the inter-war years had proceeded too far to permit its implementation.

Far from being oppressive or reactionary, separatism has impeccable liberal antecedents. But apartheid went even further than Professor Hoernlé's separation: it envisaged a life of their own for black people wherever in the country they might work and live. Dr. E. G. Jansen, Minister of Native Affairs, explained in 1950 that government policy included territorial separation but made available also opportunities for the separate development of Bantu outside their areas. However the men whose duty it was to implement apartheid at no time saw it as a suit for divorce between white and black. In 1948 Dr. Malan said that for the non-whites apartheid meant a larger measure of independence through the growth of their self-reliance and self-respect and, at the same time, the creation of greater opportunities for free development in conformity with their own character and capacity. For the Europeans, he said, it meant a new sense of security resulting from the safeguarding of their own identity and future, and for both races it meant peaceful mutual relations and co-operation for the common weal. The Bantu territories should be made to carry a larger population and the Bantu in the city centres should live in their own areas. In 1950 Dr. Jansen told Parliament that apartheid sought the development of the European and the Bantu side-by-side but not intermingled. The interdependence of the groups, he stated, was recognised, but in the European areas the interests of the European must be the dominating factor, while in the Bantu areas the interests of the Bantu must predominate.

In 1955 Dr. Verwoerd, then Minister of Native Affairs, told the Senate: "I characterise the policy of separatism as the policy of growing from one's roots, from one's own institutions and by one's own powers." In 1956, when Prime Minister Strydom was outlining Pretoria's policy in London, he quoted General Smuts: "The distinctions which are drawn in my country are, broadly speaking, designed to ensure peaceful development towards the preservation of racial and cultural identities by differentiation and by separation into different areas and groups within which each race can develop in its own way and work out its own destiny with a minimum of racial friction." In 1965, when he was Prime Minister, Dr. Verwoerd was to say: "The crux of the policy of separation is political separation. Territorial separation is important but it is not the crux of the policy of separation."

> It is in sorrow rather than in anger that we must give our
> testimony against a racial policy which is not only utterly
> unchristian (as it seems to us) but is reckless to the point of

83

insanity . . . This is a situation involving the madness of racial arrogance on the one hand, and the fury of racial indignation on the other: the *Christian World,* 24.5.56.

The Borders of National Consciousness

A line, remarkably straight and consistent, can be drawn through all these statements. From the beginning, apartheid was primarily a cultural and not a geographic concept. This was the theme of explanations of the policy that my colleagues and I were giving abroad from the early 1950s onwards . . . and I am going to interpolate here what seems to me an interesting coincidence. In February, 1962, a statement by the then Minister of Bantu Administration and Development, Mr. de Wet Nel, which I processed for publication in New York, contained the following passage: "Recent developments elsewhere on the continent show how closely tied the African is to his own community and group and nation. These are ties which take little account of political borders and constitutional arrangements. The wise planner in Africa is the man who directs them towards constructive ends. Consequently, when we speak of freedom and self-determination for our Xhosa nation, we have in mind not only the geographic area of the Transkei (the Xhosa homeland) but the four-million Xhosa people everywhere in South Africa. Our concern is not only with political borders on a map but with the borders of national consciousness which hold all Xhosas together. The Transkei will be the spring from which the national consciousness flows, but every Xhosa, wherever he may be in South Africa, will be given the fullest opportunity to share in it and to enrich it." In 1965, an article in *The Times,* London, observed: "Why should we let ourselves be governed by cartographical divisions when the divisions of language, religion and race, of ways of thinking and ways of governing are so much more potent and lasting and can form such prodigious dykes that atlases never mark. The world will not settle down peacefully in accordance with our maps."

> The situation and the problems, under the relentless rule of the Nationalist Government since it came to power in 1948, have an almost fatalistic fascination. It is hard for an observer to escape the conclusion that this is a community which is going slowly, steadily, remorselessly, deliberately towards eventual catastrophe: Erwin Griswold in *The Times,* London, 25.9.58.

There it is: the sentiment of nationality: the strength of traditions, inherited loyalties, instinctive pride and attachment which all people have

84

for the memories, manners and values which are their own. These borders of national consciousness are capable of almost unlimited extension. In the colonial era, the Englishman and his children stationed in Khartoum or Singapore were more English than the man from Birmingham. Those responsible for him created in the most outlandish places an environment to which he was accustomed–a bridge club, polo, tea at eleven and *The Tatler*–and he felt at home and was satisfied. Today, the Jamaicans of Notting Hill in London, though separated by centuries and an ocean from Africa, are essentially African. They do not speak the languages of Africa, they have not seen her shores, but the imprint of Africa is indelibly on them–even in their gestures and the inflexion of their voices. If they are to be contented and fulfilled as men and women they must have the opportunity of expressing this, their negritude.

It is the same, only much more so, with the Zulu who works in a factory in Johannesburg which manufactures transistor radios and lives in the black township of Meadowlands. He is and will always remain a Zulu; and if he and his wife and children are to prosper fully as a family it is only as a Zulu family that they will be able to do so. The notion of detribalisation–that because a man leaves the earth and occupation of his forefathers and move to an industrialised area a few hundred miles away, he thereby sheds his nature and is left naked to put on someone else's–is the greatest among the many fallacies about the development of emergent people. He will continue to be clothed in his own nature against all odds– and even against any conscious determination he may have to the contrary. The task of those who seek his real welfare is to dissuade him from this contrary determination and, wherever he is, to create the kind of environment that will enable him to be himself.

> There is no hope for the South African Government so
> long as it follows the policy of apartheid. The doctrine is not
> only immoral; it is politically and economically impractical.
> It goes against the inexorable trend in Africa and elsewhere
> in the contemporary world: the *New York Times*, 30.3.60.

Although at the beginning there was an influential body of intellectual opinion in this country which advocated total territorial separation as the ultimate goal, their plea was immediately thrown out by the court of practical politics. Total territorial separation has a long history as the solution to the problems of plural societies where the people have found it possible to get along together: Norway and Sweden, Belgium and Holland, India and Pakistan. However apartheid was a dynamically different concept–a design to enable people, even where physically intermingled, to co-exist and yet be themselves. The dependence of the white economy on black manpower and the dependence of black men for their livelihood on employment offered by the white economy would be a powerful argument against partition. However it is no argument against apartheid. On the contrary, it is the *raison d'être* of apartheid-in-practice: if there were no geographical mixing of the people there would be no need for it, the essence of apartheid (as opposed to partition) being the recognition not of cartographic borders but of those unfixed borders which men, by virtue of their nature, carry and extend with them.

> The course upon which Dr. Verwoerd and his Government
> have embarked, furthering that of his predecessors, Malan
> and Strydom, is unwavering. The goal is white supremacy
> and racial segregation–absolute and uncompromising: the
> *New York Times*, 5.2.60.

The following two extracts from my diary show how early this primary feature of the policy was being propagated abroad. They were written when I was Director of Information at South Africa House:

> *London, 1957*: This is one aspect of the land criticism. Another is that apartheid is not exclusively, or even in essence, a matter of geographical division. Geographical division is necessarily involved, but in essence apartheid is a far less mechanical concept. It is a concept of racial distinctiveness. An analogy may be helpful in understanding this idea: the difference in chemistry between a mixture and a compound. The characteristic of a mixture is that the component parts retain their identity. Wherever they may be situated physically they retain their identity. The characteristic of a compound is that the component parts lose their individuality and submit to a process which imposes on them a common identity. This illustrates the distinction between apartheid and assimilation. Those who support apartheid say that the South African society must not become a *compounded*, a *fused*, society: that each member of the South African community, whatever place he may have in it physically, must be assured of the opportunity of retaining his racial individuality and of being true to his origin. Thus the importance of the Bantu territories. The organisation and administration of Bantu elsewhere will be related to them and they will be the spiritual spring from which all Bantu . . . will be able to draw. (9)

> *London, 1958:* Apartheid does not set the races upon divergent courses. It is not the sign that stands at the forking of a road: it is represented rather by the two lines of a railway track. These, though separate, are interdependent and they carry towards a common objective–in this case, a harmonious future for the people. (10)

Apartheid is no suit for divorce between white and black. It is a marriage between co-existence and self-determination, with economic interdependence the broker and the separate heartlands the national sanctum.

Land

The first of the above two entries referred to the "land criticism". This is perhaps the most frequent criticism made of Pretoria's policy. It is also the most facile. It has reference to the fact that *today* the homelands of the black people at present within the borders of the Republic of South Africa account for some 13 per cent of the land area, whereas the black people account for some 70 per cent of the population. Inequity, injustice, oppression! cry the critics. Let's take a look at this question as it should be looked at—in fair and full perspective:

> By granting the blacks only 13 per cent of the Union's territory, and reserving for the whites most of the richest land . . . the Nationalists demonstrate at the outset a shocking lack of good faith: the *Telegraph,* London, 20.5.59.

At the end of the Anglo-Boer War, British South Africa consisted of the Cape, Natal, Transvaal, Orange Free State, Bechuanaland, Basutoland and Swaziland. This is the entity, commonly controlled from London, against which the apportionment of land, a continuing process, must be judged. It covered 765,000 square miles. The apportionment began in 1910 when the three last-named territories—black homelands— were set aside as British Protectorates (area, 293,000 square miles), and it continued with legislation passed by Pretoria in 1913 and 1936 which set aside as *Reserves* additional black homelands under Pretoria's jurisdiction (area, 60,000 square miles). The position then was that, of the 765,000 original square miles, 353,000 had been allocated to black people and the remaining 412,000 to white people. Therefore, of British South Africa as it was before 1910, the black people today possess something over 46 per cent; and that is the percentage they would have had today within Pretoria's borders had the 1910 intention that the Protectorates should be incorporated in the Union been implemented. In the event, the post-war British decision (supported by Pretoria) against incorporation—and the granting of independence to Botswana, Lesotho and Swaziland—reduced that percentage to some 13. The independence of the Transkei will reduce it to some 10; of BophuthaTswana, to some 7; of KwaZulu, to some 4, and so on. Should all the black homelands opt for independence as they are free to do, then the percentage of black land in the borders of the Republic of South Africa will be 0. But can this be regarded as a progressively more inequitable land distribution for the black people? The idea is absurd: the clear truth is that the diminishing proportion of land under Pretoria's jurisdiction belonging to black people is directly related to the measure of independence granted them. I repeat: had the course of independence for the black peoples not been followed, their proportion of the country today would have been 46 and not 13 per cent.

> Apartheid as applied in the Union of South Africa repre-
> sents an attempt, both brutal and foolish, to halt the march
> of history: Malcolm Muggeridge in the *Sunday Pictorial,*
> London, 15.3.59.

So much for the figures–and more particularly the one figure, 13 per cent, which the critics have chosen to abstract and isolate from the rest. Now for the title of the white man to the land he has. It has already been mentioned that when he arrived in the Cape in the mid-17th century, the nearest black settlements were some 500 miles to the north and some 1,000 miles to the east. Dealing with the subject a-quarter-of-a-century ago, Professor Edgar Brookes, representative of the black man in the Senate and one of the stoutest of all his representatives wrote: "Taking South Africa as a whole, what right have the Bantu to it which the Europeans have not? They are *not* the aborigines as so often termed: they are conquerors as foreign to South Africa in 1500 as Europeans were. If force confers rights on them as against Bushmen and Hottentots, it confers rights on Europeans as against them." Mr. B. K. Long, journalist and editor, wrote in his book, *In Smuts's Camp:* "The land in Southern Africa was not the land of the Bantu who were the ancestors of our natives . . . If the validity of title by conquest is to depend at all upon the treatment of the genuine aboriginal population then white title is, on the whole, considerably more valid than native title." Mr. L. E. Neame, another journalist and editor, wrote in 1952: "The whites in South Africa have as good a claim to their homeland as the Americans have to America or the Australasians have to Australasia. They founded their Mother City at the foot of the African continent while New York was still a small Dutch settlement called New Amsterdam, and more ships were entering Table Bay than sailed into the Hudson River. At one time there were nearly as many white people at the Cape of Good Hope as there were in Canada."

> It is on the creation of African ghetto states and the
> transformation of South Africa in the near but undefined
> future into a Republic that the Nationalist Government
> plans to solve the increasingly explosive racial problem: the
> *Telegraph,* London, 17.10.59.

There are other aspects of the land question. Acreage as a measure of productivity is meaningless: one acre of good soil is incomparably more productive than 10 or 100 or 1,000 acres of desert. The populations of Swaziland and Botswana are of the same order, but the per capita income of Swaziland is more than twice that of Botswana–which is 30 times its size. And the quality of Botswana land, incidentally, is similar to that of vast tracts of white-owned land in the Republic Proper. In the Republic of South Africa as a whole, 24, 7-million acres has a productive climate, and about half of this is in the black homelands. If these territories were properly farmed they would be able to support their present populations, and the increase in their populations, for the foreseeable future. The fact, however, is that traditional forms of black animal husbandry and agriculture are extremely inefficient. Despite active instruction and extension services through the years they remain so today–with the average yield per acre of grain in the homelands one-sixth of that in the Republic Proper. It is the more than 10-million tons of maize and wheat produced each year by white farmers which provides the guarantee against famine for the people of the homelands and also of neighbouring black states. The white farmers have made the Republic Proper the only exporter of grain in Africa: and every other consideration apart, and in terms alone of the supply of food, it would be reckless in present circumstances to transfer additional agricultural land from white to black hands. On this point Senator Brookes observed in the statement from which I have quoted: "The same argument applies to land occupation: as far as beneficial occupation goes, Europeans have the stronger claim."

> It is the sober truth that anyone who travels through South Africa and retains loyalty to the standards recognised, not only by the rest of the world but by most educated South Africans, will find it impossible to say a single approving word about apartheid . . . There is not a grain of common sense or humanity in the policy as it was devised by Dr. Verwoerd: Rebecca West in the *Sunday Times,* London, 27.3.60.

All these considerations must be set against the criticism that land distribution is unfair and that it denies the black people the opportunity of a decent and rising standard of living. At the same time, the present dispensation is unsatisfactory: of that there can be no doubt. The consolidation of each of the homelands (which will be dealt with later) is an urgent necessity. Land allocation in South Africa is, as has been pointed out, a continuing process, and the 1936 legislation cannot be regarded as having declared the last word on the subject.

But, finally, to be considered in conjunction with these various factors is this: that emotionally important though the possession of land may be, its economic significance is very different from what it used to be. The time when the wealth of a community was even roughly measurable by the number of acres it owned is past. Technological progress has been responsible for the change. In agriculture, yield now depends less on quantity of land than on quality of management, while the centre of gravity in modern economies as a whole has moved from the farm to the factory. The measure of a nation's wealth in the modern world is the degree of the availability to it of the technological means of production. More than 80 per cent of the goods produced in this country comes from factories situated in areas which account for some 3 per cent of the land surface. It is technological development and not the size of their territory that will determine the economic advance of the homelands; and it is their association and interdependence with a modern economy that will enable them to develop technologically. As opposed to a rigid division of population behind cartographic borders–that is, partition–separatism postulates co-operation, movement, interaction. It makes possible the acquisition of the knowledge and skills needed for the progress of black communities while safeguarding their autonomy.

Nevertheless there are those who advocate partition and an equitable division of the country's resources. One of them is Gwendoline Carter, Professor at Northwestern University and author of a book on South Africa called *The Politics of Inequality*. In an address to the South African Institute of Race Relations in 1966, one of her suggestions towards this end was "a fair share for black people of the wealth of the Witwatersrand." But this proposition of an equitable division of resources is near-impossible to contemplate in theory, let alone to apply in practice. The most important single "resource" of South Africa is unquestionably the white man's technological skill, ingenuity and capacity to conserve, plan and organise. How precisely is this commodity to be shared equally with Zulus and Xhosas? And what possibly can Professor Carter mean when she speaks of sharing the wealth of the Witwatersrand? Surely not that West Driefontein goldmine or Castle Breweries should be given to the black people to possess and operate, or that they should be split four-to-one in their favour? It is absurd. In realistic terms the means by which the ordinary individual participates actively in the wealth of a private enterprise society is by selling his labour, practising a trade or profession, operating his own farm or business, or owning a share in someone else's. Pretoria's policy (though it insists on influx control) enables the black man to sell his labour on the Witwatersrand (and elsewhere): it has been trying all it can to teach him to be a good farmer: it assists him to run a profession or a business–by making hard cash and training available and by protecting him in his own areas from the competition of economically more powerful groups; and it does not debar him from acquiring a share

90

in West Driefontein, or Castle Breweries, or OK Bazaars, or National Growth Fund or anything else the Stock Exchange has to offer. That, realistically, is what will enable him to share in the wealth of the Witwatersrand and of all South Africa–not partition, however generous, however extravagant, the land allocation.

> The prosperity and even survival of white South Africans depend on their ability to rid themselves of rulers who have shown that they are quite incapable of acting in contemporary terms. Relief everywhere would greet the news that apartheid is dead and damned: *The Times,* London, 6.4.60.

Economically, a policy which seeks to create a number of individually-viable units within the geographic entity of South Africa is untenable. The country is economically interdependent not only in terms of know-how and capital on the one hand and of manpower on the other, but also in terms of infra-structure and natural resources. The gold of the Witwatersrand, the diamonds of South West Africa, the water of Lesotho, the coal of the Transvaal, the maize of the Orange Free State, the pastures of the Transkei, the harbours of Durban and Cape Town–all these constitute together the wealth of South Africa, the opportunity for employment and the prospect of prosperity for all who live in the country. Pretoria's policy recognises this: it combines the advantages of partition and integration while countering the hazards of each. The politically-autonomous state for which it provides will be the custodian of its people's culture: it will be the heartland, but it is the body of South Africa as a whole that will provide the material needs of all her communities, white, black and brown. There is in South Africa a *common wealth* to which each individual, whatever his colour or nationality, may contribute and from which he may draw. *Equity does not demand a division among our nations of this common wealth–which is impossible: what is does demand is that each individual should be given the opportunity to make his maximum contribution and that his contribution should be fairly rewarded.* It is to this that increasing attention needs to be given.

> There is real danger that unless South Africa heeds world opinion and modifies its harsh policies the whole of Africa could be threatened with a racial violence as wasteful and merciless as the religious wars of Western Europe: the *Washington Post,* 3.4.60.

Legislation

I have outlined the circumstances in which the choice for apartheid was made in 1948, and the political, social and economic dispensation which it foreshadowed. At that time, race tension in the urban areas was acute; while in the black *Reserves* the traditional structures of society were collapsing: the sentiment of nationality of the black people was being smothered, and the leadership which they understood and respected was being usurped by unrepresentative urban élites. The first task (as Prime Minister Vorster has noted) was to sort out the muddle that had accumulated in the preceding couple of decades. For this, legislation was indispensable. It was the previous lack of decisive action, the taking of the line of least resistance, the patching-up of a problem here and the turning of a blind eye to a problem there, the muddling-through syndrome–it was this that had led to the mess, to community insecurity and to the degeneration of differentiation into discrimination. Discrimination, prejudice, suspicion, fear and confusion were the order of the day. The country was afflicted with a deepening racial malaise; and two categories of remedy had to be applied. The first was short-term and negative: the elimination by law and regulation of points of contact between the races which in the then prevailing atmosphere were points of potential conflict. The second category was long-term and positive: the establishing of a *modus vivendi* in which each community would feel secure, and in which prejudice and discrimination would accordingly diminish. The adjustment of forces lying deep in the psyche was involved: negative separatism would be necessary while, in such sensitive areas, positive separatism slowly did its therapeutic work.

The urban areas were the immediate challenge. In the generation preceding 1948 industrialisation had fast gathered momentum. People had streamed from the rural areas to the new centres of employment, and inadequate planning and inadequate accommodation had led to appalling conditions. In many of the places where they lived and bred, habitations were made of rusted iron, rotten boards, rags and paraffin tins. There were no proper water supplies, no lighting or sanitation; and the faceless misery of these urban agglomerations was well expressed in the word by which they were called–*locations*. The *locations* proliferated from Johannesburg to Port Elizabeth, Cape Town and Durban. They were swept by epidemics and exploited by rent racketeers and political agitators. Among their inhabitants there were smouldering racial animosities which erupted often into violence.

> The cause is a paralysing fear on the part of the white
> minority, particularly the Afrikaners . . . a very similar
> emotion figures in the difficulties in the South of the United
> States–with the distinction that here it is the policy of the

Federal Government to eliminate racial discrimination: the
Washington Post, 30.3.60.

Legislators toyed with the situation. They regarded the urban problem as the inevitable teething trouble of industrialisation. They supposed that in due course of time things would somehow or other right themselves; that a regulation here, an administrative control there, would suffice. It didn't: the situation got progressively worse. In the years before and during the War, the influx to the industrial areas became a flood. When the hostilities abroad ended, the *location* hostages exceeded two million, and on all sides there were predictions of an imminent explosion and national disaster.

Dr. Malan's Government designed a comprehensive programme to deal with the situation. It was backed by legislation for slum removal and for the prevention of squatting. The Group Areas Act provided residential areas of their own for the different population groups; and the Native Building Workers' Act provided for the first time for the large-scale training and employment of black artisans to build homes for their own people. One by one the *locations* were demolished, and in their place rose townships with well-built, though drab, houses and a range of amenities. The scope of the operation is illustrated by the plans for the township 15 miles southwest of Johannesburg: 23 civic centres, 75 schools, 346 miles of streets, 60 sportsfields. Before the 1950s went out, 100,000 houses for black people had been built in the urban areas; and the programme was so successful that it became a model for low-cost housing in other parts of Africa, Southern Europe and South East Asia.

> The suppressed people of Africa are also determined to fight for their existence and their rights, and if this fight is to be carried on by violence and repression a great deal of blood will flow before the issue can be resolved: the *Washington Post,* 11.4.60.

The *location* was a thing of the past: the black man had been provided with at least a decent material environment . . . but what of his psychological environment? From his close-knit tribe on which he was peculiarly dependent for his emotional well-being he had been catapulted into totally alien surroundings; and he and his two million fellows had become a hopelessly fragmented mass of humanity.

Johannesburg, 1947: Bambata looked up from the paper, but for a moment there was no sign of recognition. Then his face brightened.

" 'Nkosana!" he cried, " 'Nkosana!" I sat at the end of his hospital bed and took his hand.

"You did not know me at first", I said. "But I would have not known you either. It must be ten years since we saw one another. I did not even know you were in Johannesburg until I received a letter from my father."

"Even if you had known, it could have made no difference, not here in Johannesburg", he said. "You know that, 'Nkosana. But tell me how it goes with you and your father and the farm?" We spoke about these things and the weather and the possibility of rain. I asked how his health was and he said he was recovering.

"Then you are lucky", I said. "Many people do not recover from this disease–TB."

"Yes, I am lucky." He spoke without enthusiasm and dropped his eyes to his lap where he fidgeted with the paper.

"Your voice says one thing and your appearance another", I said. "I see you are much changed from the days when you and I were boys together."

"Yes, that is so. You are also changed. There are two lives–the boy's life and the man's life. They are not the same. One does not realise how black one is until one is a man." We went on speaking about this and that, and then he said: "Have you seen those children lying in there? They also have TB."

"Yes, I saw them as I passed. Why do you ask?"

"I just asked."

I reflected. "I am going to say something which I would say to few men, Bambata. When I saw them, I thought to myself: what crime have these children committed that they lie there like that? I asked myself: Is it their crime that they are black? That is the question I asked myself and I tell you because you are my friend and I know you are not a fool."

"There is much talk of that kind these days", he said. "Many say these things are the fault of the white man. White men themselves and Indians and our own people tell us that, and many of us, especially here in Johannesburg, believe them. It is easy to believe them and it is conforting."

"What about you? What do you think?"

South Africa has gone ahead with relating urban Africans, who have long since lost any notion of tribal affinity, with their putative tribal authorities in the reserves. This is analogous with putting everybody with the patronymic "mac" under an ethnic authority with its headquarters in the Highlands: the *Guardian*, London, 29.6.60.

"I am not sure, 'Nkosana. But I do know that it is not all the white man's fault. I am like the other black people here. I do not know what I think." He smiled suddenly. "You have seen ants when they work. They hurry here through the grass, they climb there up a tree, there they cross a stream. They make themselves into a bridge and the others cross it. They attack a worm. They kill it and piece by piece they take it home. The grown ants defend the nest from the enemy. There are many, many hundreds of these ants and yet each and every one knows what he must do and quickly and without misunderstanding he does it. But that is because of the law of the nest and the Great Mother Ant who is very fat and ugly but is nevertheless the lawgiver. And if the Great Mother is killed, then what happens? The ants outside lose their way. They cannot get home. They fall off trees and into the water. Instead of helping one another they attack one another. The worm, as he is dying, is let loose and he gets away. The little insects run in their fright in all directions their horns turning this way and that, and all is confusion. Do you understand, 'Nkosana? It is just so with the black people of Johannesburg. It is as though our Great Mother was dead." He paused, then suddenly laughed outright. "You must excuse me. How does it go with you? It would go well from what I see."

"I am not happy here in Johannesburg", I said. "There is no place for me here either and yet I must find one. I cannot go back to my farm because I am a white man and I have responsibilities which are different from yours. There are many differences between white men and black men and that is one of them, but the differences are not always what they seem to be. I listened very carefully to what you said just now, and I can tell you this: it is not only the black people who are without their Great Mother."

Bambata touched my hand and spoke very seriously: "What you say makes me happy. You give me hope, for there is hope in this." (11)

That is a long extract from my diary. I have reproduced it to give flesh and blood to the meaning of being one in a fragmented mass of humanity. It also explains why I am writing this book: it is because of my personal knowledge of the experience of men like Bambata that I am committed to the cause of separatism.

The critics said (and say) that urbanisation has destroyed the black man's values and that the white governments have put nothing in their place. The charge is devoid of meaning: a government in Europe might as well be accused of putting nothing in the place of yesterday's concept of marriage and family life. The fact is that such things are simply not "put-able": all that a government can do is to provide an environment for them. This is what separatism is designed to do: to give everyone at all wherever in the country a sense of belonging in a national community, and the right together with his countrymen to shape its destiny. For the black man everywhere that called for the re-establishment of effective focal points of national loyalty–and so the centre of gravity of policy implementation swung to the only place it could be done, the traditional homelands.

Cape Town sits among the mountains and vineyards of a

land more enchanting than Provence. It is the seat of
Parliament, and its principal manufactures are wine, fruit,
hatred and despair. Turn-over in the first has been average
this year, but productivity in the last is the greatest of the
century: James Cameron in the *News Chronicle,* 7.7.59.

They were to be the scene for revivifying the Bantu nations, but this
meant legislation. In the words of Dr. Verwoerd, then Minister of Native
Affairs: "A system which has developed over the centuries among the
Bantu, a system which is known to them–indeed, a system which is
incorporated in their own native laws and engraved in their souls–is being
taken as the starting point of development." In 1951 came the Bantu
Authorities Act which vested authority again in the authentic leadership;
in 1953, the Bantu Education Act which introduced a system of
education of, by and for the Bantu people; in 1959, legislation for
universities of their own; and in the same year, the Promotion of Bantu
Self-government Act which provided the first constitutional rung on the
ladder to sovereign independence. None of these developments in the
urban areas or in the homelands would have been possible without
legislation:

South Africa's Promotion of Bantu Self-government bill is a
peculiar compound of faith, hope and even charity. But the
faith is fanatical, the hope unrealistic and the charity
poisoned at source: the *Telegraph,* London, 20.5.59.

London, 1956: The situation can perhaps roughly be explained by these
two equations: advanced people + less-advanced people + industrialisation + laissez faire = segregation (or horizontal division) . . . advanced
people + less-advanced people + industrialisation + legislation =
apartheid (or vertical division). From these equations it will be seen that
the difference between a horizontal and a vertical division of society is
legislation. (12)

Yet it was the legislation which it passed that was the basis of universal
condemnation of Pretoria. Yes, the critics conceded, there were caste
systems, there were ghettoes, there was race prejudice and discrimination
in many countries, but nowhere else were these things *legislated for.* The
outside world had not the foggiest notion of what was going on. Brushing
aside with arrogant self-righteousness the explanations of the Pretoria
Government, it identified apartheid with discrimination and attributed to
it the very condition it was designed to remove.

The evil policy of apartheid cannot help bearing evil fruit.

96

There is a sense of tragedy hanging over that country: the
New York Times, 22.3.1960.

Articulating a Philosophy

But it must be said that people abroad were misled also by political
opponents of apartheid in this country (particularly by the opposition
press)–and by supporters of apartheid who regarded it merely as a means
for maintaining the status quo and the white man's privileged position. I
have stated that at the cross-roads in 1948 it was a direction–not a
programme or a detailed plan of action–that was chosen. The goal in
broad outline was clear to the leaders, but the advance towards it was
made in the beginning in an *ad hoc* way, and during the first dozen years
at home the whole scene was confused by the Afrikaner-Anglosan
dispute and the Republican issue. But in response to mounting questioning and condemnation abroad, it was urgently necessary on the distant
diplomatic fronts (London, Washington, the United Nations) to articulate Pretoria's policy into a coherent concept of human relations. In reply
to the challenge, the cluster of ideas that constitute separatism was
gradually given definitive expression. For instance: that separatism is a
cultural rather than a geographic concept; that the sentiment of
nationality is deep-rooted, ineradicable, in the human psyche; that borders
of national consciousness override cartographic borders; that where
diverse people live together, harmony does not depend on *individual*
rights or universal franchise but on security for the way of life of each
community; that the entitlement to sovereignty does not reside in
numbers or powers or resources, but in the right of every people to be
themselves; that separatism *is* self-determination since it confers this right
upon them; that emancipation is not achieved by giving constitutional
independence to *territories,* but by enabling *peoples* to design their own
destiny; that the "alien mould" is the inhibitor-in-chief of self-realisation;
that the most fundamental of human rights is the right of men to be true
to their origin and their kind; that a sense of identity is essential to the
dignity of the individual, and that these general principles have a universal
validity.

South Africa can only reply that foreign newspapermen are
telling lies about it. It would be hard to tell any lies that are
more damning than the proclaimed fact about the segrega-
tionist policy that is called "apartheid": the *New York
Times*, 10.4.60

97

To this articulation, incidentally, Anglosans made at least their fair contribution: and as the 1960s began, apartheid had to support it a definitive, comprehensive and coherent philosophy. It had become a full-fledged idea with a dynamic of its own.

> *Pretoria, 1962:* The leaders of Afrikaner thought have always believed that the preservation of their own way of life was as important for the Bantu as for themselves. At the same time it is true that many supporters of apartheid saw it in the beginning as separate queues in post offices and more comfortable seats in the bus for themselves. This is no oddity in the history of ideas. For people who sat round the *Place de la Concorde,* and for many other Frenchmen besides, liberty, equality and fraternity meant chopping off noblemen's heads. The majority of people anywhere haven't the time to do abstract thinking about the nature of society and human relations. They are too busy doing other things (growing mealies, driving trains) which in aggregate are just as important. And it doesn't really matter in the long run what this or that person thinks about an idea. Once released it has an existence of its own. It goes out and away beyond recall, because ideas have wings that cannot be clipped. Apartheid released the idea that South Africa's race problem could be solved on the basis of the principle that it is a good thing for a man to be himself. You can't contain an idea like that in a sign on a post office door. It doesn't matter how many of them you put up. (13)

"Apartheid" or "Separate Development"?

Nevertheless there was by this time support, even among leading members of the National Party, for dropping the word "apartheid". It means nothing more nor less than apart-ness. (The Random House dictionary defines "apart'" as "having independent or unique qualities, features or characteristics"–which represented precisely the thinking of the architects of Pretoria's policy.) The world however refused to have it that way, and within a few years "apartheid" had become perhaps the most scorned of all words in the international vocabulary. It was because of this that even ardent champions of the policy were, as the 1950s ran out, advocating the abandoning of the term and the use instead of "separate development".

In 1959, when I was on home leave from London, Foreign Minister Louw called me in and asked my view on the desirability of making such a change in our overseas publicity. I told him I was not in favour; and my grounds were as follows:

We might abandon "apartheid" but our critics wouldn't. Whatever policy, short of total integration, we might adopt and whatever we might call it, it would continue to be vilified in the outside world. The one trump card we held in the conflict was our belief in the essential rightness of apartheid. Changing its description would do nothing to still the hostility. On the contrary, it would be regarded by our enemies as a retreat and would encourage intensified attack, while at home it would be seen as a loss of self-confidence in our cause. What was needed was not that we should turn our back on "apartheid", but that we should press on tirelessly with the presentation of evidence toward its vindication.

A second point I made was that, desirable though development (in "separate development") might be, it confused the core-meaning of apartheid. This was a philosophy of human relations which asserted that different peoples could live in harmony together only if they were free to maintain those unique qualities, features and characteristics, and to order their society in accord with their own interpretation of the world and meaning of life. Development could be favourable to this idea or unfavourable. For instance, rapid industrial development might do wonders for a backward community's economy, but play havoc with its culture; and while abandoning the Westminster Model would generally be regarded as political retrogression–not development–it might nevertheless be essential for protecting the integrity of the community's traditional and organic institutions. The fact is that development is incidental to the crux of apartheid. (Perhaps Kant might have put the point as follows: The proposition that apartheid *is* separate development is *a priori* false, since its predicate falls outside the meaning of the subject. But development may or may not be an empirical adjunct of apartheid!)

However that may be, Mr. Louw said in so many words: Very well, when you get back to London, do it your way. But we agreed on a compromise-*separatism.* As the nearest exact translation of apartheid in ordinary language, it could not be regarded as a retreat nor would it confuse the central concept. The upshot of our discussion was that *apartheid, separatism* and *separate development* should be used as the context required.

99

the world and insisted upon the correctness of their policy of racial coercion against their Negro majority: the *Age,* Australia, 24.3.60.

I returned to London in good heart. The foundations for separatism had been firmly laid, the structure to be built on them had been delineated and, with the settlement of the Republican issue in sight, the way was being opened for vigorous progress. But as we shall see in Part II, unforeseen and dreadful challenges were to present themselves.

Meantime, to wrap in a wise and serene package the relationship between Pretoria and the world at this stage, I am going to quote Dr. Jack Holloway, a man with as long and as broad an experience of this country's affairs as any other. As High Commissioner, he was my chief in London and it was my good fortune to have his enlightened judgment on a great variety of complex matters, ranging from the role of gold in the monetary system to the role of liberalism in human affairs. Since he is the patron of the bi-quarterly journal which I publish and since he wrote the following words for it, I take the liberty of including his remarks in my diary. I might add that, despite the look of his name, Dr. Holloway is an Afrikaner through and through:

Pretoria, 1964: As a student under the guidance of such men as Wallas, Cannan and Dickenson at the London School of Economics, I was steeped in the liberal philosophic approach to society. Later I was director of South Africa's Office of Census and Statistics and, later again, Secretary for Finance. I was also charged from time to time with investigating a great variety of subjects such as the social condition of the Bantu, tariffs, local authorities, universities, taxation, housing. My early career thus gave me a thorough training in theoretical ideas about society, and my later career made me fairly conversant with facts and figures about it . . .

The First World War and its aftermath violently changed the climate in which the liberal philosophy had flourished. Idealism conflicted with a new set of realities whose force could not be denied; and in the home of its origins the achievements of the philosophy wilted away. It was at this stage, as with a vengeance, that it was launched abroad into the realm of race relations. In the days of its glory in Europe and America, it had been dealing with the latter phases of a long evolution and concerned relations with individuals all of whom enjoyed a basic unity of civilisation, culture, way of life and ideals. In transferring it to Africa (among other places), its proponents tacitly assumed that the same climate of affairs existed there. In so doing they were grappling with problems that had their being only in their own experience and, moreover, seeking to apply methods that were designed primarily for their own moral and intellectual satisfaction.

100

This sickness of South Africa is a symptom of a world sickness that can be cured only by the medicine of sanity, justice and tolerance: the *New York Times,* 1.4.60.

It is this which created the gulf between South African policy and its critics abroad. Our policy has been evolved, and we continue to pursue it, not because we are pig-headed or resent advice but because to us is not accorded the privilege of disregarding the inexorable human realities that surround us. These realities are no more amenable to generalised liberal theory (say, of the equality and brotherhood of man) than were those which arose from the First World War. The primary demand upon statesmanship in South Africa is to pay attention to the actual conditions which confront us, and to sort out, identify and try to understand the pieces of this giant human zig-saw. I have no doubt that such a process of sorting out is a precondition for the success of any policy in this land. Ask any practising scientist (i.e. a man who deals with the real world) and he will tell you his work cannot succeed unless and until he separates out the ingredients of the matter he is dealing with. (14)

Part two: / *Section one*
1960 to 1970–

The World Context:
   Disillusion

The West and Its Leaders

Lost Dreams

In the 1960s the Western world, disillusioned, moved towards break-down.

"We have had so many victories that we are in a difficult position. A people with political liberty, full employment and social security has lost its dreams."

The man who said that was Per Albin Hansson, one of the architects of the most famous perhaps of all welfare states, Sweden. The ambition of the socialists to transform Sweden into a state with security for all from cradle to grave was brilliantly achieved, and the victories of which Mr. Hansson spoke were manifold. Jeremy Bentham's greatest-happiness principle had been put spectacularly into practice. At the time Mr. Hansson made his remark there was no unemployment in the country, no poverty, no slums. Among the social benefits that everyone shared were free hospitalisation, free education, family allowances, old-age pensions irrespective of means, monthly grants for high-school and university students. Vacant jobs outnumbered unemployed workers five to one. Virtually every family had a car and television set; many had boats and private summer cottages. That looked like the sort of society men had been praying through the ages for: but something drastic had gone wrong somewhere. Perhaps one of the reasons was that praying was out of fashion. Having proved themselves so efficient in providing for their apparent needs themselves, Swedes had perhaps decided that it was not necessary to seek assistance elsewhere. In any case, atheism and moral nihilism were the vogue among the country's young intellectuals who dominated public discussion ... But what *was* it that was drastically wrong? In the 15 years between 1950 and 1965 the crime rate increased 97 per cent, and the actual number of crimes from 172,000 to 373,000.

Two-thirds of all offenders were under age, with youths under 20 responsible for four of every five car thefts and for half of all robberies. At the same time there was a steady growth in alcoholism, drug addiction and promiscuity. Increase in venereal disease among young people was described as catastrophic: in 1964 medical authorities reported 23,000 new cases–twice as many as six years before. Professor Knut Sveri, head of Stockholm's Institute of Criminal Science, saw the basic causes in the weakness of family ties, loss of parental authority and the welfare state itself. Poverty was no longer the cause of stealing, he observed. Sweden was facing a new kind of lawlessness which spread with rising standards of living. He called it "welfare criminality".

In Britain–the largest of the welfare states and their conceptual originator–the people by the mid-1960s were no longer having it so good. The master-builder of Britain's welfare state, Lord Beveridge, had warned them some 15 years before. In 1951, in an article in *The Spectator* he had expressed his dismay at the immorality of a populace "all too ready to assume that, without much personal exertion, it is their entitlement to draw their share of an inexhaustible common fund from centralised authority." He wrote: "Can a country whose destiny (in part at least) is in the hands of a people so irresponsible and so ignorant hope to be well-governed?" His warning was not heeded, and now–in the mid-1960s–left-wing socialist Anthony Wedgwood Benn is speaking of "discontent expressing itself in apathy or violent protest which could engulf us all in bloodshed." And Tory Angus Maude is writing of the necessity to protect parliamentary democracy from "the virtual certainty of an ultimate outbreak of popular violence."

In the United States, education, science, ingenuity and the machine have produced wealth quite beyond comprehension. By the mid-1960s the country's annual national product is moving towards 1,000,000,000,-000 dollars; and in 1968 an army of poor camp in a shanty-town near the monuments to Washington, Lincoln and Jefferson, called *Resurrection City*. In the last ten years the population of the United States grows 10 per cent: the incidence of crime, 88 per cent. The income of gangster organisations is reckoned in tens of billions–from protection rackets, gambling and traffic in women and drugs. The successful politician is the man with money, with the right public relations firm, the polished image, the ability to capitalise on grievances and emotions. The President of the United States of America may not move freely among the people for fear of being killed. He and his Ministers must move through by-ways and back-doors: decoys are sent out to draw the assassin's bullet. "We hold these truths to be self-evident: that all men are created equal, that they are endowed by their creator with certain inalienable rights; that among these are life, liberty and the pursuit of happiness."

In France at this same time–the mid-1960s–discord and hatred threaten another revolution. But the French revolutionaries now are not oppressed peasants or factory workers but students of the Sorbonne versed in the arts and humanities. Their objective is not to improve the lot of their fellow men: the Government's offer to reform education and raise wages merely incites them further. They are not reformers but anarchists. These young men and women of the Sorbonne–well-educated, well-read, privileged–have laid bare the fangs of naked intellect. It is no coincidence that their comrades in anarchy are ex-mercenaries from the Congo: with no other guide than reason, the intellect would as soon consort with violence as with virtue. We have it on the authority of that mild-mannered Scottish philosopher, David Hume: "When a passion is neither founded on false suppositions nor chooses means insufficient for the end, the understanding can neither justify it nor condemn it. It is not contrary to Reason to prefer the destruction of the whole world to the scratching of my finger."

Can you believe it? None of this is fiction: it is all fact; in fact, it is the basic facts. The four countries mentioned here are the home, respectively: of the Nobel Prizes for Peace and so on; of parliamentary democracy; of free enterprise, and of liberty, equality and fraternity. These are main pillars of our Western culture, but the rot in them has been hidden from the ordinary man's eyes by the froth of pseudo-liberal effusions.

We are going to take a closer look now at America and then Britain.

(1) THE UNITED STATES

Golden and Other Gods

In America as the 1960s open only one of its two faces is at all visible: it is bright, it is golden. Two Americans personify the golden myth: a golden girl and a golden boy: Marilyn Monroe and Jack Kennedy. Marilyn, body and lips lusciously curved: the ultimate symbol of sex: of sex, exploited, yes, but as yet unperverted: the poor little American girl making gloriously good. Jack Kennedy, young, handsome, courageous, intelligent: the American boy whose dad made good and is showing the world that massive wealth may also produce men dedicated to public service and the cause of mankind; charismatic, chimeratic.

The success of Marshall Aid in Europe has fired still further America's zeal to reshape the world. The ancient heart of Western civilisation, weak to death and imminently threatened, has been restored by infusions of American strength. The first of America's post-war crusades has succeeded beyond all expectation, and achievement seems to have no limit. Africa, Asia, the Near East, the Far East: all can be transformed. The earth–and space–are waiting for America. Optimism is unbounded and rhetoric unrestrained. Idealism is inflated and loyalties proliferate to mankind, democracy, racial integration, universal peace, the conquest of space, the advancement of the more backward members of the human race. Congress votes billions of dollars of aid for the emergent nations. Experts are assigned to the furtheest corners of the earth to teach the techniques of government and progress; young Americans sally forth with the Peace Corps to point the way for Asians, Africans, Arabs to the good life. Jack Kennedy speaks in his inaugural address of "taking up the torch of the first revolution, the American revolution for liberty and human rights". He vows to beat the Russians and put an American on the moon before the decade is out. America races on to reach the unreachable goals. The people share the inspiration: the two great parties–the Democrats and the Republicans–take the same course, switch lanes at the bends. You can't distinguish them from the grandstand . . . until Senator Barry Goldwater in 1964 changes the nature of the Republican running and for a time brings into focus the foreground of American affairs.

Pretoria, 1964: An article written by a little-known author, Charles Brower, and called *In Defence of Squares* has won wide attention in the United States. With the ridiculing of the square, Mr. Brower notes, the sneer has replaced the grin on the face of America and laughter has been replaced by Mort Sahl's cackle of despair. Mr. Brower suggests, to counteract this "great nothing of cynical sophistication", the formation of a new society, the Society of Squares–SOS. He cautions, though, that it might have to go underground for a while to avoid being trampled to death by the rat-packs of cynical saboteurs . . .

Now, was the nomination of Senator Goldwater in July an SOS that went out to save a civilisation? Because we have it from historian Toynbee that, of the world's 21 notable civilisations, 19 perished from no other cause than evaporation of belief within. In any case, the rat-packs Mr. Brower predicted have been in full cry. A leader of the rat-pack, London's *New Statesman*, writes that the significance of the Goldwater candidacy is its threat to the paramountcy of reason. I think many of the Senator's followers would accept that analysis. Kneeling for so long at the feet of Reason, they are revolted at what it has brought them. Senator Goldwater's candidacy–win or lose–means that at a time when reason itself is being automated, American people are once more in search of other gods. (15)

Some Americans, it turned out, *were* in search of other gods: many were: indeed, 25-million voted for Senator Goldwater. But it was not enough–not nearly: having been caricatured by the media (his own word was "crucified" when he spoke to me about it) he was overwhelmed at the polls. Lyndon Johnson was firmly back in power. In the months that followed, any doubt that the election might have raised was swept aside. Everything again seemed possible. Secretary of State Dean Rusk spoke of "a worldwide democracy–victory for all mankind, a worldwide victory for freedom." More specifically, Defence Secretary McNamara said that all America's boys would be victorious in Vietnam and back home for Christmas, 1965.

But year after year the Vietnam War continued: and as one after another of Senator Goldwater's recommendations were belatedly implemented, a credibility gap wide as the ocean that separates the United States from South East Asia opened between the American people and their Administration. Opposition to the war was expressed in violent protest and demonstration around the nation and on its campuses. Draft-dodgers were the new folk-heroes and their behaviour was made to seem moral by the backing the churches gave them. Patriotism was one of many of the civic virtues in a state of collapse. And while Washington fought for a world of law and order, women feared to travel alone on the underground in New York at night. It was reported by a leading broadcast network that the Mafia paid more to the country's policemen in bribes than the government did in salaries. Profits from drugs, pornography and lewdness reached all-time highs. Dolls–inanimate dolls, that is– were put through their sex paces on the New York stage: the Lord's Prayer was banned from public schools. Malcolm Muggeridge commented from across the Atlantic: "It is the inevitable mark of the decadence of our society. As our vitality ebbs people reach out for vicarious excitement." The pseudo-liberal apologists declared that all this was emancipating: that the movement towards individual freedom, self-expression and permissiveness could not and should not be reversed. Administration spokesmen maintained the pretence of the Great Society: they were speaking still in the second half of the 1960s of "independence from the dregs of mankind's past of ill-health, poverty, ignorance and short life: independence from fear and hatred and from the degradation of racial discrimination."

Civil Rights

The Civil Rights Movement began in 1954. In 1965 it was finally victorious: all legislative discrimination against the Negroes was removed, and the law provided them with opportunity equal to that of every other American. The crowning triumph was the voting rights bill which assured Negroes effective use of the franchise. While the passage of that bill was being celebrated in Washington, the worst Negro riots in the country's history occurred in Los Angeles: 34 people were killed, 3,800 were arrested and damage to property was estimated at 175-million dollars. It was the first eruption of its kind: in the hot summers that followed, the flames of Negro frustration were to sear the night sky of many another American city. In May, 1965 President Johnson said it was apparent that legal freedom was not enough: "In spite of the court orders and the laws, the victories and the speeches, for the Negroes the walls are rising, the gulf is widening." The President said he did not know the full reason for this, and that an answer could not be found in the experience of other American minorities. They had made a successful effort to emerge from poverty and prejudice: but, he noted, success and achievement did not change the colour of a man's skin. Commenting, Stanley Burch reported for the *Johannesburg Star:* "The dreams of the Negroes range from an America where white and black are utterly and harmoniously mixed, to an America with an all-black state that excludes all white men with the furious pride of segregation in reverse. Their methods range from turning the other cheek, to terrorism; their weapons, from prayers and hymns to sawn-off shotguns."

In July, 1967 the first national convention in the United States of Black Power was held in Newark. Resolutions passed called for black universities and black national holidays; proposals were made to boycott black magazines that accepted advertisements for hair-straighteners and bleaching creams. The entire emphasis was on blackness: delegates who used the term Negro were shouted down. The following month Martin Luther King (soon to be assassinated) called for commitment to "the sense of negritude" and to "Afro-American unity". The convention of the Southern Christian Leadership Conference which he was addressing passed a resolution recommending "a sane doctrine of negritude–through art, music, and all other media–that will obliterate from the mind of the black people any vestige of inferiority." In 1968, 2,000 students at Howard University staged a sit-in and drove the university's administrators from their offices. Ninety per cent of Howard's 8,000 students were black. For more than a century Howard had groomed the sons of slaves, their grandsons and great-grandsons for entry into white middle-class society. To be a "Howard man" was, through those generations, the height of academic and social ambition for countless young Negroes. But now they no longer wanted to be groomed for entry into middle-class white society: they demanded that Howard should henceforth "relate to the black community the way that Harvard and the Massachusetts Institute of Technology relate to the white community." Summing up the mood, black intellectual Nathan Hare explained: "Assimilation mortifies the ego of the black man. Integration and equalisation are not

110

the same thing. Trying to act like white men and adopting their customs has failed. Liberal reform over the centuries has led nowhere. Integration is not a desirable end in itself, and accordingly black people are moving under Black Power towards self-assertion."

Influential individual white Americans were also re-assessing the desirability of integration. One of them was Mr. George Kennan, Pulitzer Prize winner and former American Ambassador in Moscow. In June, 1968, he spoke on the subject at historic Williamsburg in Virginia. He said that it was necessary that the Negroes in America should have their own local political communities "where their people can express themselves collectively and gain both authority and responsibility", and that this was in line with what certain Negro leaders were themselves advocating. He said that Negroes could not now make their way into the American system: that as individuals they could not compete in a political set-up which they neither understood nor respected and for which they were ill-prepared. He went further: he said it was necessary to restrict the migration of Negroes into American cities–either by persuading them through economic incentives to stay where they were, or by direct administrative control.

However the Administration kept to its conviction in the possibility of a single harmonious American society capable of accommodating all its kinds of people. As in Britain, so in the United States, the thought that race might have something to do with black-white tension was shunned like the plague: consciousness of race and a desire for the recognition of ethnic identity was the infectious product of sick minds. And the issue was fuzzed by official jargon: "ultimately", wrote the United States Information Service in July, 1967, "it is likely that the plight of the urban Negro is but one more aspect of the long and difficult process, known as the industrial revolution. This is a total process, affecting the countryside as well as the cities, and like all total processes, it brings massive disruption."

The Thread of Credibility

Washington's commitment to undifferentiated equalitarianism at home was, under the Democrats and despite all evidence to the contrary, unalterable. There was much evidence also of failure to reach global goals. American aid and ideas had been fed into the emergent world with the same generosity, the same enthusiasm and the same high purpose as they had been fed into war-torn Europe. But the essential conditions for successful transfusion from the United States to the Third World did not exist. The cultures of donor and recipients were too different, and a high

111

degree of incompatibility marred the operation. Where there were indications of new vitality, they were superficial. Organic structures on which the systems of the emergent people depended were broken down. The lifestream which was the legacy of their own experience was thinned: the springs of organic activity were weakened: the reaction was rejection of the donor and its tissues. Emancipated communities abandoned democracy: totalitarian governments tightened their control: the European states, restored to strength by Uncle Sam, sought their own advantage at his expense—and North Korea seized an American man-of-war on the high seas. And yet, in 1967, Mr. Joseph W. Barr, Under-Secretary of the Treasury in Mr. Johnson's Administration, was still saying: "Once again Americans are carrying out an exclusively creative revolution. Where Americans once fought a war of independence, they now fight for independence from war. They seek independence from war not just for themselves but for everyone without exception. They seek a world community of nations that will be as averse to destruction and as orientated to creative change as was, and is, the American society started by our war of independence."

Seventeen seventy-six to nineteen sixty-seven: the indestructible dream!

And now as I draft this chapter I read in the popular press the posthumous fate of the Golden Girl and the Golden Boy. We know that both were dead some dozen and more years ago: Marilyn Monroe on August 4, 1962, we were told, by her own hand: Jack Kennedy on November 22, 1963, by the hand of an assassin, Lee Oswald. That is what we were told, though there was soon much speculation about the accuracy and the completeness of the information we were given. Now the popular press provides us with details as they are to be published by Anthony Scaduto in the *Oui* magazine of the *Playboy* organisation. Scaduto claims (according to a press release on the article) that Robert Slatzer, a former husband of Marilyn, told him that she had said soon before her death that she was angry because Bobby Kennedy (also later assassinated) had broken a promise to marry her. She threatened to call a press conference but was dissuaded by Slatzer on the ground it would be dangerous for her. According to Scaduto, a wire-tapping expert, Bernard Spindel, told him he bugged Marilyn's telephone on orders of Jimmy Hoffa, former President of the Teamsters' Union, who was sent to prison following an investigation by Bobby, then Attorney General, on charges of mail fraud and tampering with a jury. At the time of the alleged wire-tapping, Hoffa wanted to obtain recordings to use against Bobby. These tapes (so the story goes), subsequently stolen from Spindel, were potentially so embarrassing that Bobby unsuccessfully offered Spindel a large sum of money for them. One tape was a record of a telephone conversation on the morning Marilyn died, in which an unidentified

112

caller asked: "Is she dead yet?". Scaduto alleges: "The evidence of the murder was suppressed to protect John and Robert Kennedy. Almost certainly both had been her lovers." He maintains certain Los Angeles police officials admitted privately that their files contained a 723-page document on microfilm labelled "Marilyn Monroe–Murder."

The truth of this story is irrelevant: adultery, murder, assassination, bribery, miscarriage of justice, abuse of executive power, tapes and bugging. The lie is no less indicative of the mood of American disillusion than the truth would be. The story has been read by millions, and many are prepared and conditioned to believe it. They do not dismiss it as fiction. Was ever a golden age so debased, a vision so violated?

Such is the common measure, known to all today, of the disintegration of America's post-war public idealism. In 1967, I wrote:

> *Pretoria, 1967:* Actual events at home and abroad, the true nature of men and the world, are cutting to the quick of Washington's creed, but there is no abatement in the zeal or the inconsistency of the American mission. From the pens of ghost-writers and the mouths of national spokesmen the cascade of eloquent clichés continues. Their spray obscures the black rocks of reality that loom behind. But for how long? The threads of credibility are stretched to snapping point. (16)

Mr. Nixon

On November 5, 1968 the threads of credibility in the Democratic Administration snapped. Richard Nixon was elected to the White House: and his performance at home and abroad resulted in his re-election with a huge majority four years later. During that period, when the United States was once again an effective world leader, great changes occurred in the international scene. As 1973 began there was an even-keel look about world affairs. Then out of the blue came Watergate. The leadership of the United States was crippled: Mr. Nixon was paralysed then destroyed. On an evening in September, 1974 I heard a report over the radio that Melvin Laird, former United States Secretary for Defence, had said that Mr. Nixon had lost contact with reason. I was unable to sleep that night, and in the small hours I made the following entry in my diary:

> *Pretoria, September, 1974:* Watergate was, in the lawyer's terminology, the proximate cause of Mr. Nixon's resignation. For an event so historic, for a reversal of fortune so extraordinary, for a personal tragedy so deep, we must seek the ultimate cause.
>
> In July, 1973 Congressman Gerald Ford, then Republican floor leader

113

in the United States House of Representatives, declared: "The successes achieved by President Nixon are most remarkable. On many fronts and through many separate initiatives, he has patiently laid the groundwork for the first real peace in the world since 1913. We may indeed be on the edge of a generation of peace." A year later, this same man was mocked and disgraced–the butt of second-rate editorial writers and cartoonists along the circumference of the world. We sense them still running through Roget's synonyms to outdo one another in describing what Mr. Nixon did to his office ... debase, defile, degrade, corrupt, prostitute, violate, rape and much else besides. (We don't have our own Roget with us just now).

What *was* the ultimate cause of a reversal of fortune so extraordinary? It was the vengeance of the pseudo-liberal estblishment that began the downfall of a man they despised, feared and hated. They hated him not only for what he was himself but also because his term of office coincided with the collapse of their illusions. It was this: abetted by the *ersatz* fervour of a loud section of America's people for holy crusading: their belief that morality is a commodity for processing, export and internal consumption like any other ...

When Mr. Nixon was returned to the White House he pledged to restore order at home and the reputation and authority of America abroad. This he did. Within the United States he reconstituted the Supreme Court which had assumed to itself the authority to fashion American society along pseudo-liberal lines. In matters such as civil rights and desegregation, he substituted practical for doctrinaire approaches. He removed the cuffs from the hands of law-enforcement officers, and revived the notion that consideration was due to the victims as well as the perpetrators of crime. The mood of level-headedness he set was reflected through wide sectors of the nation, and not least in the fall-off of extremism among the black and student communities.

Long before he entered the White House he was the sworn enemy of communists in his country and their pseudo-liberal fellow-travellers. They scorned him for this: and as, when in the White House, he piled success upon success for his unromantic policies, their scorn turned to hatred–and their hatred was sharpened by their own impotent and gutless opposition to his progress. They shrank from fair and open confrontation with a man who could mine the harbours of North Vietnam, could honour at the risk of Super Power conflagration his commitment to Israel, could order a worldwide nuclear alert of his armed forces to prevent Russian intervention in the Middle East, could set forth upon a mission to the Arab world, to NATO and to Moscow when already the jackals were tearing at his jugular vein.

But that came later. Meantime the pseudo-liberals skulked in their Ivory Towers, behind their Presses and their Networks. His fellow intellectuals ostracised Henry Kissinger for throwing in his lot with the President. As

114

Mr. Nixon moved to the pinnacle of his power, the American political writer Thomas Molnar observed in 1971 that the burden on Western statesmen would become ever more onerous because of the domestic hatred unleashed against them by the cultural revolutionaries. Nevertheless Mr. Nixon reached the pinnacle of his power when in November, 1972 he was given a vote of confidence by the people seldom paralleled in American history.

The pseudo-liberals thought no doubt that their time had still not come. But in fact it had, because during the election campaign a group of supporters of the Republican Party had made a clumsy attempt to eavesdrop on their political opponents in a complex of buildings in Washington called Watergate. As this was made known, moral fervour aligned itself with pseudo-liberalism: frustrated national zeal turned inward upon itself: a general inquisition began . . . and the storm was agitated from its place in a teacup to the outermost frontiers of the United States and the world.

Mr. Nixon used every means, constitutional and unconstitutional, to disperse it. He covered up and he lied–we know, even, that in private conversation with his colleagues he cursed and swore. Honesty might have saved him from destruction. That we do not know. But Mr. Nixon knew the calibre of his opponents and the means for his destruction at their disposal: and we can but assume that he decided that honesty was not the best policy: not the best policy, that is, for enabling him to continue the work so well begun of securing peace for mankind and saving it from disaster. Who is fit to pass judgment when the issue is such as this?

The President's persecutors believed they were. But it is their conduct, not his, that reeks to the ionosphere of hypocrisy and ruthlessness: the conduct of those who in the name of integrity wrought their own mean vengeance, who brought him low and kicked him in the groin as he fell. Mr. Tom Stacey, London journalist and publisher, had diagnosed a nation tearing at its own entrails–and this is what made the nauseating stench. The British commentator, Malcolm Muggeridge, observed that it was television that finally broke the President: but the manipulators of the mass media who claim that they were acting from noble motive in the public interest are guilty of a deceit more insidious than any Mr. Nixon perpetrated. We do not question the capacity of privately-owned media in a free society for doing good. Their capacity for doing bad is no less: but the fact is that either way the good or bad they do is supremely incidental to their main objective, which is the securing of readers, viewers and listeners–through (in many cases) sensationalism and for (in all cases) profit. It is the same media who masquerade today as the upholders of morality in American public life who were main instigators of what historian Max Lerner described on the eve of Mr. Nixon's Presidency as "a Babylonian society, a late sensate period in which all the codes have been broken": main instigators of an idolum in which journalist Paul

Zimmerman noted that "nudity, eroticism and obscenity have become prime weapons in the hands of the artist as humaniser." The tearing by the inquisitors at the entrails of their President is, of all things, late-sensate, Babylonian, nakedly obscene. After his resignation, beaten and finished, they kept him still on the rack of their revenge and cried out in protest when he was pardoned.

The burdens of the world Mr. Nixon could carry. He walked lightly as recently as June with Mr. Brezhnev-the leaders of the West and the communist world together-beside the Black Sea, although already his physical step was beginning to falter. He could, perhaps, have borne his own guilt: he could not bear alone its mortification which his nation inflicted upon him. But in the depths of this great tragedy there is the possibility of a redeeming paradox. Like Mr. Nixon, we are aware of the means of destruction over which the pseudo-liberals dispose: but it could be that in this final act of vengeance they have spent themselves and killed their own cause also-because they brought to the White House a man more conservative than Mr. Nixon was or ever could have been. In acting as the repository, the garbage can, of their warped and thwarted ideals, Mr. Nixon has made straighter the highways of American life. In his strength he served the world: even in his weakness, his country.

When President Ford was sworn in he declared: "In the beginning I asked you to pray for me. Before closing I ask your prayers again for Richard Nixon and his family. May God bless and comfort his wonderful wife and daughters, whose love and loyalty will forever be a shining legacy to all who bear the lonely burdens of the White House. May our former President, who brought peace to millions, find it himself." Amen. (17)

That was my reaction the night I learned Mr. Nixon had lost contact with reason.

United States and Africa

When John Kennedy (Democrat) replaced General Eisenhower (Republican) as President in 1960, he gave official expression to the intellectual view of America's relations with Africa which had meantime taken shape. As we have seen, this view envisaged the winning of the new black states for the West on the assumption that they shared America's allegiance to democracy and to a free and open society devoted to common welfare and the protection of civil liberties and minority rights. This had a direct bearing on policy towards Pretoria. Professor Rupert Emerson of Harvard wrote in 1963: "If the United States pleads neutrality and looks the other way when South Africa elbows its African majority aside, can it expect better than a suspicious neutrality when it seeks to rally Africa's people to the free world's standards?" Professor James Coleman of the University of California wrote at this time that most persons outside South Africa regarded the situation there as pregnant with impending disaster: the prospects of an ultimate racial holocaust were made virtually certain by the intransigence of the overwhelming majority of Europeans on the principle of white supremacy.

Upon assuming office President Kennedy identified himself with such views: according to Professor Vernon McKay of Johns Hopkins University: "the Kennedy-Rusk-Williams team accepted the pre-eminence of African interests in Africa and injected a valuable New Frontier spirit into our relations with African leaders." Chief United States Frontiersman at this time was the third of the above-mentioned trio, Mennen Williams, incumbent of the recently-created post of Assistant Secretary of State for Africa, which was to become the focus of official American approval of the emancipated black states and of abhorrence of apartheid. Mr. Williams left no doubt about whose side he was on: not necessarily on the side of the angels or the democrats, but assuredly on the side of black Africa. On his initial fact-finding mission to the continent in 1961, he proclaimed "Africa for the Africans" (and subsequently wrote a book with that title). While supporting the cry of one-man-one-vote for the Republic, he reversed America's view on the suitability of democracy for black Africa and defended the emergence of black dictatorships. "Africa which has just emerged from colonialism", he stated, "cannot be expected to vault into 20th century democracy and stability." It was Mr. Williams, when serving later in the Johnson Adminstration, who was responsible for banning the United States Navy from South African ports: and in a television interview in 1966 he said it was the policy of the United States to bring down the Pretoria Government.

He returned to party politics and was succeeded by Mr. Joseph Palmer, a career diplomat whose service in Africa dated back 20 years to when he was consul in Nairobi. Mr. Palmer proved a quieter and more balanced man than Mr. Williams but no less confirmed in his abhorrence of apartheid. In 1968 he told the Foreign Affairs Committee of Congress that: Africans were increasingly sceptical about the prospect of non-violent change in the Republic: there was no evidence that Pretoria contemplated a significant programme of change in its domestic policies that would facilitate fruitful relations with the rest of Africa; and there was little basis for confidence in the South African Prime Minister's outward-looking policy. In October of that year Mr. Palmer came to South Africa and met the Prime Minister. He was quoted in one report of the interview as saying that the talks had been fruitful. Immediately he issued a sharp correction: the talks had been frank, not fruitful! For even a

117

moderate and reasonable man in the Democratic Administration it was improper to have fruitful relations with Pretoria.

Washington's regularly expressed "abhorrence" of apartheid during the eight years of Democratic rule in the 1960s was compounded of several things: a conviction that the policy, as it was understood, was wrong: a theory-shallow knowledge of African conditions based on the opinion of academics: competition with the Soviet Union for the support of black states: pandering to aggressive black opinion at home, particularly in the counter-productive circumstances of the Civil Rights Movement. In addition there was resentment that influential men in the United States–black and white–were increasingly advocating separatism as a solution of their own race problem. These are factors which contributed to the Democratic Administration's attitude to Pretoria; and over the years it added up to little less than incitement to black people across and within its borders to overthrow the status quo in the Republic.

Illuminating in this context was a book published in 1968, *The Discipline of Power,* by George Ball who was previously second-in-command of the State Department under Dean Rusk. He argued that United States policy towards Pretoria was creating a siege psychology and that, instead of mindlessly adhering to the idyllic formula of a multiracial South Africa, Washington should be looking for useful options for the country. He maintained that Washington's current South African attitude reflected "our own sense of guilt at home" and a desire not to affront the Civil Rights Movement. It also reflected in his opinion America's interest in the votes of black Africa which were needed on such issues as blocking Red China's admission to the United Nations. Mr. Ball disputed whether America had anything to gain from trying to curry favour with the new non-white states. The developing nations of the southern half of the world should not, he advised, be treated by Washington as if their political and economic idiosyncrasies had a large and decisive impact on the world balance of power.

In the year that Mr. Ball's book was published Mr. Nixon entered the White House. The following year he adopted a policy towards South Africa, recommended by Dr. Kissinger, which came to be known as *communication.* Its main elements were: rejection of violence, recognition that America's ability to influence affairs in South Africa was limited, avoidance of unnecessarily hostile rhetoric, and an endeavour to act as honest broker between the races and as a catalyst in inter-racial contact. In 1970 Mr. Nixon told Congress that over the past decade America had not had a clear conception of its relationship with post-colonial Africa and its particular problems: all too often the United States had told the black nations only what it thought they wanted to hear. Dealing with the general problems of black Africa, the President made the following points: that arbitrary boundaries drawn by the colonial powers left many

118

African countries vulnerable to tribal strife: that foreign ideologies had often proved notoriously irrelevant and tragically wasteful as designs for African progress: that outsiders could not prescribe the political framework most conducive to African growth: that each country faced its own problems, and that solutions to them must spring from its own experience: that Africans were confronted by the formidable task of strengthening their sense of identity and preserving their national culture as their societies made the transition to modernity. Speaking specifically of tensions between black Africa and the white-ruled South, Mr. Nixon said: "The 1960s have shown all of us that the racial problems in the southern region of the continent will not be solved quickly. These tensions are deeply rooted in the history of the region and thus in the psychology of both black and white. These problems must be solved, but there remains a real issue in how best to achieve their resolution." Mr. Nixon went on to observe that there was much to be gained "if we and others can help to devise ways in which the more developed African states can share their resources with their neighbours." (The Republic is the most developed state in Africa, and official spokesmen said subsequently that the President was in fact referring to it.)

In the course of this statement Mr. Nixon condemned apartheid: but for him there was no contradiction here, since his paramount foreign policy objective was to establish a pattern of co-existence among nations even when they were divided by the deepest ideological differences. In the two remaining years of his effective administration he concentrated on achieving such a pattern with Moscow and Peking and in the Middle East. Whatever plans he may have had for a similar operation in Africa were thwarted by Watergate. However he had already rescued relations between Washington and Pretoria from the dangerous deadlock of the Kennedy and Johnson years, and he had created the climate for contact, communication and detente in Africa.

BRITAIN

The Trackless Tram

You remember that bandwagon to utopia which I encountered in Britain in the 1950s? Well, it turned out to be not a bandwagon at all but a trackless tram–with multiple controls, reversible directions, HAPPINESS on the destination-board, and no licence plates. Suddenly, with scarce a warning, it transported Britain during the 1960s to the point of political, social and economic dissolution–and rode into the ground the high hopes of the previous decade of moral leadership in the world, a harmonious commonwealth of nations and a contented populace at home.

The degree to which Britain's circumstances had changed was brought home stunningly in a speech made by Mr. Dean Acheson, former United States Secretary of State, at the end of 1962. He declared that Britain had lost her empire but had not found a new role in world politics. He said: "Her attempts to play a separate power role–that is, a role apart from Europe, a role based on a special relationship with the United States, a role based on being the head of a Commonwealth which has no political structure or unity or strength and enjoys a fragile and precarious economic relationship by means of the sterling area and preference in the British market–this role is about played out. Great Britain, attempting to work alone and to be a broker between the United States and Russia, has seemed to conduct a policy as weak as her military power."

Those brutally hard words dismayed some Britons and enraged others. Mr. Selwyn Lloyd, Foreign Secretary and Chancellor of the Exchequer in Conservative Governments, answered valiantly. He counter-attacked: "It is true that our strength and influence in certain cases have been undermined by the actions of some Americans. I say so bluntly . . . On the topic of United States leadership I will be frank: for a long time the United States role in the world outside was regarded by the Americans as that of the great champion of theoretical liberal principles. The supporters of any subversive or insurrectionary movement anywhere in the world were given freedom of the American press and platform. How the Kremlin must have been delighted to see the United States' friends and allies undermined in this way." Those remarks by so eminent and balanced a British statesman must have gone a fair way to liquidating whatever might have been left of the special relationship. And Mr. Lloyd "utterly rejected" Mr. Acheson's main contention: The British Commonwealth, he declared, was a unique association of free nations with many common ties capable of vast influences for good; and "our military might may have relatively diminished, but our power to influence has not, provided we ourselves have the necessary will power to maintain our standards and to share them."

It was a brave defence by a man who through many years of distinguished service had known the meaning of patriotism: but the truth is that, for the time being at any rate, Britain no longer had the necessary will power of which he spoke. *The Spectator* faced the truth: it commented that Britain's inability to find a new world role was a plain reality which anybody who had studied her policy since the War had to admit. First the Commonwealth and then the special relationship with America had proved delusory; and an instability had been brought into Britain's political life which would last until efforts were directed towards the construction of "that larger unit." The larger unit was the European

Economic Community: but within months of *The Spectator's* comment, General de Gaulle vetoed Britain's entry. "Within the space of a single lifetime", commented Professor Max Beloff, "Britain has been transformed from being the centre and power-house of a world empire into an unsuccessful candidate for admission into an embryonic federation of Western Europe." The last of the international hopes was dashed, and political instability at home increased apace.

By the mid-1960s many in Britain were conceding that the Westminster model had failed in the emergent world. But that wasn't the real problem for Britain: the Westminster model was failing in Westminster. A hundred years before, Walter Bagehot–illustrious editor of *The Economist* and author, in 1867, of *The English Constitution*–predicted that it would. Commenting on the extension of the franchise, he wrote in 1872: "In plain English what I fear is that both our political parties (the Conservatives and the Liberals) will bid for the support of the working man; that both of them will promise to do as he likes if he will only tell them what it is; that, as he now holds the casting vote in our affairs, both parties will beg and pray him to give that vote to them." That was bad enough. Even worse, Bagehot foresaw a political combination of the working classes as such for their own ends. This would mean nothing other than "the supremacy of ignorance over instruction and of numbers over knowledge." In the mid-20th century Lord Beveridge, one of the great liberals of the age, suggested that the franchise should be made contingent upon the passing of some intelligence test, and thus abandoned the right of the populace as a whole to vote. For him there was a clear contradiction between universal franchise and effective democracy. "We have somehow", he said, "to carry on an aristocratic tradition in Britain without the aristocrats."

Was Bagehot, then, right or wrong? Both, perhaps, depending on the presence or absence of a factor not so far mentioned. Despite the extended franchise, Britain managed pretty well during the first half of this century. She held her empire together, daringly transformed parts of it into independent Dominions, patrolled the seas, increased her riches, projected from her island home to the world a model of stable and reasonable government, and fought two world wars–the second of them with unsurpassed courage and national purpose. That is the factor: national purpose–and in the 1960s it was no longer there. The lesson would seem to be that democracy based on universal suffrage can work as long as the various groups in the population have a loyalty to the nation and common weal that overrides their separate and conflicting interests. There was no such loyalty in Britain in the 1960s, and groups asserted themselves ruthlessly against one another.

Group conflict was exploited by outside forces. In 1966 Prime Minister Wilson told Parliament: "The House will be aware that the

121

Communist Party, unlike the major political parties, has at its disposal an efficient and disciplined industrial apparatus controlled from Communist Party headquarters. No major strike occurs anywhere in this country in any sector of industry in which that apparatus fails to concern itself." A main question in the last two general elections in Britain has been: who rules–Parliament or the unions? The issue has not yet been settled.

The indiscipline in Britain in the 1960s, the lack of respect for authority, the general permissiveness are assumed to be contemporary phenomena. Certainly modern conditions had their part . . . but consider this passage which appeared in 370 B.C. in Plato's *Republic:* The people arise against their oppressors and triumphantly declare the victory of Democracy over Tyranny and Plutocracy. In the first flush of victory they kill many of their opponents, send a few more into exile, and then settle down to show the survivors how the world should really be governed. In order to retain the goodwill of the masses, they are obliged to do something the tyrants and the oligarchs can dispense with. They must flatter the mob, and as a result all standards are debased by an increasing amount of vulgarity. Manners too are coarsened because there is no-one to show them any better; and soon it becomes apparent that just as the mad pursuit of wealth must eventually destroy oligarchy, in the same way the excess of liberty must destroy democracy. And then there is another period of decline: for, in such a state, anarchy gains until it presently finds its way into all private houses and even ends by getting hold of the animals. Fathers get accustomed to descend to the level of their sons, and the sons behave with insolence towards their fathers as they no longer have any fear of them. The teacher begins to stand in awe of his pupils, and as a result the pupils despise their teachers. From that moment on, young and old are equal, and the young are ready to compete with the old in word and deed, while the old feebly imitate the young. In the end all horses and donkeys begin to march along with the rights and dignities of free men, and everything is just ready to burst with liberty. And what is the result? That the excessive increase of this so-called liberty causes a reaction in the opposite direction: for an excess of liberty, whether in nations or individuals, seems duly to pass into slavery. And the most aggravated form of tyranny arises invariably out of the most extreme form of liberty, for the moment liberty becomes licence dictatorship is near.

Race in Britain

As the 1960s drew to a close the pretence that immigrant problems had nothing to do with race exploded. In 1968 a leading member of the

Conservative Party, Mr. Enoch Powell, cast his particularly clear eye at the situation and concluded that his party, the Government party and Parliament were confusing themselves. In a speech in Birmingham he called for an end to coloured immigration and for encouragement to coloured immigrants already in Britain to return home. "We must be mad", he said, "literally mad as a nation to permit the annual inflow of some 50,000 immigrant dependents." He said the present situation was like watching a nation "busily engaged in heaping up its own funeral pyre." He said: "As I look ahead I am filled with foreboding. Like the Roman I seem to see the River Tiber foaming with much blood." This was startling language (the Tory chief forthwith sacked Mr. Powell from his Shadow Cabinet), but it is clear enough why he used it: Mr. Powell, professor of Greek, wartime brigadier and former Government minister, meant to brand into the consciousness of the people the reality of the darkly-looming prospect. Clearly, the British public were already much aware of it. Letters in their scores of thousands arrived in bulging mailbags at Mr. Powell's doorstep, and but for a dozen or two they all supported him. Public opinion polls showed 90 per cent and more of the people behind him. At long last a man of substance had presented the British people with an alternative to the unthinking wishfulness of the political parties–and this was their response.

The pretence was over–explicitly. The London *Daily Mail's* political editor wrote an article headed *Now the Double-Talk Has Really Got to Stop.* The fact was, he declared, that too many black and brown people had poured into Britain without the Government doing anything to stop them. The arrival of thousands of Ugandan Asians had proved to be the last straw. Never since the War (wrote the editor) had there been a reaction so strong or influential: there was in Britain today a contagious sense of persecution, "and it goes back to one word–Race." Cartoonists competed with editorial writers to give expression to the public outburst. One drawing after another showed white Commonwealth citizens being kept out of Britain by colored officials–bloated-looking blacks, rapacious-looking Indians. Once upon a time cartoons with racial themes were pretty bad in some South African newspapers, but (observed a London correspondent) not even the worst of them was ever quite like this. (Once upon a time was a generation ago, before apartheid, when the prospect of integration turned tolerance in South Africa, too, to fear and hatred.)

In 1971 the Conservative Government introduced into the international vocabulary on citizenship the term *patriality:* it featured large in immigration legislation presented to and passed by the House of Commons. The legislation declared that a citizen of the Commonwealth, one of whose two parents or one of whose four grandparents was born in Britain, had a right to enter the country when he pleased, to leave when he pleased and to stay as long as he pleased. It was the most comprehensive measure of its kind ever put forward by a British Government. From an immigration point of view, it ended the distinction that previously existed between the Commonwealth and the rest of the world. In future, people entering Britain from the Commonwealth would have no greater rights than the most remote of foreigners coming to the country. Commonwealth and foreign-country immigrants would alike be aliens. To get into Britain they would have to have work permits for specific jobs in areas where there was no pressure on housing or social amenities. In addition, the legislation made provision for state aid to immigrants who wished to return to their homelands. Professor Hugh Tinker, Director of the Institute of Race Relations, expressed the view "that present trends suggest that compulsory repatriation of non-white immigrants is only five or ten years away in Conservative thinking."

The open multi-racial heart of a worldwide multi-racial association of nations had stopped beating. After having dealt for generations with people of colour in distant countries that spanned the globe, Britain believed as the post-war era began that the building of a single community of widely diverse people was a desirable and realisable proposition. The coloured people came in large numbers from the distant countries to live among Britons–and in the space of two decades the belief collapsed. It was a development of world significance, and its nature was delineated by the new concept of patriality: it was the ethnic tie, more than any other qualification, that had been made the passport from the Commonwealth to Britain. In dramatic fashion, Britain had reversed a dominant assumption in post-war international thinking, and had re-affirmed the overriding importance for a congenial and harmonious society of kith and kin.

At the time of the debate on this legislation, the following paragraph appeared in the press: "We have our homelands with their own nationals. Of course we can absorb a certain number of strangers, but it is impossible to absorb the vast numbers we have let in. And the reason is that they do not want to be absorbed. What do people calling themselves multi-racialists really envisage–a sort of hybrid race? It is a legitimate question to ask, but one waits for the answer." That paragraph appeared in the press not of the Republic but of Britain. The homelands referred to were England, Scotland and Wales: the man who put the question, Sir Wintringham Stable, former judge of the High Court of Britain.

Relations with Pretoria

As the 1960s opened, Prime Minister Harold Macmillan made a tour of British dependencies in Africa. Four years before, the Suez disaster had occurred. Prime Minister Anthony Eden, in co-operation with the French, had decided to halt militarily the challenge of Colonel Nasser to long-established European interests in the Canal zone. However, before the operation could be consolidated it was thwarted by the opposition of the Labour Party in Britain and of the Eisenhower Administration in the United States. It was a devastating blow to Britain's international prestige and a glaring exposure of her lost ability to intervene effectively in international affairs. She was humiliated before the world: and pressures upon her, especially from Washington, to divest herself of her imperial role were intolerably intensified. On this point, Mr. Selwyn Lloyd (in his reply to Mr. Dean Acheson) subsequently observed: "Mr. Acheson might have remarked that towards the end of the 1939–45 war and since 1945, the American obsession against colonialism has made the pace of constitutional advance too fast and has led to countries' becoming independent before they had the skills and resources to look after themselves. This has produced conditions, especially in Africa, which have unnecessarily weakened the Western position. Whatever Washington may have intended, there is the knowledge in Britain that in Iran, in Egypt, in the Middle East, in Africa and Asia, America's influence has on a number of occasions been cast against Britain."

Following the Suez catastrophe, the Conservatives' plans for de-colonisation were radically foreshortened–from decades to years. They adopted an approach, in general style and timing, indistinguishable from the Socialists'. There was only one substantial difference between the two parties: it was the more understanding attitude which the Conservatives until then had adopted to Pretoria; and that was the party political context in which Mr. Macmillan set out on his African journey in 1960. There was indignation among the Socialists that the Union (as it still was then) had been included in his itinerary: it amounted, they declared, to the lending of respectability to the abhorrent policy of apartheid . . . There was no need for their alarm: Mr. Macmillan yielded on this issue also: the current flowing against Pretoria was too strong for a pragmatic politician to resist.

> The rest of the Commonwealth can have little "common interest" with a revival of Nazi beliefs in race superiority or with a cultural and political outlook that revives that of the European exploiters of the days of the slave trade. And if he

125

On February 2 the British Prime Minister and his party were met at Cape Town's airport by Dr. Verwoerd. The following day, Mr. Macmillan addressed the members of the Union Parliament.

He said that the wind of change was moving through Africa and that African nationalism was something which policy would have to take into account. He said that in countries inhabited by several different races it had been Britain's aim to find the means by which fellowship could be fostered between their various parts. Her policy was non-racial: it offered a future in which Africans, Europeans, Asians, the peoples of the Pacific and others with whom Britain was concerned would all play their full part as citizens in the countries where they lived and in which feelings of race would be submerged in loyalty to new nations. "As a fellow member of the Commonwealth", he declared, "it is our earnest desire to give South Africa our support and encouragement, but I hope you won't mind my saying frankly that there are some aspects of your policies which make it impossible for us to do this without being false to our deep convictions about the political destinies of free men, to which in our own territories we are trying to give affect. I think as friends we ought to face together–without seeking to apportion credit or blame–the fact that in the world of today this difference of outlook lies between us."

Nationalist South Africa is becoming a police state and moving towards qualification for the description of being the Nazi Dominion and the home and high temple of racialism in a Commonwealth which, if it is to fulfil its ·destiny, must be multi-racial: the *National and English Review*, May, 1957.

It was a bolt from the blue. Dr. Verwoerd had not been given an advance copy, as is customary, of Mr. Macmillan's speech. Without warning, he was confronted with this statement which spelt out so clearly a parting of the ways. I reproduce Dr. Verwoerd's reply, which he made immediately, in verbatim fashion–since I see it as a summation of his extraordinary personality and, more, of the attitude in the desperate struggle in which it was involved of the nation he represented:

All that I wish to do is to thank you very heartily for coming to South Africa and putting before us here your point of view. I am glad you were frank. We are a people who are capable of listening with great pleasure to what others have to say even though they differ from us. I think it is an attribute of civilisation that one should

be capable of discussing matters with friends with great frankness–
and even in spite of differences, great or small, remain friends after
that and be able to co-operate in all that remains of mutual interest.

> If South Africa's membership of the Commonwealth is used
> to shield her from the disgust of the British Government
> and people there will be a growing demand for her
> expulsion: the *News Chronicle,* London, 6.4.60.

May I say that we can understand your outlook on the picture of
the world and on the picture of Africa in that world. I also do not
find fault with the major object you have in view. South Africa has
the same objects: peace, to which you have made a very considerable contribution, and for which I also wish to thank you today: the
survival of Western ideas, of Western civilisation: throwing in your
weight on the side of the Western nations in this possibly increasing
division that exists in the world today. We are with you there.
Seeing Africa as making possible balance between the two world
groupings, and hoping to develop the mind of man as it exists in
Africa in the above-mentioned direction–that too can be of the
greatest value in your search for goodwill between all men and for
peace and prosperity on earth. It is only a matter of how that can
best be achieved. How can Africa be won? There we do not see eye
to eye very often.

You believe, as I gather, that policies which we deem not only
advisable for South Africa but which we believe, if rightly
understood, should make an impact on Africa and the world, are not
to the advantage of those very ideals for which you strive and we
strive too. If our policies were rightly understood, we believe
however that it would be seen that what we are attempting to do is
not at variance with the new direction in Africa but is in fullest
accord with it . . .

We look upon ourselves as indispensable to the white world. If
there is to be a division in the future, how can South Africa best
play its part? It should both co-operate with the white nations of the
world and, at the same time, make friends with the black states of
Africa in such a way that they will provide strength to the arm of
those who fight for the civilisation in which we believe. We are the
link. We are white, but we are of Africa. We have links with both
and that lays upon us a special duty, and we realise that.

> The Commonwealth must remain a multi-racial society
> with no ifs and buts. What matters at the moment is that

127

South African policy is an open denial of what the Commonwealth stands for. It is not susceptible to adjustments. All temptations towards appeasement should be rejected: the *News Chronicle,* London, 8.10.60.

I do not wish to pursue this matter any further, but do wish to assure you that in the Christian philosophy which you endorse, we find a philosophy which we too wish to follow. If our methods should be different, let us try to understand one another, and may we at least find in the world at large that trust in our sincerity which must be the basis of all goodwill and true understanding . . .

I thank you from the depth of my heart for your presence in South Africa. I bid you on behalf of the Parliament of South Africa, Godspeed on your return. May you find in Great Britain less problems to deal with than we, unfortunately, have here.

In Cape Town on Wednesday, two Prime Ministers of the British Commonwealth made speeches; and it may be that events to come will cause the exchange to take on certain historic significance: the *New York Times,* 5.2.60.

Here in Cape Town on February 3, 1960, was a confrontation between two notable men, both gracious and civilised but differing diametrically on the nature of politics and political leadership. Five years later, in 1965, Dr. Verwoerd himself spoke in Parliament about the difference.

When the Prime Minister of Britain, Mr. Macmillan, was in South Africa some years ago, he tried to explain to me on a particular occasion what his political philosophy was. He said that one imagined in vain when one was in power that one could influence the destiny of one's nation or of nations or the trend of history: that no government could do so. All it can do is to ensure that it remains in power: it can then govern the country, and it will find that what would have happened in the ordinary course of events will happen in any event. A government is like a boat which is in the middle of a river. It is carried along in mid-stream by the streams of public opinion, and there is very little that the government can do about it. All that it can do is to see to it that it remains in power, and in order to be able to do that it has to see to it that it does not strand on either the left bank or the right bank. When it sees, therefore, that in the broad stream of public opinion opposite ideas are gaining so much ground that they threaten to

128

force the boat on to one of the banks, it must see to it that it remains in mid-stream, even if in order to do so it has to adopt some part of its opponents' policy in order to get to the middle of the stream of public opinion again.

Mr. Macmillan said this to me because he knew that I was advocating the establishment of a Republic and that I believed in a fixed colour policy, and he wanted to bring it home to me that I would not be able to achieve these aims because I was heading upstream and that history would take its course. Well, my reply to him was that if the boat was simply kept in the middle of the stream by an opportunistic government just so as to be able to remain in power, such a government might well succeed in steering clear of the banks, but that it overlooked the fact that there might be a waterfall ahead and that it might be overtaken by a greater disaster than would have been the case if it merely stranded on one of the banks. I said that I preferred to run upstream: that I preferred to set a course for myself rather than be carried along willy-nilly by the stream: that I believed that in that way I would be able to exercise some influence over the course of history and that I would then be in a position to ensure the fulfilment of the desire of that section of the nation whose support I enjoyed. I mentioned by way of an example the establishment of the Republic. We left it at that.

I think this is as clear an explanation as there could be of the nature of the encounter between this nation and its sincere and respectable critics abroad.

The Commonwealth Issue

Thirteen months after Mr. Macmillan's Cape Town speech, Dr. Verwoerd was in London for the Commonwealth Conference. The establishment of the Republic was imminent, and he was there to plead for its continued membership, as a Republic, in the Commonwealth. I know from my personal experience that this was his ardent purpose: and since his sincerity on this point has often been questioned I am going to describe here the personal experience of which I speak:

> Apartheid before Sharpeville left a sickening taste in the mouth. The cruelties it involved were clearly indigestible however much the difficulties of the white minority could be understood. Apartheid after Sharpeville, however, looks like becoming an emetic which may make it difficult for the

129

Commonwealth to prevent South Africa being spewed out: the *Telegraph*, London, 6.4.60

I first met Dr. Verwoerd in early 1959, a few months after he had become Prime Minister, when I was on home leave. The meeting was in his office in the Parliament buildings; and it happens that it was an auspicious day: the Bill for the Promotion of Bantu Self-government was to be presented to the House. The Prime Minister asked me why I wanted to see him. I replied that I was Director of Information in London, and that I felt pretty foolish when people asked me what kind of man my Prime Minister was and I had to admit that I had never met him. Dr. Verwoerd smiled, saying it was a good point. He invited me to sit down and to ask whatever questions I chose. For some half-an-hour he spoke to me with great frankness. He discussed among other things the pros and cons of Commonwealth membership: and included in the cons was his view that Pretoria's relations with London might be easier if South Africa was out of the Commonwealth, whether a Conservative or a Labour Government was in power. He had at that stage an open mind on the subject. (And I interpolate here a remark I made as the interview closed. It was a hot day and the Prime Minister was sitting in a white shirt with his large back to a window. I asked him whether he didn't think it presented an easy target for anyone who might like to take a pot-shot at him. He replied with a smile that that was the kind of risk a man in his position couldn't afford to worry about.)

Subsequently he decided that the Republic should remain in the Commonwealth if it could, the overriding reason being the need to cement national unity at home. I don't know when that decision was taken, but before 1960 was out I received instructions to do everything in my power to create a public opinion in Britain favourable to our continued membership. Part of the publicity programme I then initiated was the purchase of column one, page two, each second week, in the London *Sunday Times* to present South Africa's case. (It cost £1 per word–the most expensive copy I ever wrote!) During the fortnight or so that Dr. Verwoerd was in London I was in daily contact with him, and I was aware that he was straining every nerve of his being to have the application for continued membership of the Commonwealth succeed. On the evening of one of the days that the discussion of the application was in progress, I spoke with him for a few minutes at the Lord Mayor's Party at the Guildhall. He looked tired and disappointed. "I have been speaking to them and speaking to them", he said, "but they simply will not listen. I can't understand it." Dr. Verwoerd had such limitless conviction in the rightness of his own course and such awesome powers in marshalling and presenting his arguments that it was incomprehensible to him that others, having heard him, should not be persuaded. In the event, as the world knows, the opponents of Pretoria–the non-white member states and Canada, represented by Mr. Diefenbaker–remained adamant. They insisted on the right to intervene in Pretoria's policies–and on March 15, Dr. Verwoerd withdrew his application.

> The operation is over and the unhealthy limb has been removed. Now the Commonwealth can be expected to live and grow with vigour as an association believing in the equal worth of all races: the *Guardian*, London, 16.3.61.

In an address to the South Africa Club in the Savoy Hotel two evenings later, he explained why: "Our attackers (at the conference) wanted the communique to contain the formulation, as a principle of the Commonwealth, that its multi-racial character must apply to the internal policies of constituent members. It would have to apply in such a way that full integration could be the only form that would do justice to such a principle. This would not only constitute interference in domestic affairs but would also mean the disappearance of the rights of the white man and of the minority coloured groups in South Africa. Both the honour of South Africa and the practical considerations involved for South Africa made the decision to withdraw inevitable . . . And now what lies ahead? For the United Kingdom to hold together in her own way, if she can, the new and changing Commonwealth of increasingly non-white nations. She can attempt to do so without the embarrassment of South Africa with her policy of creating full but separate opportunities for white and black . . . For South Africa and the United Kingdom and the other old friends this means new opportunity. They must seek to develop in other ways, untrammelled by the former problems, great bonds of friendship and co-operation to their mutual advantage. We need each other. With friendship unimpaired and so many interests so intertwined to our mutual benefit, this is wise policy and will, I trust, become wise practice. We will leave London satisfied that what happened had to be, and that our countries and their leaders remain better and more understanding friends than ever before."

> Perhaps the shock of withdrawal will prove to be the catalyst which will set going in South Africa a reaction against present policies and produce in time a change for the better: the *Telegraph*, London, 17.3.61.

In the years that followed, one after another of Britain's emancipated colonies opted for Commonwealth membership. Regularly their Presidents and Prime Ministers met from all corners of the earth in conference in London. No matter all the disparagement, Britons told themselves, this alone was proof enough of the success of the venture. But I think they failed to take account of a prime motivation of the new leaders. The majority of them were men driven, often obsessively, to win prestige and status for themselves (and their countries), to put themselves on the international map, to have their names written into history. It was the reaction to a subservience of centuries: and the Commonwealth provided a ready-made, limelit platform. The Presidents and the Prime Ministers, one suspects, travelled to Marlborough House less to partake of the nourishment of international co-operation than to catch the Fleet Street headlines and the cameras of BBC and ITV.

It was believed that the new association of nations would be held together by its common history and the common institutions it had inherited. Mr. John Strachey declared in 1963 that "the stamp of the British culture pattern is, in varying degrees, upon each and all of these fantastically different countries." But increasingly the members of the new Commonwealth went their own way, rejecting the Westminster model, establishing their own kind of institutions and joining other international blocs. This was rationalised in London in terms of the Commonwealth's tradition of "limitless elasticity" . . . but elasticity is not limitless: stretch elastic too far and its power to draw and hold together is sapped and finally exhausted. The greatest of all the Commonwealth virtues had been seen as bridge-building between different colours and different races. However *The Economist,* earlier a champion of this view, remarked in May, 1963: "Even the belief in the Commonwealth as the pointer to a multi-racial world society of to-morrow has, to say the least, fallen into doubt." And in April, 1964, it wrote: "The Commonwealth, with nations in every stage of economic and cultural transition scattered all over the globe, cannot generate the beginnings of the new model international institutions needed to organise the peace, above all, between East and West."

Nonetheless, successive British Governments kept to their Commonwealth commitment: and it was relentlessly exploited by the emergent members. They battened on the guilt complex, widespread in Britain and particularly prevalent among the Socialists, towards their imperial past. They took whatever was offered, contending that it was due compensation to ex-colonial people. They showed no gratitude, and no understanding of Britain's problems: they criticised and rebuked her: some severed relations with her: they made common cause with her political and economic rivals: they alienated her from her natural friends: and all the time they increased their demands, satisfied–because of the commitment–that they would go on being met. And so through the years they were: Britain continued to give precedence to the preservation of the Commonwealth to the damage of her economy, her freedom of action and her relations with others.

132

The crime of South Africa: Overshadowing the Commonwealth Prime Ministers' Conference in London are the problems of Southern Africa. President Kwame Nkrumah of Ghana is one of the significant voices urging Britain to take more decisive action: the *Daily Mirror,* London, 13.7.64.

However there was, after all, a limit to the commitment–and about 1968 it was reached. The Socialist Government itself gave effective notice that at last the one-sided game was up: it was made clear that Britain would not be dictated to on the Rhodesian issue, and that she would not be forced against her own interests to take coloured immigrants from Africa or any other Commonwealth country. Her decision to link her destiny and find her future in an association with Europe was now explicit–and the Commonwealth Office in London was absorbed by the Foreign Office. The first post-war phase of the Commonwealth had ended: and it is at least to the credit of the new members that they were quick to grasp the implications. The Malaysian Prime Minister, Tunku Abdul Rahman, summed up their changed attitude: "The Commonwealth must no longer be regarded merely as a forum to take it out on good old Britain for having bossed it over us once upon a time." Britain, declared the Tunku, was no longer carrying on with her protective role but was withdrawing from her commitment to her Commonwealth friends. He warned that a void was being created and that unless Commonwealth members "put their heads together" to fill it, the association would disintegrate to their detriment. The old posture (a revolver in Britain's back) had gone: and in the new one (putting heads together) it was possible that the Commonwealth might prove a useful, though not significant, influence in world affairs.

It was Mr. Edward Heath, leader of the Conservative Party, who in December, 1968, defined the one and only pattern for Commonwealth survival: "The independence of each of its members should be respected. Their internal affairs and individual responsibilities should be matters for their individual decision alone. And jointly they should consider only those matters freely agreed upon as of mutual interest. There can be no other basis for fruitful consultation between member countries today." That is precisely the stand Dr. Verwoerd took at the conference in 1961, that the Commonwealth then rejected and that led to South Africa's withdrawal.

133

The Protectorates and the CAF

There were two aspects of Britain's decolonisation during the 1960s which had major importance for Pretoria's political philosophy and for inter-state relations in the sub-continent: one was the granting of independence to the three Protectorates of Bechuanaland (as Botswana), Basutoland (as Lesotho) and Swaziland: the other was the collapse of the Central African Federation of Southern Rhodesia, Northern Rhodesia and Nyasaland.

I have explained earlier that when the Union was created in 1910 by Act of the British Parliament, the three Protectorates were excluded from its borders, while other black homelands–such as Zululand and the Transkei–which were closely associated with one or other of the four constituent provinces of the Union were included within them. However at the time it was the intention of both London and Pretoria (and was provided for in the South Africa Act) that the Protectorates, too, in due course should be incorporated; and negotiations to that end were in progress between the two Governments at the outbreak of World War II. In the years following the war the prospect of incorporation steadily receded because of changes of attitude in both capitals.

In Pretoria there was growing support for the concept of independence for all of South Africa's black nations; and in 1963 Dr. Verwoerd declared: "The incorporation of the Protectorates is against my Government's policy of separate development which has as its objective the political independence of Bantu nations." But it was as long as four years before that that this change of policy was being considered–and I happen to have been present at, I think, its very beginning. It was in London: Foreign Minister Eric Louw was to speak to the South Africa Club there; and as was his custom he discussed at a meeting in the High Commissioner's office the draft speech. Since it was my responsibility to process the speech, I was present. There was a passage in it expressing the view that the incorporation of the Protectorates would be more to their own advantage than to the Union's. It was suggested at the meeting that the granting of independence to these countries would set a most potent precedent for our own policy: in the circumstances was it wise any longer to press for incorporation? Mr. Louw said he would consider the matter. Late that afternoon, as I was waiting to have the speech duplicated, he telephoned me from his suite in the Dorchester Hotel and instructed me to take out the passage in question. And so, for the first time, was the incorporation issue dropped by Pretoria.

In the event–with the granting of independence to the Protectorate

134

between 1966 and 1968–the potent precedent was set. Nations such as the Zulus and the Xhosas have, by any measure, as great a right to their own nationhood and sovereignty as the Batswana, the Basutos or the Swazis; and to have denied them independence when it was given to the Protectorates would have been an altogether unjustifiable and untenable anomaly. The die had been cast with a vengeance for a free and separate nationhood for each and all of South Africa's black peoples: history had played havoc with London's intentions, turning them inside out and standing them on their head: London's opposition to apartheid–expressed in the grant of sovereignty to the Protectorates–had underwritten apartheid and entrenched Pretoria's own programme. It was the British Government which struck the first and mortal blow at the idea of a single, multi-racial South African state, and it established the practical conditions for an association of independent states which Pretoria's Bantu Self-government Act of 1959 had envisaged.

It was because of its opposition to apartheid that Britain in the post-war years adopted the policy it did towards the Protectorates: and it was to demonstrate that there was a viable alternative to apartheid in Africa that it created in 1953 the Central African Federation of Southern Rhodesia, Northern Rhodesia and Nyasaland: this was to be the evidence for the theory that differences in race, culture and creed could be submerged in common loyalty to a new, emancipated state.

It did not work out like that. The black people of Northern Rhodesia (under Dr. Kaunda) and of Nyasaland (under Dr. Banda) feared under the federal dispensation domination by richer, more progressive, white-ruled Southern Rhodesia. Every effort that Britain could make to hold the federation together was made: but there was discontent, friction and violence: after ten years, in 1963, the experiment was abandoned; and Northern Rhodesia (as Zambia) and Nyasaland (as Malawi) were left to go their own separate ways towards independence. As an alternative to apartheid the CAF was a disastrous failure. But more than that: as in the case of the Protectorates it positively reinforced the Republic's philosophy: for no sooner had he turned away from Salisbury than Dr. Banda turned towards Pretoria. Although the Republic was also white-ruled and incomparably stronger than Rhodesia, he was confident that there was no danger in an association with Pretoria because the policy of separatism which it defended against the world was the ultimate guarantee of respect for his country's sovereignty and identity. The two countries began to work together in a variety of fields; and among the first of their joint projects was financial and technical assistance from Pretoria for the building of Malawi's new capital at Lilongwe. Diplomats were exchanged; and in 1971, as we shall see, Dr. Banda made a state visit to the Republic.

The consequences of Britain's antagonism towards apartheid in the

135

granting of independence to the Protectorates and the establishment of the CAF were a classic kick-back of history.

Rhodesia

Another consequence of the break-up of the CAF was the dispute it precipitated between Salisbury and London, culminating in the unilateral declaration of independence by Prime Minister Ian Smith on behalf of Rhodesia on November 11, 1965. From the beginning there was deep sympathy in the Republic and a sense of close involvement with the stand taken by Mr. Smith and his followers. For a decade Anglo-Afrikaners had anxiously observed the headlong drive towards independence in Africa. As it surged through the continent evidence accumulated–in the Congo, Ghana, Nigeria, Uganda, Tanganyika (as it then was) and elsewhere–of the disorder and danger it could bring. But it was not stopped or steadied. Unreasoning sentiment in the Western world, the calculation of the communists and the ambition of the Afro-Asians gave it new momentum. In the United Nations the forces behind it came together, built up pressure and then flooded on: first West Africa, then East Africa, then Central Africa: and in the mid-1960s Southern Africa was threatened with inundation. There was desperate need of a holding wall, and Mr. Smith's UDI provided it. Just to the north of the Republic, someone responsible for law, order and progress in Africa had had the guts to face the world and cry halt.

Here was the source of sympathy, and admiration, among Anglo-Afrikaners for Mr. Smith's stand: and their sense of involvement was heightened by a common interest in demonstrating the inefficacy of the international sanctions which through the years had been threatened against the Republic and had now been imposed against Rhodesia. Rhodesia was to provide sanctions with their second great test. The first had been when they were imposed against Mussolini's Italy after the invasion of Abyssinia in 1935–and failed. But now they looked an odds-on favourite. This was quite a different proposition from the previous generation's. There were only 220,000 white Rhodesians and their resources were small–supported mainly by men on the land growing tobacco. Their mother country was their enemy-in-chief. They were greatly outnumbered within their own borders by black people, and to the north a score of black states sought their destruction. They had no access to the sea of their own, and in the capitals across the seas there was sympathy for their cause only in little Lisbon. It looked a good thing for sanctions. No-one was going to be seriously hurt by imposing them, and international morality burgeoned and blossomed. It is true that unlike

Mussolini, Mr. Smith had no aggressive intentions. It is true that Rhodesia was peaceful and well-governed. It is true that she had ruled herself for 40 years and had been promised independence. It is true that her black people had a better life than their fellows in emergent Africa. That was all true enough. But what about the vote? Did each man have one: and was not this the overriding issue, the touchstone of morality and political decency–indeed, of Christianity–in the second half of the 20th century? It must have been. There was no dilly-dallying on this occasion. Stringent measures–economic, financial, industrial–had long been prepared in London. They were applied forthwith, and the assembled states of the world (bar two) supported them. In December an oil embargo–that most feared of all sanctions' weapons–was imposed, and by January the great victory seemed at hand. At a meeting of Commonwealth Prime Ministers in Lagos Mr. Harold Wilson said that the fall of the Salisbury Government could be expected within weeks; and in Westminster he gave Parliament details of the new multi-racial regime about to be introduced.

Those who desired the destruction of white government's in Southern Africa were exultant. In January the editor of the liberal *Rand Daily Mail* declared that the doubts about the effectiveness of sanctions had at last been exploded: in particular it had been shown that an oil embargo could be imposed without a naval blockade. A course had been plotted in Rhodesia (he wrote) which might well be a blueprint for action against the Republic, and he advised Pretoria to capitulate, to abandon apartheid, "to use the breathing space we still have to bring into being a more equitable and acceptable social order."

However, by mid-1966, it was clear that sanctions were not destroying but were invigorating the Rhodesian economy. (In the years to follow she was to have one of the highest growth rates and one of the lowest inflation rates in the world.) Not in the political or the economic or the psychological field had they achieved their ends–and in their fundamental purpose they had failed. This purpose is the avoidance of the use of force: but in April the British Government had sought and obtained the authority of the Security Council to operate a blockade against Beira. It was at this point that Mr. Wilson's sanctions policy was shown to have broken down: the evidence is in the Charter of the United Nations: Article 42 says that a blockade may be instituted only if economic, communications and diplomatic sanctions have proved inadequate. However Mr. Wilson claimed that by obtaining the blockade resolution Britain had forged a new instrument of international peace. Others saw this as no new legal concept but as a demonstration of the age-old proposition that there is one law for the weak and one for the strong: the gunboat is a weapon as ancient as the pretexts for using it.

Sanctions had been subjected to two tests and on both occasions they

137

had failed: against Mussolini who was an aggressor and against Ian Smith who was a keeper of the peace. They failed for two reasons. The first is that international morality is riddled with hypocrisy and does not have the power to overcome self-interest and bind nations in common action. The second reason for the failure of sanctions has been the strength opposed to them: in the case of Italy it was material and military strength; in the case of Rhodesia, the strength of the spirit.

From 1966 onwards talk of sanctions against the Republic steadily diminished: and for this Anglo-Afrikaners are deeply indebted to the Rhodesians. Pretoria helped by refusing to have any part in the sanctions campaign; and in 1967 it sent elements of its police to the Zambesi to strengthen Rhodesia's security forces in their action against the incursion of terrorists among whom were South African blacks–members of the African National Congress–bent on making their way to the Republic to commit subversion. But none of this–neither sympathy, nor admiration nor common action–represented at any time an endorsement by Pretoria of Mr. Smith's policies. (The year before UDI Dr. Verwoerd had told Parliament: "The domestic affairs of Rhodesia are none of our business: who should constitute their government is the business of the voters of Rhodesia. We shall co-operate with whomsoever the machinery of that State places in power"). To corroborate this crucial point for an understanding of the strain that was to develop in relations between the two countries, I propose to quote from a series of entries made in my diary from the time that UDI was declared. All of them were contained in the journal, *RSA World*, which circulates in influential quarters in Salisbury:

Pretoria, November, 1965: Rhodesia's destiny is to become part of a community of Southern African states. In some of these states there is a white hegemony; in some there is, or will be, a black hegemony; and in some there is, or will be, a sharing of political rights between white and non-white. Rhodesia's position will be that of a shared-rights state. (18)

Pretoria, February, 1967: White dominance over the whole of Rhodesia would be contrary to the Republic's own policy to which she is irrevocably committed, contrary to what is both expedient and right, contrary to what she believes to be the requirements of Africa in this last third of the 20th century, and contrary to her determination to establish good relations between men of all colour in the sub-continent. Powerful white South Africa has rejected white dominance: can anyone suppose that it could be perpetuated in Rhodesia? This is not a viable option, and those Rhodesians who have not yet done so will have to understand that a solution must be sought elsewhere. (19)

Pretoria, December, 1967: It is, no doubt, reasons like these that caused Mr.

Vorster to remark the other day that the Rhodesian situation was "the fly in the ointment" in this part of the world. His ointment of co-operative co-existence is working wonders, but if it is to go on working the fly must be extracted. South Africa says it must be done. But it is not for South Africa to say how it should be done, and even less to perform the operation. It is Mr. Smith who holds the forceps. (20)

Pretoria, July, 1969: For white Rhodesians to suppose that they can shape a future for themselves within the confines of the Zambesi and the Limpopo is an alarming illusion. (21)

Pretoria, November, 1974: Concern in the Republic at the statemate in Rhodesia is widespread. It does not arise from a reluctance to go on doing—indefinitely if necessary—whatever can be done to help Rhodesia solve her predicament, but from the conviction that there is no possibility of a solution merely in maintaining the status quo. The Republic itself rejected the status quo 15 years ago when it legislated for the autonomy of its various Bantu nations. (22)

Pretoria, May, 1975: It was essential from the declaration of independence in 1965 that there should have been an immediate advance to new territory. Whatever course was taken would have involved risk: but to mark time on quick-sand, however boldly, was to invite disaster. (23)

The final acts in the liquidation of Britain's empire in Africa—the granting of independence to the Protectorates, Zambia and Malawi and the dispute with Salisbury—served to delineate Pretoria's political philosophy and to reveal its relevance for the whole sub-continent.

CHAPTER NINE / 1960 to 1970–

World Movements

(1) THE UNITED NATIONS

South West Africa

By the end of the 1950s three emancipated African states–Sudan, Ghana and Guinea–had joined the United Nations. In 1959 Foreign Minister Eric Louw declared in the General Assembly: "I speak from this rostrum as the representative of an African state in the fullest sense of that term, and it is in that capacity that I today welcome those fellow African states that have acquired independence during the past two years and also those who are on the threshold of independence. It is in the spirit of a common African heritage that, on behalf of my country, I offer our friendship and co-operation."

Those on the threshold mentioned by Mr. Louw were to be numbered in scores. By 1975 the membership of the United Nations had increased from the original 58 to 144: but the new members brushed aside offers of friendship and co-operation, and proceeded systematically to distort the design and the purposes of the world body as formulated in San Francisco. Using their overwhelming numbers as a bloc voting machine, they shifted the centre of gravity of the organisation from the Security Council to the General Assembly, and there sought to establish a supranational authority with jurisdiction binding upon members. The dispute with Pretoria over South West Africa typified their manipulation of the principles of the Charter and the general unscrupulousness with which they set about achieving their ends.

The second paragraph of the Charter requires members to develop friendly relations among nations, and declares that these must be based "on respect for the principle of equal rights and self-determination of

140

peoples." The principle enunciated here does not refer to self-determination of states but of peoples. Now, in South West Africa the population, though it numbers only some 800,000, consists of eight main peoples very different in ethnic origin, culture and language. The largest of them are the Wambos (some 350,000); the second-largest, the whites (some 125,000). Before the coming of the whites towards the end of the last century, the history of these indigenous peoples was marked by strife, bloodshed and enslavement. In recent years Pretoria, as the mandatory power, has been leading each of them to self-government, with a view to enabling them to determine among themselves their relationship with one another and the over-all constitutional shape of the Territory. Despite the terms of the Charter, the United Nations has throughout rejected self-determination of peoples and insisted on independence for the Territory as a whole as a unitary state on a one-man-one-vote basis.

Coupled with this constitutional issue was the United Nations charge against Pretoria of maladministration of the Territory. In 1960, at the instigation of the UN Committee on South West Africa, Ethiopia and Liberia (the two black states who had been members of the League of Nations) brought the charge before the International Court of Justice in The Hague. It was a culmination of the attack that had been coming from all quarters of the globe for 15 years; and the indictment against Pretoria was of oppression, exploitation and *male fides*. Backed by world opinion, the accusers anticipated a walk-over victory: but by the time oral hearings began in 1965, Pretoria had presented the Court with minutely-detailed information on every social and economic aspect of the life of South West Africa's peoples. Ethiopia and Liberia had no answer to such evidence, and vigorously opposed Pretoria's invitation to the Court to visit the country and see for itself. Of all the world army of critics, not one appeared in the witness box to substantiate his accusations. For the first time Pretoria's policy had been removed from the forums of emotion and placed on trial before a bench of judges. The evidence against it was wanting: the charge that the policy was "arbitrary, unreasonable, unjust and detrimental to human dignity" was abandoned: the charge that it was oppressive either in effect or intention was abandoned–abandoned by the complainants themselves.

However this was not the end of the case as it should have been. Having been obliged to drop the charges of actual or intended oppression, the complainants formulated a new one: that Pretoria's policy violated what was termed "an international norm of non-differentiation." The norm, they argued, had been established by the international community at the United Nations (that is, by the majority in the General Assembly). What this amounted to was an attempt to convert the United Nations into a world legislature and a norm into international law–in terms of which it was proposed, in this particular case, to convict Pretoria. But the

141

threat in this stratagem to national sovereignty generally was unlimited: tomorrow might there not be a norm against immigration restrictions, the day after against tariff protection? At 4 P.M. on July 18, 1966, national sovereignty was at the brink: two hours later it was, for the time being at any rate, on safe ground: the judgment delivered by the Australian President of the Court, Sir Percy Spender, had put it there. It declared that humanitarian considerations did not generate legal rights, and that the function of the Court was to apply the law and not make it.

In the world's highest tribunal, after proceedings lasting six years, it had not been possible to support the charges against Pretoria's policy, and the danger to national sovereignty had been deflected. However the matter was still not allowed to rest. The Afro-Asian bloc, backed by men of the West such as America's UN Ambassador Arthur Goldberg, pressed their vendetta. A resolution of the General Assembly later that year terminated the mandate and called on Pretoria to withdraw from the Territory. This she refused to do on the ground that the resolution was invalid. The issue was again brought before the World Court, now duly reconstituted with a Pakistani as President. Pretoria proposed when the case opened that, to settle the matter once and for all, a plebiscite should be held to ascertain from the peoples of South West Africa themselves whether they wanted to be administered by the Republic or the United Nations. The proposal was turned down and the Court went on to rule that the Republic was in illegal occupation of the Territory–by a majority of 13 votes to two. The two dissenting votes were those of the judges from Britain and France; and London's *Daily Telegraph* described the Court's ruling as "a political decision that will change nothing".

That was in 1971. In October, 1972 UN Secretary General Kurt Waldheim, recently appointed to replace U Thant, sent a seasoned Swiss diplomat, Dr. Alfred Escher, to South Africa to negotiate as his personal representative with Pretoria. After a 16-day on-the-spot investigation of conditions in South West Africa and exhaustive discussions with Prime Minister Vorster, he signed a document in which he accepted the principle of regionalism as an essential element in self-determination. With that principle so authoritatively endorsed, what justification could there now be for the world community's attack through a quarter of a century on Pretoria's administration of South West Africa or on its general policy of separatism? The answer: Dr. Escher was relieved forthwith of his duties, and negotiation with Pretoria was terminated. Neither paragraph two of the Charter, nor the failure of the indictment at the World Court in 1966, nor the finding of the personal representative of the UN Secretary General was enough to stem the campaign of the Third World–communist coalition. As for negotiations, it was prepared to abide only by those the outcome of which was favourable to its own ends.

Through the years the Western nations tolerated, and not infrequently abetted, the attack at the United Nations on Pretoria. By so doing they opened the way wider for the Third World attack on themselves, and hastened the decline of the world body into disrepute. By the early 1970s its performance had become a farce, with the emergent states (the less-developed countries, the LDCs as they came to be known)–the clowns-in-chief. For instance: in 1972 a United Nations conference on the Human Environment was held in Stockholm. This, America and her co-sponsors supposed, was of all subjects one upon which all countries could co-operate for the betterment of mankind. But immediately it was converted into a bitter political conflict. The Brazilians condemned it forthwith as a conspiracy concocted by the haves against the have-nots. Their argument was that the rich had got rich by polluting their environments, and that they now proposed to prevent the poor from getting rich by prohibiting them from polluting theirs. This would have the side-effect (it was argued) of enabling the rich to continue their monopoly of the use of the raw materials of the poor–since for the poor to process their raw materials would cause pollution. The First World was not intent upon helping others but merely, by these Machiavellian means, on exploiting them. "Are not poverty and need the greatest polluters?" cried Prime Minister Indira Gandhi of India. "There are grave misgivings", she said, "that the discussion of ecology may be designed to distract attention from the problems of war and poverty." The LDCs contrived even to bring apartheid into the discussion: ecological or not, it was certainly a pollutant. This conference on the environment declared as its first principle: "Man has the fundamental right to freedom, equality and adequate conditions of life, in an environment of quality which permits a life of dignity and well-being, and bears a solemn responsibility to protect and improve the environment for present and future generations. In this respect, policies promoting or perpetuating apartheid, racial segregation, discrimination, colonial and other forms of oppression and foreign domination stand condemned and must be eliminated."

Two years later the United Nations held its World Population conference in Bucharest. It had long been apparent to objective observers that a main obstacle to increasing the per capita income of the LDCs was their rocketing population growth. The two countries with the largest of all populations, China with 800-million and India with 550-million, had in fact long before initiated birth control programmes of their own–China, a good bit more effectively than India. But agreement to hold an international conference on population control was regarded as a substantial advance: UN Secretary General Waldheim claimed that it represented "a turning point in the history of mankind". Before the conference, a guideline plan of action had been drafted. It proposed to reduce by 1985 birth rates in the LDCs to 30 per thousand as against a projected 34 per thousand, and to make available information about family planning, and the means for it, to all who might be interested. This seemed moderate and reasonable enough–but not for the LDCs and the communists. The President of Rumania, the host country, opened the conference by declaring: "the division of the world into developed and underdeveloped countries is a result of historical evolution and is a direct consequence of the imperialist, capitalist and neo-colonialist policies of exploitation of many peoples." He called for a new international economic order, and rejected "a pessimistic outlook on population growth". The Indian representative denounced what he called "the colonial denudation" of the East and the "vulgar affluence" of the West. The Chinese representative saw the very idea of population control as fundamentally subversive of the Third World. Its bright future could be spoilt only by the imperialists (the West) and the hegemonists (the Soviets)–and population control was their wrecking device. The upshot of the conference was a Third World demand that economic growth in the West should cease, and that the wealth of the world should be redistributed.

In this, as in all other similar issues, the Third World had the support of the West's massive guilt complex. Soon after the Bucharest conference, a statement by Professor Renè Dumont of France was given front-page treatment by an official UN publication, *Development Forum*. Entitled *Plunderers of the Third World,* one passage read: "*Eating little children:* I have already had occasion to show that the rich white man, with his over-consumption of meat and his lack of generosity towards poor populations, acts like a true cannibal, albeit indirect. Last year, in over-consuming meat which wasted the cereals ·that could have saved them, we ate the little children of the Sahel, Ethiopia and Bangladesh. And this year we are continuing to do the same thing with the same appetite". The LDCs exploited the guilt complex to the hilt. Thus, at the World Food Conference in Rome in 1973, the Indian spokesman declared: "It is obvious that the developed nations can be held responsible for their (the LDCs') plight. Developed nations therefore have a duty to help them. Whatever help is rendered to them now should not be regarded as charity but deferred compensation for what has been done to them in the past by the developed nations."

The attack was pressed by the Third World with exhilaration during 1974 at the United Nations and elsewhere. The General Assembly approved in December a charter of *Economic Rights and Duties of States.* It provided for the right to nationalise property and to pay compensation according to national and not international law, and for the formation of producer cartels (on the model of the one operated by oil producers) as a means of accelerating the development of the poor nations. It also called for a faster redistribution of wealth from the rich to the poor, and a greater transfer by the developed nations of their technology and productive facilities to the LDCs. Pretoria and Israel were gagged in the General Assembly and threatened with expulsion; and as 1974 ended, Peking was saying that the "new majority" had written a brilliant chapter and that it was "sweeping ahead with full sail as the boat of imperialism and hegemonism founders."

In November, 1975, the American representative at the United Nations spoke in the General Assembly of the contribution which the nature of the attack on Pretoria had made to this state of affairs. Ambassador Daniel Patrick Moynihan condemned African countries for what he described as "selective morality" in their attitude to Pretoria, and said it was threatening the integrity of the world body. This danger, described by General Smuts in 1946, was now recognised by the United States–some 30 years late.

(2) COLLECTIVE MEASURES

Plan for Invasion

Boycotts, embargoes and blockades–and the threat of them–figured large in the action against Pretoria of the United Nations and other of the country's opponents. In the event, they turned out invariably to be counter-productive: but in the first half of the 1960s (and until, in particular, the failure of sanctions against Rhodesia) they were regarded as potent weapons, and the extensive use of them was widely urged. The temper of the times was well illustrated by the publication in March, 1965 by the Carnegie Endowment for International Peace of a 170-page document entitled *Apartheid and United Nations Collective Measures*. It contained a detailed analysis of the prospects of a blockade and invasion of the Republic, of the forces that would be required, of the casualties that could be expected and of the costs. The study was edited by Miss Amelia Leiss, then a member of the Carnegie staff; and among her collaborators were Major Sam Sarkisian, of the U.S. Military Academy at West Point; Vernon McKay, of the Johns Hopkins School of Advanced International Studies, and a State Department Adviser; Professor W. O. Brown of Boston University, and W. A. Hance of Columbia University.

> We will have to throw our whole weight into a campaign to end apartheid. By universal denial of arms, international

145

ostracism, economic pressures and unequivocal commitment against apartheid, the West can make a last vigorous effort to remove this oppression without military intervention. There is still a little time left: the *New Statesman,* 31.5.63

Their report envisaged a show of force against South Africa: if that did not succeed, a blockade; and ultimately, should it prove necessary, a full-scale invasion. Given South Africa's long coastline and vulnerability to air attack, it would seem most ·logical (stated the report) that a United Nations show of force would be primarily an air and naval operation, "and the psychological impact of such an operation might be even greater if there were well-publicised incorporation of some ground units in these forces–implying the intention of going beyond a blockade if necessary." It was estimated that 25 warships (including submarines and an aircraft carrier), 100–200 aircraft (principally fighter-bombers) and 6,000 ground troops would be needed in the initial phase. Should that fail, a naval and air blockade would be instituted; and the effectiveness of the blockade would be measured by its success or otherwise "in persuading South Africa to alter its political and social structure along the lines insisted upon by the United Nations." The final resort would be direct military invasion. For this, naval and air forces would have to be stepped up, at least 100,000 UN military men would be needed, and the cost would be some 95-million dollars a month. The air and amphibious assault phase might be expected to last up to two weeks, with complete control of the country being secured within four months. Casualties among the UN forces were estimated at between 19,000 and 38,000 killed and wounded. "As the fighting continued", declared the report, "the non-whites would have stepped up their own campaign of terror and violence. As South African forces lost control over the internal security of the country–as they inevitably would if full-scale fighting with UN forces continued–the principal present obstacle to effective insurgency movements within the Republic would have been removed."

Such was the outcome of what the authors described as "an objective examination of the implications of one of the courses open to the United Nations": a blueprint produced by a famous Peace Endowment for war, chaos, anarchy, bloodshed and terror.

That was the assessment in 1965. Seven years later it had undergone radical change. In February, 1972, an article entitled *Southern Africa: No Hope for Violent Liberation* appeared in the liberal American journal *Africa Report,* published by the African-American Institute. The author was Lewis H. Gann, a senior fellow at the Hoover Institution of Stanford University. He described the Republic as the only sub-Saharan state with an industrial and logistical infra-structure strong enough to maintain an up-to-date system of land, sea and air defences. The Republic alone could field a balanced force, with a modern navy, air force arm and army complete with armoured units. In a time of crisis it could certainly mobilise 200,000 men or more. Moreover its industrial potential was such that it was capable of manufacturing instruments of war as varied as the Rl rifle, the Panhard armoured vehicle, the Impala jet trainer, the Cactus air defence system, computers, etc. It had also come to an agreement with France for the production of Mirage fighter aircraft. And "while the South Africans disclaim any intention of manufacturing nuclear weapons, they now probably have the technical capacity to do so." Accordingly, in the view of Mr. Gann, the Republic is well placed to fight a conventional war against any enemy or combination of enemies, barring the Soviet Union or the United States. A seaborne invasion would be a giant enterprise, more difficult in certain respects than the landings in North Africa or Normandy in World War II. An invader would have no industrial base with adequate supply and port facilites within thousands of miles of the Cape. Hence a seaborne assault force would have to be marshalled in distant ports such as Rio de Janeiro or Dakar. The author expressed the opinion that the Soviet Union could knock out the Republic with sea-to-land missiles carrying nuclear warheads. However that would not solve the problem of "liberating" the country–an operation which would require military occupation and administrative control. "The Soviets at present lack the maritime experience to carry out such a task which would involve them in an enormously risky operation far from the periphery of their empire–a venture totally opposed to the cautious step-by-step strategy favoured by Soviet planners." Mr. Gann concluded that in all likelihood no power but the United States at present commands the whole array of airlift, amphibious and engineering capacity, in addition to the tremendous concentration of firepower, required for the completion of such an enterprise; and "the South Africans are convinced that the Americans will never wage war in the Antipodes." Hopes for a military solution thus, in this expert's view, seemed illusory.

The Sports Campaign

By the time the 1960s were out, the faith previously placed in other sanctions–economic, diplomatic, cultural and academic–had proved no less illusory. Much more effective was the campaign to ostracise Anglo-Afrikaner sportsmen. This is an issue which has been discussed through the years in every home in the Republic, and there is perhaps none that has caused more confusion or frustration.

> A polite and reasoned refusal to enter into new sporting arrangements might well have a more galvanic effect on

South Africa than dozens of votes in the Security Council. For sporting contacts with the outside world are those which South Africans cherish most: the *Telegraph*, London, 8.4.60.

It is often said that undue attention is paid to sport in the Republic. Countless headmasters have found it necessary to warn succeeding generations of schoolboys that, important though sport and the competitive spirit may be, examination passes are more so. It is a predictable passage in their prize-day speeches. But the predilection remains: there are few Anglo-Afrikaner youths who would not eagerly swop a first-class matric for rugby or cricket colours. It is the same in later life. The young man who succeeds in industry, the sciences or professions is respected: but that very special admiration is reserved for the Springbok, and all eyes follow the wearer of the green-and-gold when he passes. Even the pop star cannot compete in the esteem of most of the young with the fellow who smashed a hundred in an hour or kicks the deciding penalty in the last minutes of the match. Nor is the national trait confined to the young: old men (surely not able to see that far) you will observe at any big occasion at Newlands or Ellis Park. Why is it? The sunshine and the green turf: the space that makes football and cricket pitches, golf courses and tennis courts a feature of the country's cities, towns and villages: the tradition passed on from father to son, so that as soon as he can toddle he is given bat, ball or club? No doubt: and there is also the Republic's success in sport: there are few games in which it cannot hold its own or better the rest. This naturally is a source of pride; and in the first couple of decades after the war it had a special national significance. At a time when politically the country was being besmirched, attacked and ostracised, its sportsmen maintained with other countries bonds of friendship and respect, and in the sporting arena at least they were able to meet the challenge of the world and show their mettle. Political opponents detected the psychological importance of all this, and set about exploiting what they believed might be a fatal weakness. Their intensive campaign to boycott Springbok sport was more than a bid to extend the nation's isolation. The deeper purpose was to strike at the morale of the people: they were to be persuaded that it was not only ideologues and pressure groups that were against them but also the ordinary folk of Lords, Twickenham, Wimbledon and similar places in other countries where through the generations Springboks had been enthusiastically welcomed.

The white South African may not care about the freedom of speech, movement or opinion. But he cares profoundly about freedom to beat the world at hurling the discus. The Government's sop to these animal priorities has, predict-

148

ably, been succeeded by still greater repression of more relevant freedoms: the *Sunday Times,* London, 20.8.67.

The instigators of this campaign had no interest in sport or sportsmen, white, black or brown. They were not at all concerned with the straight bat or the clean heel: they were rough-riding politicos, and many of them anarchists and revolutionaries. Their objective was, and is, an undifferentiated, equalitarian world society. They used sport in a bid to foist this kind of society, in the first place, on South Africa: and their great achievement has been the recruiting into their ranks in many countries of people who have none but the best intentions.

The primary reason for this success (believe it or not) was the inadequate terminology with which our part of the world is cursed and to which I referred at the beginning of the book. The white nation here has neither a distinctive name of its own nor a distinctive name for the state which is its home. Accordingly when in the past an invitation was sent to a team representing the white nation to play, say, cricket in Britain or rugby in New Zealand, the team which accepted the invitation was officially called a "South African" team. And when a Test Match was played at Lords or wherever in Britain, it was described above the scoreboard in foot-high letters: "England versus South Africa". Note the anomaly, please: the English are but a part of the British population, whereas a "South African" may be a Bushman, an Indian, a Coloured, a Bantu or an Anglo-Afrikaner. The Englishman has a name to distinguish him from other members of the British population: the white South African has none to distinguish him from other members of the South African population. ("Anglo-Afrikaner" is my own term to get round this difficulty.) The rugby set-up in Britain pinpoints the anomaly even more clearly. There, teams which take part in the European Five-Nations Competition are composed of Englishmen, Scots, Welshmen and Irishmen–with Frenchmen composing the fifth. It is accepted without question that each of these nations has every right to be represented in international sports by members drawn from its own ranks: yet the white nation in South Africa is denied that right. It is a proposition totally opposed to logic and fairplay, and consistent only with the political objectives of those who seek to submerge the identity of the white nation and to liquidate its control over its own destiny.

To white South Africans, sport is one of the anodynes to the strain of living in their fear-ridden, rigidly controlled caste society: *The Times,* London, 17.2.68.

But what is the historical position? It is that among the various nations of South Africa there is one that has its origins in Europe. It has preserved its European heritage and maintained its identity through 300 years, and

149

it is this–not the country in which it lives–that constitutes and circumscribes its nationhood. In its nature it is European; by definition its national representatives are chosen from this nation, and in the case of sport they are popularly known about the world as Springboks. That is the position: and it is as unreasonable to require an Anglo-Afrikaner, or Springbok, team to include a Xhosa or a Zulu or an Indian, as it would be to require an English team to include a Scot, a Welshman or an Irishman . . . or a French team to include a German, Italian or Dutchman . . . or a Canadian team to include a representative from the United States or Mexico. "South African" is no more descriptive of the Anglo-Afrikaner than "British" is of the Englishman, "European" of the Frenchman or "North American" of the Canadian. Pardon me if I appear to labour this point: but the plain fact is that misunderstanding of it lies at the very heart of the confusion and bitterness which this wretched sports conspiracy has caused.

First among the conspirators was a Coloured teacher, Dennis Brutus, a clever revolutionary. Having been banned under the Suppression of Communism Act, he transferred himself and his boycott organisation to London in the early 1960s, and concentrated in the beginning on the Republic's exclusion from the Olympics. One of his deputies in the early days of his agitation was John Harris, convicted of murder and executed for the death–and injury–he caused when he planted a bomb in the concourse of the Johannesburg railway station in 1964. One of Brutus's star pupils was Peter Hain. Hain, as a schoolboy, attended the cremation of Harris who was his hero. "We are here to say farewell to John Harris whom we all loved", he said at the funeral. He quoted from Scripture: "Blessed are they who are persecuted for righteousness' sake, for theirs is the Kingdom of Heaven." From London, Hain was later to play the leading part against Springbok tours of Britain, Australia and New Zealand. One of Brutus's accomplices was Abdul Minty, of the Anti-Apartheid Movement in London, who was to say: "Even when South Africa has integrated sport we will not be satisfied: we want a black government." Among the organisations which supported Brutus's movement was the Supreme Council for Sport in Africa, agent of the Organisation of African Unity; and everywhere the allies of Brutus were the communists and their fellow travellers–those witting and unwitting tools of Russian imperialism for which, the Kremlin has all along known, Southern Africa would be a decisive world prize.

> The Springboks, representatives of apartheid, had to be protected by barbed wire at Cardiff Arms Park. The white minority can dominate South Africa only by use of para-military forces, pass laws and oppression. They have to protect themselves in their white laagers. Without barbed

wire and guns their society would collapse. It was appropriate, therefore, that the Springboks had to play with wire to protect them: the *Guardian,* London, 15.12.69.

Such was the alliance against Pretoria, abusing sport for naked political purpose. Its first major success was the expulsion in 1961 of South Africa from international soccer. In the years that followed, Britain, Australia and New Zealand cut their long-standing cricket ties with the Springboks. Springbok rugby tours of Britain and Australia were occasions for protest, demonstration and anarchy. The visiting players, on and off the field, were constantly harassed, taunted, insulted, spat at. In Swansea, agitation provoked a mass fight: 30 people were taken to hospital–one, a policeman, with a stab wound in the chest. As Opposition Labour Party leader in New Zealand, Norman Kirk said in 1972: "In a democratic country there is an inalienable right to freedom of speech, art, writing, cultural and sporting pursuits." The following year as Prime Minister, he ordered the cancellation of the impending Springbok rugby tour. The persecution of Springboks was extended round the world, to all fields of sport and to men and women. Golf star Gary Player had to be given police protection along American fairways; tennis star Brenda Kirk was hounded by hooligans in Australia. When Socialist Gough Whitlam became Prime Minister of that country he refused transit facilities to all Springbok teams. Black and communist states threatened to cut their sporting ties with whatever country allowed its representatives to play against the Springboks. One government after another, one sporting body after another, yielded to the blackmail–with a notable exception. The British rugby authorities refused to be cowed. Every effort was made to coerce them into calling off the Lions tour of the Republic in 1974. They would have nothing of it: the secretary of the tour committee, Mr. Albert Agar, explained: "We won't give in to threats. There are so many people threatening things in the world today, and it is time someone stood up to the threats." In reprisal, the Wilson Government instructed its diplomats in Pretoria to have no social contact with the Lions, while junior minister Joan Lestor apologised in person to the Zambian and Kenyan governments. But it was the Springboks' closest and most esteemed sporting rivals, New Zealand and Australia, who under socialist governments had turned most sharply against them. Their attitude was inconsistent and unprincipled: while they rejected the right of the white people in South Africa to sporting representatives of their own, they looked with favour at home upon, respectively, all-Maori and all-Aborigine teams.

With extreme reluctance therefore *The Daily News,* which like most New Zealanders holds apartheid abhorrent,

151

believes that the time has come for this country to sever all sporting relations with South Africa until the Republic's team selections and attitude to race conform with accepted international views: the *Daily News*, New Zealand, 2.1.71.

The Olympics

However it was at the Olympics that the starkest account of the betrayal of the spirit of sport was written: an account, though, with a twist ending that would have delighted De Maupassant. "All Peleponnasus", we are informed, "was at peace for the duration of the Games. All wars great and small between states and cities were suspended. Those who a few days before were mortal enemies on the battlefields would now contend for laurels in the Stadium of Olympia." So writes history of the Olympic Games which date back, at least, to 776 B.C. The ancient Games indicate the mood of the founders of our civilisation: today, 2,750 years later, the modern Games indict its present condition. It was in 1896 that the Olympic Games were revived by a Frenchman, Pierre de Coubertin. Springboks participated regularly from 1908–and it was in that year that sprinter Reggie Walker won the first of their 16 gold medals. For half a century at the Olympics, as at other international gatherings, the Springboks were respected participants. But by the end of that period profound changes were occurring in the world. The culture of Greece, Rome and Christianity, so long dominant, was being challenged. Those who shared nothing of its experience or ideals were determined to crush its leadership and authority. The white nation in South Africa was a prime objective of the attack: and, tragically, the challengers at the gates were championed often by Western men. Some of them claimed to be Christians: two of them were priests. Around 1960 Father Trevor Huddleston and the Rev. Michael Scott organised protests against Springbok participation in the Games. They were joined by the Brutuses, the Harrises, the Hains, the Mintys, the Afro-Asians and the communists. By 1964 the pressure of the challengers was such that the Olympic congress in Lusanne declined to extend an invitation to the Republic to compete in Tokyo. This was in face of the fact that non-white South African athletes had already been chosen to go there.

> Do we as a nation really want to play games against another nation which oppresses most of its people because it believes that a man who is not white is an inferior being?: the *Canberra Times*, Australia, 19.9.68.

The sporting authorities in the Republic refused to accept defeat. At meeting after meeting in the ensuing years they calmly put their case: as a result a special Olympic delegation consisting of three men and including a Nigerian was sent to South Africa in 1967 to investigate the situation. Their report to the International Olympic Committee stated: "The overwhelming evidence from administrators and competitors of all communities in Olympic sport in South Africa is that the country has worked out an acceptable basis for a multi-racial team to the Mexico Olympic Games." Following receipt of the report, a majority of members of the ICC decided to issue an invitation to South Africa . . . and here there is a notable parallel with the World Court decision on South West Africa of 1966. After taking evidence and objectively weighing the facts at issue, the World Court–like the ICC–found in favour of South Africa and rejected the contention of the challengers–Ethiopia and Liberia. But prejudice and political blackmail took over, and at the United Nations the verdict of the World Court was rejected. The same happened in the case of the decision of the ICC: prejudice and political blackmail took over: the decision was rejected, and the invitation was withdrawn. Commenting, the head of the Olympic Movement, Avery Brundage, said it was no reflection on the Republic or its policies but on the chaotic state of the world.

> I find a source of great pride in the fact that, as a sporting nation, Australia has cut off ties with South Africa. That they did, in my opinion, allowed us to hold up our heads in the sporting world, where once we should have bowed them in shame for helping proliferate a policy that shows man at his most loathsome: Mike Gibson in the *Sunday Telegraph*, 24.3.74.

The exclusion of athletes from this country did not save the Mexico City Games from disruption. For days on end the police were engaged in controlling rioters: racialism seared the occasion: on the podium receiving their medals, Negroes from the United States raised their fists in the Black Power salute. In 1970 the Republic was expelled from the Olympic Movement, and accordingly was not present at the Munich Games two years later. There, at the last moment, it was a contingent of white and black athletes from Rhodesia who were sent away. But that did not save the Munich Games from disruption either: indeed subsequent events were a brutal exposure of the hypocrisy that it is among white men in Southern Africa that racism resorts. On September 5, when the Games were in full swing, Arab terrorists first held hostage and then murdered 11 Israelis.

Through it all the contention of the Republic's sporting authorities was that "international tournaments can be staged in our country without friction or demonstration and with full harmony": those were the words used on one occasion by the Republic's representative at a meeting of the

International Lawn Tennis Union; and in the case of tennis the claim was proved to the hilt at a series of major tournaments–including the World Federation Cup–held at Ellis Park in Johannesburg. In the case of athletics, at the First South African Games, held also in Johannesburg in 1964, there was full harmony–but only one foreigner competitor, Peter Snell of New Zealand. At the Second South African Games in Bloemfontein in 1969, there was full harmony–and 126 foreign competitors. At the Third South African Games in Pretoria City in 1973, there was full harmony–and 635 foreign competitors. They came, many of them in defiance of their own governments and sporting bodies, from 27 countries to participate–white, black, brown and yellow–in open competition with representatives of all the national groups in South Africa–Caucasian, Bantu, Coloured and Asian.

> Apartheid will not be overcome in a day or merely as a result of the banning of South African sports tours. But such campaigns do concentrate the force of world disapproval, and demonstrate to all South Africans just how repugnant the system of apartheid is regarded by world opinion: the *Guardian,* London, 10.9.71.

Pretoria City, 1973: The Games were opened by State President Jim Fouche–and from that moment it was apparent that something exciting beyond expectation was about to happen. The opening ceremony was no extravaganza. There were no runners carrying torches, no massed bands or ceremonial marches. The setting was not a glittering arena but a simple hall. By the same token, though, the audience were not remote spectators. They were immediate participants–all 4½-thousand of them: the visiting competitors, the VIPs and the ordinary people who had been early enough to get a seat. The Pretoria boy in the back row, the Japanese girl balancing miraculously on the bar, shared the mood. It was like intimate theatre. There was a roar of approval when the brilliant American gymnast, Miss Kim Chase, was awarded a gold medal and a kiss from Mrs. Fouche. South Africa was expressing its appreciation to her and to the other 634 competitors from abroad for having come. This was the secret of the informality, spontaneity and fellowship. The men and women from the 27 countries were not merely distinguished guests. They were friends among us: their acceptance of our invitation at this time proved it. It was the same throughout the tournament. Whatever the event there was goodwill and fairplay in the arena and on the stands. At the boxing, when a doubtful decision went against a black contender in favour of a white, white members of the audience stood and booed. The white South African winner of the 400 metres ran an exhibition lap at the insistence of black spectators. It characterised the prevailing spirit: throughout the Games there was no single untoward incident. It was in the Republic of South Africa, home of apartheid, that the spirit of the Olympics rose from the ashes of Mexico City and Munich. (24)

And strange though it may seem to others (and delighted though De Maupassant would doubtless have been at such an ending), there was in truth no contradiction in it. It is no mere coincidence that the triumph of the Games followed upon the granting in 1972 of self-government to five black nations in South Africa. With the security of each of them secured, the traditional goodwill between the peoples of South Africa was again expressing itself, and at the Games Stadium in Pretoria City it was extended to embrace men and women of all kind and colour and creed from all around the globe.

Here is the result of the world conspiracy against South African sport: it has promoted, within the pattern of separatism, the sporting activities and opportunities of all sections of the country's population; and it has marked out the course to be followed in the years ahead. In sport, as in all aspects of the country's life, each national group must be free to act for and among its own people. In sport, as in politics, finance, commerce, each must be free to have its own representatives; but this does not in any way preclude, whenever the occasion requires it, co-operation and team-work among them. The Anglo-Afrikaner will defend at all times his full entitlement to have his own sporting representatives, the Springboks: but in the same way as the English rugby player joins with the Scot, Welsh and Irish to represent multi-national Britain, so will the Anglo-Afrikaner join with the black man, the Coloured and the Indian to represent multi-national South Africa.

(3) THE CHURCH

From Heaven to Earth

Ours is a Western Christian civilisation. Christ is at the centre of Western Christian civilisation. He came into a world of decay and despair. The achievements in human effort, thought and government in the preceding centuries had been prodigious, but they had culminated in spiritual bankruptcy. Superhuman intervention was seen as the only hope of salvation, and was fervently prayed for and prophesied by the Jews. Christ intervened: and it is a matter of historical fact that civilisation was saved by him: by Christ recognised as the son of God, born of the Virgin Mary, crucified and raised from the dead. His way of redemption was not political doctrine or government reform but the transposition of the norms and aspirations of individual men: humility for pride, spiritual riches for material wealth, moral courage for physical strength, forebearance for aggression. He sanctified peace and gentleness. It was the beginning of his message for successive generations of men: gentle Jesus, meek and mild, look upon a little child. Peace I leave with you, my peace I give to you. In the world you will have tribulation, but be of good cheer for I have overcome the world. Christ, the means of grace and the hope of glory: this is the force that moved through history. Often misunderstood and abused, it nevertheless took command of a civilisation in retreat, turned it about and converted it into a grand forward march, modifying every aspect of the life-style of Western man.

It is not surprising, therefore, that the disintegration of the culture of the modern Western world that I have been writing about coincided with a sudden weakening, then distortion, then perversion of Christian teaching. It was in the immediate post-war years that revolutions in politics, communications and theology combined to accelerate the process, though their beginnings were evident long before. It was in 1884 that the Fabian Society was formed, leading on to the welfare state and the worldwide British revolution. It was about the same time that the internal combustion engine was discovered, leading on to the motor car, the aeroplane, the space-ship. And already in the 19th century also, growing numbers of churchmen were shifting their focus from heaven to earth.

Remember that bandwagon, that trackless tram, I encountered in Britain in the 1950s? Well, when it was getting under way in the previous century certain clerics were among its first eager passengers. They and the Benthamites owed allegiance (then) to quite different gods: nonetheless Graham Wallas referred to "the tradition of a working alliance" between evangelical Christianity and non-religious liberalism; and Gladstone observed that the non-conformist religious sects were the backbone of political liberalism. It was a pretty expedient get-together: the churchmen were useful to the liberals' political purposes, and the liberals to the churchmen's social purposes. Meanwhile the churchmen's own teaching that true liberty was possible for the individual only within the compass of God's ordinances was dumped somewhere among the baggage: on the route map which they now espoused there were no boundaries or barriers or halts. They got their shorter working hours, higher wages and washrooms–and that piece about true liberty got more and more buried at the back. Various distinguished men of the cloth issued warnings. John Newman, for instance, described liberalism as the badge of a school "of a dry and repulsive character." And he observed with some perspicacity that "liberalism is not very dangerous in itself, though dangerous as opening the door to evils which it does not itself either anticipate or comprehend."

By and large though to most observers general progress looked astonishingly good. Then, post–World War II, came the implementation of a politics of security from cradle to grave; probes into space–to the moon and far beyond–and the final destruction in the popular imagination of a heaven either "up there" or "out there". The outcome of this conjunction of developments was a theology which rejected alike the need for and the possibility of God. Some of the new theologians, trying to clarify this bewildering new state of affairs, succeeded only in compounding the ordinary man's confusion. Dr. Paul van Buren set forth a version of Christianity in which there was no such thing as a God and in which Christ did not survive his crucifixion: nevertheless he believed that the language of the New Testament and the Creeds should continue to be used to describe some psychological experience which Christians are able to have. Dr. Thomas Boslooper likewise believed that we should continue to recite the affirmation that Christ was born of the Virgin Mary, but that in doing so we should not mean by these words that he was in fact born of the Virgin Mary. Some of the new theologians were less ambiguous. Dr. Harvey Cox, author of *The Secular City,* minced no words about God's new location: he was to be found in the picket line. Men, he wrote, must be called away from their fascination with other worlds–astrological, metaphysical or religious–and be summoned to confront the concrete issues of this one. Christianity must engage people at particular points, not just in general: it must build peace in a nuclear world, contribute to justice in a world stalked by starvation, and hasten the day of freedom in societies stifled by segregation: "it entails our discernment of where God is working and then joining the work. Standing in a picket line is a way of speaking: by doing it a Christian speaks of God." For Dr. Thomas Altizer, God is neither in heaven nor in a picket line nor anywhere else–very definitely not: "God is dead, literally. He died in the physical Christ. The dead God was resurrected in an empty form by Christianity. When this form of Christianity collapsed, then the reality of the death of God became manifest. We are not simply saying that modern man is incapable of believing in God. We are saying that God has disappeared from history. He is truly absent, not simply hidden from view, and therefore he is truly dead."

In the 1960s this remarkable controversy as to whether God is alive or dead raged through the United States, and to a lesser extent through Britain and Europe. It was fascinating, boring, distressing, shocking, scandalous or blasphemous according to the individual's point of view: but its real significance was that it pinpointed the endeavour of men who supposed themselves to be Christians to bring their religion to terms with the modern age. The notion of a heaven or a hell beyond the girdle of the sun being no longer tenable, the new theologians were turning to the earth and its people as their real point of reference and the ultimate object

157

of their concern. Between the New Testament and modern man there was a credibility gap, and they were attempting to bridge it by secularising Christianity. They were abandoning the central Christian purpose of bringing man into touch with his Maker, and now saw it as their duty to improve the lot of men by active, day-to-day intervention in the mundane affairs of society: in the words of one of them they were "immersing themselves in the new world of the secular city."

Immersion in the secular city included challenging the laws of the land. Dr. Eugene Carson Blake, a leading American Presbyterian, declared: "Law is not God. It has always from the first been a basic Christian conviction that there are times when a Christian ought to break the law, any law." Activist clergymen proceeded to decide for themselves which laws were fit to be obeyed and which broken. Leaving their pulpits for "social action", they organised restive slum-dwellers, supported striking workers, marched with civil rights campaigners, harassed members of their Government. When they stayed in their pulpits they castigated American participation in the Vietnam conflict, or called for immediate action against Rhodesia. They informed young Americans that it was for them to determine the kind of war in which they would fight and advised them on ways of dodging military service.

The secularisation of Christianity was evident not only among individual theologians and clerics but even in the most ancient and conservative of Christian Churches–the Roman Catholic Church. An example is the Pope's Easter Encyclical in 1967. Among its pronouncements were these: The development of peoples has the Church's closest attention–particularly the development of those who are striving to escape from hunger, endemic diseases and ignorance, of those who are looking for a wider share in the benefits of civilisation and a more active improvement of their human qualities; private property does not constitute for anyone an absolute and unconditional right. If certain landed estates impede the general prosperity because they are extensive, unused or poorly used, or because they bring hardship to peoples, or are detrimental to the interests of the country, the common good sometimes demands their expropriation; it is unacceptable that citizens with abundant incomes from the resources and activity of their country should transfer a considerable part of their income abroad; it is unfortunate that a system has been constructed which considers profit as the key motive for economic progress, competition as the supreme law of economics and private ownership as the means of production with an absolute right that has no social obligation; the economic dictatorship of free competition in trade should be avoided. Freedom of trade is fair only if it is subject to the demands of social justice; if today's flourishing civilisations remain selfishly wrapped up in themselves, they could easily place their highest values in jeopardy, and sacrifice their will to be great to their desire to possess more; only worldwide collaboration will succeed in overcoming basic rivalries and in establishing a fruitful and peaceful exchange between peoples. For this there must be an end to isolation and the creation of an effective world authority ... World authority, social progress, property, trade, income, investment: such were the terms of the message of the oldest of the Christian institutions on the occasion of the commemoration of Christ's death and resurrection.

Mr. M. B. Martin, author of *Jesus Now* and formerly a Jesuit professor at the Pontifical Biblical Insitute in Rome, writes of a new form of ecumenism in the Church of Rome which originated in Latin America and is finding increasing vogue throughout the Western world. Utterly committed to their cause and prepared if necessary to perish in their efforts, these new ecumenists declare the existing social, economic and political systems of the Western world to be dehumanising, irremediably unjust and religiously intolerable for any genuine Christian. According to their argument, atheism is essential for understanding class struggle and oppression: and communion with God means abolition of private ownership. Mr. Martin maintains that responsibility for the impact and appeal of their doctrine must be shared by the Vatican administration who have too lightheartedly pursued a dialogue with Marxist theoreticians and communist governments. Vatican documents have introduced a volatile note into basic questions such as private ownership of the means of production, the nature of political rights and sovereignty and, most important, the teaching authority of the Church.

The World Council of Churches

However it was in the co-ordinating body of the Protestant Churches–the World Council of Churches–that the secularisation of Christianity was to reach its widest and most excruciating (Malcolm Muggeridge's word) limit. The WCC was established in 1948. It happened to be the year in which the National Party and apartheid took over in Pretoria: but in the beginning the WCC was less concerned with external affairs of this kind than with healing the age-old divisions within Christendom, and with doing humanitarian work such as bringing relief to many of the world's hungry and homeless people. However after some dozen years an abrupt change in its motivation occurred–and it coincided with the admission into the Council's ranks of Churches in the communist countries of Eastern Europe. At the WCC General Assembly in New Delhi in 1961 Soviet-approved Orthodox Churches from Russia, Rumania, Bulgaria and Poland became full members. The man who led them into membership was Metropolitan Nikolai, second in the hierarchy of the Russian Orthodox Church and an avowed enemy of the United States. (Earlier he had accused the American army of committing atrocities in Korea, including the crucifying of North Koreans and the burying alive of women and children.) Claiming a total of 70-million adherents, the new members immediately altered the Council's balance of power: their representatives on its committees and commissions gave them a virtual veto over resolutions which they disapproved–and any censure of behaviour in communist countries they strongly disapproved.

William Fletcher, a Soviet expert at the University of Kansas, wrote that the purpose of the participation of the Eastern Churches was to ensure that the Council's actions would conform to the interests of the Kremlin. Events corroborated his view. In 1962 the WCC condemned America during the Cuban missile crisis. In 1966, at a conference in Geneva, it openly committed itself to revolutionary change. In 1968, while the civilised world expressed spontaneous revulsion at the Soviet invasion of Czechoslovakia, the WCC remained silent until Russia's goals had been won. In 1970 it established a fund to support draft-dodgers and deserters from the American armed forces in Canada and Sweden. In 1970 it sent medical supplies and equipment to the communists in Vietnam. In September, 1972, it condemned the West German police for "callous disregard" and "violent action" in their unsuccessful bid to save the Israeli hostages at the Olympic Games.

Meanwhile, apart from these political activities, the WCC was propagating a new way of living. In July, 1968, it held its Fourth Assembly in Uppsala, Sweden. It was the largest meeting in the 20 years of its existence: 200 Churches were represented, and it was claimed that never before had spokesmen of so many varying Christian beliefs gathered under the same roof. The working sections into which the conference was divided pointed to the nature of its deliberations. Four of the six of them were concerned, respectively, with economic development, justice in international affairs, the place of religion in a secular age, and the evolving of what was called a new life-style. For the rest, according to one observer: "the programme was skilfully designed to bring the Churches clear into the open on the great public issues of our time. The customary theological and doctrinal discussions were pruned to give place for the emergence of genuine revolutionary and constructive thinking which the World Council hopes will place the Christian Churches in the van of leadership in the search for a new style of human living."

The emphasis was on this new life-style and on the part of youth in shaping it. All young people were not revolutionaries, stated one Council document, but it was undeniable that a new style of life particular to the young was spreading over the world, together with the secular, technological civilisation. "Youth", the document declared, "has a right to participate in decisions in schools, universities and business. Young people are right to challenge authority when it is not authentically earned." There was wide approval of permissiveness and protest. One report condoned extra-marital sex. Compiled by a committee of delegates under the chairmanship of a Swedish woman, the key passage on the subject of sex read: "Too often chastity is thought of simply in terms of abstinence or of keeping intercourse within marriage. But chastity is surely more concerned with the way love is expressed." Another section of this report dealt with protest. Christians were urged to adopt the use of protest songs to force authorities to act. It was recommended also that Christians should engage in "symbolic destruction of property and sabotage" as a means to obtaining freedom.

On this point, the Vatican and the WCC joined voices at a conference which they sponsored in Beirut in the same year. In a document that came before the conference, the methods that Christians should use to force change were spelt out: "Christians will naturally attempt to achieve necessary change by non-violent means. But they cannot be accused of illegality and irresponsible violence when they confront and defy illegal, irresponsible and violent regimes." But with God discounted and his commandments erased, where is the guideline to necessary change? Peking and Moscow also urge revolution in the name of justice. Which man's conscience is to judge between what is just and unjust? Mao? Brezhnev? Carson Blake?

The aspect of the WCC's activity most closely related to South Africa and most revealing of the nature it has assumed began in May, 1969, in Notting Hill, London. What was called a "consultation" was held there by the Council's Committee on Race. The meeting recommended boycotts against corporations doing business in the Republic and, if necessary, support for resistance movements, including revolutions. That was the start of the WCC's Programme to Combat Racism. In 1970 it opened a fund with 200,000 dollars to support 19 revolutionary movements. Most of them were active in Southern Africa; four of them were avowedly pro-communist, armed, trained and directed by Russia and China; and they included the South African ANC (African National Congress), PAC (Pan Africanist Congress) and SWAPO (South West African People's Organisation). These organisations, cloaked in Christian respectability by the WCC, were not engaged in conventional warfare but in intimidation and terrorism among innocent–and predominantly black–civilian populations, murder, arson, torture, and the maiming of animals as well as human beings.

Influential voices abroad were raised against the granting of Christian sanction to such activities. Germany's *Die Welt* wrote: "Christian faith and terrorist power are incompatible." London's *Daily Telegraph* wrote: "Once it was missionaries who received our funds for their dispensaries

161

and schools. Now it is obscure, many-lettered organisations which plant explosives by night and are enemies, conscious or unconscious, of all peace and prosperity." In a letter to *The Times,* London, Malcolm Muggeridge asked what the upheavals planned by the terrorists had to do with advancing the Kingdom of Christ. "Is Kenya more Christ-like because Jomo Kenyatta now rules over it? Or the Congo because President Mobutu is now in charge? It is difficult to think off-hand of any regime in the world which, in Christian terms, does not deserve to be overthrown. Why then should African freedom fighters be favoured?" Generally, observed Muggeridge, no issue that he could recall in some 40 years of journalism had lent itself to so much mental and moral confusion and sheer humbug as the South African one; and "into this unedifying maelstrom of mixed motives and confused purposes, the World Council of Churches drags the name of Christ. How excruciating."

Such protests had no effect: year by year the WCC reinforced its financial aid and moral support for the "freedom fighters". Moreover Carson Blake, General Secretary of the WCC (and the man who advocated the breaking of laws in the United States) extended the new Christian vision to include blessing for massive acts of sabotage. It was good that the revolutionaries were planning to blow up Cabora Bassa. True, Cabora Bassa was Africa's greatest dam and hydro-electric project: it could bring a higher standard of living and hope to countless black people in Mocambique and neighbouring states: but it was being built by an international consortium in which the Republic was a major partner: it was a symbol of racism: it should be removed from the face of the earth-and so also the hydro-electric project on the opposite side of the sub-continent, on the Kunene River between South West Africa and Angola. The WCC had by now gained its own new-Christian momentum. Carson Blake was replaced by Philip Potter, a West Indian, who declared: "I am prepared to face chaos and anarchy if that is what it takes to bring about the necessary change in the world."

Potter understates his case. The WCC is not facing chaos and anarchy, it is actively inciting them; and the changes which the WCC deems necessary cause the Christian's conscience to shudder for the fate of the world and his faith. One of Potter's lieutenants is Canon Burgess Carr, a Liberian who is General Secretary of the WCC's affiliate, the All African Conference of Churches. He is a leading exponent of the theology of violence. He says that it was only after the Jews were liberated from Egypt that they were given the commandment: "Thou Shall Not Kill"; and in describing Sharpeville as the Good Friday of Africa, he declares that "in accepting the violence of the Cross, God in Jesus Christ sanctified violence into a redemptive instrument for bringing into being a fuller human life."

It is difficult to be restrained in the presence of such blasphemy. Christ, the gentle man of peace, died as he did to sanctify suffering for the sake of others, and to offer individual men release from their sins. On that account, even the General Secretary of this organisation of African Churches is not beyond redemption.

Of all the Churches in the world it might have been expected that the English-language Churches of South Africa would break with the WCC (the Afrikaans Churches did so 15 years ago). They have adopted instead the two-faced stance of dissociating themselves from support for violence while remaining members of the World Council. No amount of rationalising can conceal this equivocation: their continuing association with the WCC–these Churches most closely involved–has strengthened alike the hand of the revolutionary movements and the Council's leadership. Shortly before his retirement as General Secretary, Carson Blake told the press: "People have charged us with supporting rapists or terrorists . . . as for the fact that some of the liberation groups might be communist, I don't know. But we have not lost a member church by granting these funds." It is a disgrace to Christianity that the English-language Churches in the Republic should have enabled him to make this claim.

But we must not lose perspective: the Republic of South Africa is incidental in all this. The secularisation of Christianity, the theology which rejects a resurrected Christ and denies the existence of God, will, if it prevails, destroy our culture and bring to all mankind the doom from which 2,000 years ago Christ saved it.

CHAPTER TEN / 1960 to 1970–
Black Africa

The Fall of Freedom

As 1964 opened with the recent grant of independence to Zambia, the decolonisation of Africa north of the Zambesi–except for the Portuguese territories–was virtually complete. It was seven years since the African revolution had begun with Ghana's independence in 1957; and of that event one commentator wrote: "The joy in Great Britain is no less profound than in Russia and the United States. Idealists in every country have hailed the event with rapture." Those were the seven fat years. During that period 30 and more new states in Africa had come into being, and their Presidents and Prime Ministers had the eyes and ears of the world at its heart. They were respected and intimately trusted: Kwame Nkrumah was the first man outside the British Royal family to be informed of an impending royal birth. Because the new states were backward, poor and inexperienced they were given limitless encouragement and moral and material support. And although they were backward, poor and inexperienced they were given an influence which they exerted even on the greatest of powers. Their African revolution was seen as an inexorable force. "The tide of national consciousness now rising in Africa" is how Mr. Macmillan described it: in its spring it would sweep all before it and, in particular, leave no trace upon the continent of white control. This, it was believed, was not only on account of the weight of black numbers: it was also because the black man had right on his side. The socialist dogma held that in capitalist countries the workers could do no wrong, and that in colonial countries the white man could do no right. For the communist countries the proletariat possessed a monopoly of wisdom and virtue; and in the eyes of all the world the black people were altogether morally superior to their rulers. These were the seven fat years

164

and no group of nations could ever have had it so good. But within a decade of 1957 freedom in Africa had risen and fallen. In no period of history had so many constitutions been written out, or so many torn up. The earlier euphoria in the West, coinciding with its own changing condition, was replaced by deep disenchantment concerning Africa; and commentators abroad strove to find the answer.

The mass circulation *Life Magazine* was one of them. It wrote in 1966 that the United States now seemed to have been wrong in assuming, as it pressed for the dissolution of colonial empires after the War, that democracy would be the natural substitute for white rule. America had feared that Africa would go communist: "but we might have done better to fear other things." In Europe the *Swiss Review of World Affairs* (published by the renowned *Neue Züricher Zeitung)* analysed the collapse of African freedom. It had been generally thought, it wrote, that democracy could be established "with a little goodwill and substantial financial support." However it had become evident that the necessary voluntary consent of the people could not be achieved, because "the mental prerequisites do not exist." Sir Alec Douglas-Home, previously British Foreign Secretary and Prime Minister, told Americans that very few of the new African countries had the apparatus essential for the basic tasks of government.

Others rationalised black Africa's failures. As the Westminster model was rejected by one country after another, British socialist John Strachey observed that this was to have been expected: "The immense difficulties which some of the newer members of the Commonwealth face in the political field was forcibly brought home to me in Africa last year (1962) when I was informed that the only possible translation into many African languages of the term 'Leader of the Opposition' was 'Chief Enemy'." U Thant, Secretary General of the United Nations, declared in London in the same year: "The notion that democracy requires the existence of an organised opposition to the Government of the day is not valid." There were many other rationalisations. Co-operation with communism by the new black states was rationalised in the name of non-alignment and national freedom: the Congo disaster was rationalised on the ground of inadequate preparation for independence by the Belgians: maladministration was rationalised by the worn-out notion (comfortable enough for the non-participants) that good government is no substitute for self-government: lack of elementary justice was rationalised by the argument that the same standards could not be expected in Africa as in old-established countries: graft and nepotism were rationalised as being part of traditional African behaviour: poverty, misery and disease for millions of black people were rationalised as a necessary price for freedom. The coming of the military dictators was rationalised: like Nkrumah a handful of years before these new dictators were now the saviours of their people.

165

The GM Model

There was some truth in these rationalisations—and not least in the recognition that the parliamentary system which the idealists had insisted they should have was altogether unsuited to the temperament of Africa's people. But other basic causes of Africa's poor performance were ignored. One of the chief among them was that sophisticated techniques of production—what has been called the General Motors model—are no better suited to emergent Africa's economic development than the Westminster model is to its political development. The GM model may well increase national income in emergent countries, but it does less than nothing to enlist the enthusiasm of the people. It is necessarily established, directed and managed by foreigners because men with the skills for this kind of operation are not yet available locally. The natives are not active participants but passive agents, obeying orders, drawing wages—and having the illusion created for them that progress can be achieved without initiative. The GM model not only distracts attention from the overriding importance of agriculture but draws people physically from rural to city areas, and gives rise to expectations which the people of no emergent state will in the foreseeable future be able to enjoy. Worst of all, the GM model is one which is beyond the capacity of emergent people to assimilate into their own culture: foreign aid can be effective in stimulating real growth only if it fertilises the grass-roots of the recipient society, and if treatment is adapted in each case to the cultural soil of the community concerned. If not it will stifle or force growth, distort or obliterate it.

These are consequences even when the GM model is introduced with worthy motives: but generally motives have been ulterior. Aid of this kind was given more often than not to further the purposes of the donor rather than to answer the real needs of the recipients. The objective was less to promote progress than to buy political favour and to entrench influence. Expedient considerations set the qualifications for aid—the disposition of the élitist leaders instead of the requirements of the people—and often the least-deserving were the richest beneficiaries. Moreover, in concentrating wealth within the narrowest sectors of the community, the GM model incited rival élitist cliques to compete for political power and thus to lay their hands upon these limited sources of affluence. In this way Western concepts of economic development combined with Western concepts of political development (parliamentary democracy, the nation-state and anti-tribalism) to destroy the structure of black society, to dry up the springs of organic community activity and to bolster the position of unrepresentative nationalist leaders.

American historian Cornelis de Kiewiet* summed up the situation in 1970 in an article written for the *Virginia Quarterly Review*. Among his conclusions were these: Western techniques of modernisation have limited validity for African conditions, and the assumption that they would spread their benefit through the whole of the emergent community was an illusion: the modern world in these African countries is a vessel too small and inelastic to contain those who wish to enter it: their leaders must refashion the shape of the future by retracing their steps into the past, and if they are not to be thrust back into actual colonialism, they must adjust to the pace of colonial growth–of infinitely tedious social and economic pioneering: prosperity in the new black states is an island surrounded by stagnation, and the spoils of political power are the quickest and sometimes the only road to affluence: international assistance must discover what it never possessed–the insight and the imagination needed for the comprehensive modernisation of Africa.

The Non-Revolution

Mr. Macmillan's winds of change struck back at black Africa. They blew apart its inherited forms of government. They tore down the myth of artificially-inseminated economic development and laid bare the basic poverty of the new states. They fanned rivalry between them and tribal and ethnic hostility within them. In obliterating colonialism, they demolished the anti-colonial cause which united them. The course of decolonisation in Africa and its aftermath comprehensively contradicted the expectations of the idealists . . . and behind it all lay a massive fallacy. It was this: the winds of change did not originate in Africa but in Europe and the United States. Nationalism as known in Europe was foreign to Africa; and the African Revolution which Mr. Macmillan implied and the rest of the world assumed did not–and has never–occurred.

A revolution springs from an idea: liberty, equality, fraternity; or the inalienable rights of the individual, or the supremacy of the proletariat. It involves the whole of society and comprehends its restructuring into a radically different life-style. There was nothing of this kind in Africa. There was not even a spontaneous and widespread dissatisfaction with the colonial status quo (not least because it offered greater security than the earlier dispensation), and no eruption of common purpose to achieve

*Cornelis Willen de Kiewiet, whom I shall be quoting again, was born in Holland and educated in Johannesburg. In 1939 he became a US citizen, in 1941 Professor of Modern History at Cornell, and in 1951 President of Rochester University. His books include *A History of South Africa* (1941) and *An Anatomy of South African Misery* (1956). He is a sharp critic of apartheid.

some other status. The demand for emancipation was confined to a negligible proportion of the people, and even then it was conceived abroad–among the Fabian socialists in Britain mainly. "Independence" was simply not understood by African tribesmen: there is the story of the one in the Congo who, upon being told about it, asked whether it was to come by road or rail.

Resistance by the ruler is implicit in revolution. However there was no resistance in Britain, which country set the pace and pattern of decolonisation. Britain did not protest but promoted the movement. She did not regard her abdication–as any ruler in a revolution would–as a defeat but as a rousing victory for herself and mankind. What was involved here was not the outraged sense of injustice of the revolutionary but the sense of guilt of the ruler for past offences real or imagined. On this point Professor de Kiewiet declares:

An Africa without colonialism was an Africa profoundly changed by that fact alone. It was an Africa free to act, and capable of gaining a strength which it could itself command. Thus it was that the steps that led to independence and the documents that confirmed it were received with far more consent than criticism. History had begun to smile kindly upon a continent so long and bitterly deprived. Who then could frown? Criticism and scepticism were muffled as unfriendly toward the high purpose of independence. The contradictions and insufficiencies so blatantly discernible in the colonial past were ignored or minimised, almost as if they had not flowed massively across the dividing line between subjection and nationhood. There was an unexamined persuasion that Africa had acquired a new symmetry and coherence and continuity. Objective minds were thrown off guard, as hope and enthusiasm subtly imparted a sense of imminence and certainty to the future they wished to see emerge. A sense of guilt about the past fused objective and moral judgments into a single state of mind. Not on one side of the Atlantic alone, a mood of penitence was overtaken by a mood of self-exoneration, because such a generous gift had been made to the future. The gentle transition to independence was a windfall of history, a blessed anomaly that purged the future of rancour and resentment. Feelings of generosity and rectitude hid an arrogance that overestimated the worth of the gift that had been made, and underestimated the burdens that had been placed on unready shoulders.

Here, Professor de Kiewiet noted, was the root of the conviction that the order of things in South Africa was doomed. If time was at last on the side of the new Africa, it could not equally be on the side of South Africa.

In a presumed contest between a black African and a white South African tempo of change, the odds were against the dragging pace and the anachronistic direction chosen by South Africa.

There was no revolution in Africa. The emancipated "nations" knew nothing of the binding force of a shared struggle for a common ideal. Their freedom was not won in the heat of conflict but written out for them between the cold corridors of Westminster. Nor were they nations: they were agglomerations of people owing their identity to nothing more than borders on a map–as arbitrarily drawn by the colonial administrators as were the charters, drawn by legal draughtsmen, which presumed to give them independent nationhood. These emergent black states had the advantage neither of ethnic unity, nor of the emotional cohesion forged by revolutionary seizing of power, nor the stability of a well-prepared and orderly transfer of power from trustee to ward.

In these circumstances is the explanation of much of what has happened in black Africa in the past 20 years. Having won independence in the way described, the militants among the élitist black leaders endeavoured to evoke, after the event, the revolutionary fervour which did not precede it. They substituted revolutionary rhetoric for the reality of revolution. One of the first acts of the Organisation of African Unity in 1963 was to establish a Liberation Committee. However the members of the OAU were already liberated: the Committee's mission was therefore necessarily confined to liberating others–their "brothers" in the white-ruled countries of the South. But revolution cannot be experienced vicariously; and unity based on hostility to others cannot inspire constructive action. Instead of establishing and moving out together towards positive goals, the members of the OAU wasted their precariously limited resources, dissipated their energies and fouled their perspective by pursuing their anti-white vendetta. A good future for Africa cannot be found except in co-operation among all its communities, black and white, underdeveloped and developed. In its rejection of this course, the OAU exacerbated the problems loaded upon black Africa by the misguided judgments, the sentimentality and the expedience of the Western world. There have all along been moderate men among the black leaders, understanding the restricting realities of emergent Africa and advocating pragmatic policies. However they were out-shouted and out-voted by the militants–though even the militants, in large measure, can be excused: it was the West that invented black nationalism and its revolution; that was responsible for the myth of black Africa's "symmetry, cohesion and continuity", and that invested its leaders with the false sense of their importance.

, And what of the ordinary black people in all this–those patient, good-humoured and courteous people? It is tragic that the disciples of decolonisation should have raised in them expectations so false of rapid

169

progress and enrichment; and criminal for the prophets of freedom–including those who call themselves men of God–to incite them to violence. They were taught to try to destroy the white man in Africa, but co-operation with him offers the best hope for their release–slow though it will inevitably be–from impoverishment and backwardness.

Professor de Kiewiet mentioned the possibility of the emergent states "being thrust back into actual colonialism": and at the same time–early 1970–it was advocated as necessary by a leading British journalist, Mr. Peregrin Worsthorne. In an article in London's *Sunday Telegraph* he expressed the view that before the 1970s were out, millions of Asians and Africans would have died through famine, war and massacre. "The problems facing great areas of the underdeveloped world", he wrote, "are proving fundamentally different from what we thought they were going to be, not so much growing pains as death agonies, not so much problems of economic growth requiring advice and assistance as basic problems of political cohesion requiring external intervention and control. In the years ahead, the experience of self-government in Africa and India may well carry with it a level of tragic inhumanity, a scale of human suffering, a degree of disorder and chaos which will make it unacceptable to the rest of the civilised world. In such circumstances it may only be a question of time before the truth dawns that nothing short of a return to colonialism can prevent a renewed descent into barbarism."

How does Pretoria regard such an assessment? The Afrikaner's was the first of Africa's nationalisms: he was involved for three years at the turn of the century in a total revolutionary struggle for independence: he was Africa's pioneer opponent of colonialism; and Pretoria today rejects colonialism in whatever form, from whatever quarter and in whatever part of the continent. Nevertheless, the opinion on the subject of two men so far apart politically as Professor de Kiewiet and Mr. Worsthorne points to the precariousness of independence in black Africa: indeed, large areas of the continent already face the threat of recolonisation by Russia. The best hope for thwarting it is for the black states to plan their progress realistically within their capacity, to co-operate regionally and, where possible, to associate and interact with a developed society. Because of the existence of such a society in the Republic, this last and decisive advantage is available at least to those of them in Southern Africa.

The Indian in Africa

Among the consequences of the fall of freedom in black Africa was the hardship, and worse, it brought for tribal and ethnic minorities in many

170

countries. One case of this, the treatment of Indians in East Africa, is of particular interest to us.

A major problem in coming to any sort of balanced judgment of the respective merits of various race policies is the different circumstances in which the policies operate in different countries. Thus, for Anglo-Afrikaners, a comparison of actual conditions in their country with those in others seems time and again to them to redound to their favour. The critics see it otherwise: for them there are other factors which rule out or reverse the conclusion drawn from the comparison. For instance: the Anglo-Afrikaner claims in support of his policies that housing, hospitalisation, education, social services, wages, standard of life and general amenities of living for non-whites in South Africa are substantially superior to those in Africa at large. The critic replies that, taking into account South Africa's much greater wealth, they jolly well should be–that they should be considerably more superior than they are. The Anglo-Afrikaner points to the hardships suffered by the Negro in the United States and the Jamaican in Britain. The critic, while admitting the hardships, points out that there is an essential difference in that South Africa is the black man's own country. The Anglo-Afrikaner points to the gross discrimination–racial, tribal, caste, religious–practised in countries around the globe. The critic replies, while acknowledging the truth of this, that whereas countries elsewhere oppose discrimination (however ineffectually) by law, Pretoria makes it the basis of her social organisation. So the argument goes, and has gone for 30 years: each side accuses the other of unreasonableness and ulterior motive and no common ground is discovered. Perhaps the explanation is that the areas of race relations indicated here are not, in fact, comparable: but the recent fate of Indians in South Africa and East Africa provides one that is.

In South Africa and East Africa alike the Indians are an immigrant community. They were brought to East Africa at the turn of the century to help build the railroad from Mombasa to Kampala. Others followed; and through hard work, diligence, thrift and mutual assistance within their community, they prospered. They became the owners of small trading establishments in the rural areas, and of bazaars, department stores, garages and hotels, in the towns. They worked as carpenters, mechanics, artisans, bank-tellers, clerks and book-keepers–and in the process made a large contribution to the development of East Africa's economy. After independence in the early 1960s, the new black governments in Nairobi, Kampala and Dar es Salaam proclaimed their belief in a non-racial society. However the Indian is innately different from the African; and the maintaining of his difference within an exclusive, co-operating community of his own had been the source of his success. He could not assimilate with the African if he chose, and he did not choose. When at independence he was offered a British passport, he eagerly took it. He saw it as a means of safeguarding his separate way of life and as an insurance against an uncertain future. Not un-naturally the governments in East Africa resented this attitude: and the new generation of blacks, anxious to move into better-paid and more privileged jobs, regarded the Indians as barring their progress. Rancour between the two communities escalated: the non-racial ideal evaporated: Indians were denied the opportunity to work, they were harassed and, under Amin in Uganda, persecuted and expelled *en masse*. Although they held British passports, the British Government was reluctant to take them in because of the effect their presence would have on race relations in an "open" society (and proceeded to introduce into its immigration legislation the "patriality" principle I have described).

So much for the fate of Indians in non-racial states.

Then there is the world's apartheid state. Indians were first brought to South Africa in the 1860s as labourers on the sugar plantations of Natal. Others followed, and for the same reasons–as in East Africa they prospered and multiplied. In South Africa–as in East Africa (and Britain) today–there was for a long time antipathy in plenty against them: and through many decades successive governments tried to eliminate the problem by repatriating them to India. Various arrangements with the Indian Government–notably in 1927–were made with this in view, and financial assistance was offered by Pretoria to those who chose to leave. In the event, a negligible number did: despite the tensions, they preferred life in South Africa. Meanwhile South Africa's traditional attitude to race relations of live and let live was taking specific form in apartheid. At no time had there been any attempt to break the Indians' customs or to wean them from them: they were left in peace with their temples and mosques, their strange ceremonies, food and dress. Resentment towards them rose from other causes–from their intrusion into white commercial and residential areas, and from the political implications of their fast-growing numbers. With the implementation of apartheid, these causes of friction were progressively removed. Like other groups of the country's population, the Indians were to be a self-contained, self-governing community with areas of their own and institutions of their own. Whereas the exclusiveness and mutual support of their community was held against them in East Africa (and Britain), it would be converted by apartheid to their own advantage in South Africa: whereas their foreign ways were disliked elsewhere, they would be welcomed in South Africa as contributing to its rich human diversity. In the past, few Indians left South Africa despite the inducements to do so. Today none leave, and there is no longer any government inducement to them to go because, under apartheid, they are welcome to stay. In 1961 the Minister of the Interior stated in Parliament: "The Indians are here and the great

172

majority of them are going to remain here. We must realise that they are South African citizens and as such are entitled to the necessary attention and necessary assistance. Today we say unequivocally that the Indians in this country are our permanent responsibility."

When that statement was made, Indians in South Africa owned 181 industrial undertakings. In 1974 they owned 626, including more than 100 clothing factories. This accounts for some one-sixth of all factories in Natal. In 1974 they established their own bank, the New Republic Bank: and at the opening ceremony the Minister of Finance, Dr. Diederichs, congratulated them on their enterprise: in contrast with other race groups in the country, their success had been achieved with little or no assistance from the State. "Your achievement in industrial ventures", he said, "proves in no uncertain way that the Indian's natural aptitude for business has found another outlet outside the wholesale and retail trade. The South African Indian, as a member of one of the permanent population groups (now moving towards the million-mark) of the Republic, has a destiny to fulfil in this country. His undoubted talents must be developed to the full and should feature prominently in the broader South African economy."

There, discerning Reader, you have the comparative lot of an immigrant community in non-racial states and in an apartheid state. All the conditions are present for a fair comparison: is it unreasonable to claim that the making of it redounds resoundingly to the credit of Pretoria and its policies?

Part two: / Section two
1960 to 1970–

The Pretoria Theme:
Engagement: The Fight and
Win for Survival

The Punishment

A Time of Crisis

The 1960s were the Republic's crisis decade. A series of climacteric events occurred, any one of which might have seemed enough to break the nation's will to pursue its chosen course. At home one trauma followed another: from abroad, the pseudo-liberals–their hope for a new world order in ruins–sought to compensate their frustration by pressing their attack on apartheid. According to historian Cornelis de Kiewiet, a sense of guilt about their past fused objective and moral judgments into a single state of mind–and it found expression in the persecution of Pretoria.

> *Pretoria, 1967:* 1960 was proclaimed "Africa Year". The storm drove in and there was no horizon beyond the tomorrow. The thunder rolled. In Cape Town British Prime Minister Macmillan described black nationalism as an irresistible force. In the euphoria of their new freedom the African states promised 1963 as the year of South Africa's liberation. There were boycotts around the world, threats of sanctions, plans for armed invasion. The United Nations rang with denunciation of South Africa and wild accusation. The lightning struck: at Sharpeville, at the Rand Easter Show where the first attempt was made on Prime Minister Verwoerd's life, at the Johannesburg railway station where the terrorist bomb exploded.

>> As one feels pity for a wounded man, whatever his political opinions, so one must also feel compassion for a wounded country, and South Africa is indeed a wounded country: the *New York Times*, 10.4.60.

175

What was there beyond today? There was no certainty, no safety but only the determination of a small nation to defend itself, and its faith. Again the lightning struck: on September 6, 1966 the Prime Minister was assassinated at his desk in Parliament. Momentarily there was a darkness deeper than at any time in the years before. In striking to death the Prime Minister the assassin had liberated his life's work. The darkness was dispersed and the heavens cleared. (25)

Those first six years of the decade: the odds were terrible! Let us take a look at the chief among them, and at the manner in which they were overcome:

Sharpeville

On Sunday, March 27, 1960, I looked down from my office on the fourth floor of South Africa House in London upon a mass of people in Trafalgar Square. They were standing shoulder to shoulder–10,000 and more of them. These were not rabble-rousers. It was a chilly day. Many wore overcoats, some caps, some hats, most were bare-headed. These were middle-aged, middle-class, respectable people: average British citizens who had come at the behest of the Labour Party to protest about Sharpeville. But they seemed to me more worried and curious than angry. Through the past six days they had read innumerable lurid reports and seen many bloody pictures on their telly. The South African Police had opened fire on a crowd of black people, and 69 of them had been killed and many others wounded. Was this, at last, the eruption of the volcano, the bloodbath, their media had been telling them for a dozen years was inevitable in South Africa? What did it all mean? What could they do about it?

> The death of at least 66 Negroes following demonstrations
> against apartheid in South Africa is a warning inscribed in
> blood on the wall: the *Washington Post,* 23.3.60.

That was the mood of the mass of people as I judged it. And the calling of this huge demonstration in the heart of London was an example of the political exploitation against Pretoria of the genuine concern of ordinary people. The Labour Party, in opposition at this stage, had lost the decolonisation initiative to the Conservatives. They had been comprehensively out-manoeuvred the previous month by Mr. Macmillan's wind-of-change speech in Cape Town. This, surely, was unfair: emancipating black people was surely one of the proudest of all socialist babies–now it had been kidnapped by the Tories. It was very necessary that the British public should not be deceived: that they should know that the Labour Party was the *real* champion of the oppressed. So it is highly improbable that the socialists on the platform at Trafalgar Square that Sunday would have given their audience a full and fair account of what happened at Sharpeville, even had they been able to. And they were not able to, since the facts were unknown to them.

> For there is over that land a dark shadow which afflicts all men both there and elsewhere who feel the weight of great problems concerning the fate of millions; and a sense that the awful culmination of Calvary has yet to come: the *Sunday Times*, London, 17.4.60.

The previous Wednesday–two days after the shooting–I had had a long-standing engagement to talk to the men at a military establishment in the Midlands. I passed through a reading-room with my host on the way to the lecture hall, and on the tables were half-a-dozen newspapers with full-page photographs of sprawled bodies on the ground of the dead and wounded. As I faced the officers, I believe they were more embarrassed for my sake than angry. They were thinking: "What can the poor bastard say?" What could I say? The facts were not known to me either. No-one knew them then: and another part of the Sharpeville tragedy is that distorted reports were circulated round the world by people who did not know. One of them was the ex-Bishop of Johannesburg, Ambrose Reeves, who supported the rumour that the police had used dum-dum bullets. It was not until evidence was placed before the courts of law and until the months-long and exhaustive investigation of a judicial commission of inquiry was published that a fair assessment could be made of the events at Sharpeville. And the events themselves could not, and cannot, be judged except with knowledge of the wide–the worldwide–context in which they occurred. The forces that came together and erupted that day in the normally well-ordered and peaceful black township near Vereeniging in the Transvaal were many, varied and complex. Included among them were: the international agitation against Pretoria; the gathering momentum of decolonisation in Africa; the pledge by the Pan-Africanists to overthrow, by 1963, the Pretoria Government and to include the Republic in a United States of Africa, and the competition for the support of South Africa's black people between two local urban-based nationalist organisations. Agitation against control of the influx of black people into the city areas–the "pass laws" which had been a focus of resentment for half a century and longer–was no more than what lawyers might call the proximate cause of the trouble.

> Such may be the fruits of Sharpeville. Like the first flash of lightning, they may herald a period of darkling calm: but after that comes the thunderstorm. The world prays that civilised and Christian people in South Africa will turn back before it is too late: the *Sunday Times*, London, 27.3.60.

The first of the rival black nationalist organisations was the African National Congress. It had been formed soon after the founding of the Union in 1910. In the post-war years the ANC took the lead in championing the cause of what it described as "a united South African nation constituted of the heterogeneous tribes of Africa, and of the ending of foreign domination and foreign leadership." Communist influence was strong. As far back as 1936 the Secretary General of the ANC was a communist, J. B. Marks. In 1949 the Secretary General of the South African Communist Party, Moses Kotane, became Secretary General of the ANC. The ANC worked closely with the Indian National Congress, the Congress of Democrats (a white communist-front organisation) and the South African Coloured People's Organisation. This, and the fact that the ANC under Albert Luthuli was considered too moderate, led to a split in the movement and to the formation in April, 1959, of the exclusively black Pan Africanist Congress. It was the very time that the Bill for the Promotion of Bantu Self-government was before Parliament in Cape Town: and here, dramatically counterposed, were the alternative courses before South Africa. One led constitutionally to autonomy for each of the country's black nations; the other, to the revolutionary establishment of a single South African state which was to be incorporated in a United States of Africa. It was Kwame Nkrumah's vision, his megalomaniac illusion–a United States of Africa extending from the Cape to Cairo, from Morocco to Madagascar, of which the Republic was to be the jewel. The Republic must be liberated so that it could be possessed; and once it became the possession of black Africa, it would provide the riches for the development of the continent as a whole.

> Undoubtedly Mr. Calwell's speech fairly expressed the feelings of most Australians on the recent outburst of violence and repression (in South Africa), and it may have done more than that. It may have helped to demonstrate to our Asian neighbours that we are not wholly uninterested in the rights and even the lives of colored people: *The Age*, Australia, 1.4.60.

178

As 1959 ended, circumstances from a variety of quarters conspired towards a heightening of militant black expectations. In October a body called the Bishop's Committee (recently formed by Bishop Ambrose Reeves of Johannesburg) announced the launching of a campaign against the pass laws. In December the Pan Africanist Congress decided to take "final and positive action" against these laws as the first phase in its programme for overthrowing the Government. In January, 1960, the Labour Party in London announced that, as a symbolic act, it would support a campaign to boycott South African goods, and that it had taken this decision in direct response to an appeal from the ANC, the South African Indian Congress and the South African Liberal Party. Early in February, Prime Minister Macmillan made his speech in Cape Town in which he spoke of the need to come to terms with black nationalism. Later that month the ANC, in co-operation with the Bishop's Committee, announced a plan for mass demonstrations throughout the Transvaal towards the end of March against the pass laws.

The PAC was in danger of being out-manoeuvred and out-paced. On March 18 its leader, Robert Sobukwe, told a press conference that the first major protest organised by his movement against the pass laws had been set for the following Monday, March 21. The protest required that black people should present themselves *en masse* at police stations, and request that they be arrested because they were not carrying their passes and did not propose at any time in future to do so. During the intervening week-end pamphlets were distributed in large numbers among black workers in various parts of the country. One stated: "This is the call the African people have been waiting for. It has come! On Monday, March 21, 1960, we launch our Positive, Decisive campaign against the pass laws in this country." Another stated: "In 1960 we take our first step, in 1963 our last, to freedom and independence." The pamphlets were headed: "Calling the Nation! No bail, no defence, no fines."

> The South African Government's moral credit in the world
> has sunk to its lowest point. No episode since Hitler's time
> has aroused such universal execration: the *Guardian*, Lon-
> don, 7.4.60.

The PAC laid their plans well, particularly in Sharpeville. Sharpeville is, and then was, a neat township with homes for families and single-quarters on the outskirts of the industrial town of Vereeniging. At the time it had a population of 38,000; and the total complement of its police station was one white sergeant, eight black sergeants, two white constables and 27 black constables. There was a branch of the PAC there, and as from Friday evening its officials began their campaign. The

179

pamphlets were spread about, and the inhabitants were persuaded to stay away from work on Monday, to leave their reference books (their "passes") at home and to present themselves for arrest at the police station. On Sunday night, persuasion became intimidation: PAC supporters went from home to home, forcing their inmates by threats and violence to join the groups of demonstrators who were beginning to move through the streets of the township. The drivers of the buses which took the people to work were rounded up and told that they were not to report for duty the following morning. Telephone communications were broken. Women whose menfolk were being molested went to the police and asked for protection for themselves and their children. In the small hours of Monday morning, the police were engaged in dispersing the demonstrators: no less than 18 separate clashes between police and demonstrators, led by young PAC hooligans, occurred between midnight and 5 A.M. when the streets were cleared and order was restored.

The trouble started again as people leaving for work were intercepted by intimidators. At about 7 A.M. there was a turbulent encounter between a column of several thousand demonstrators and a police detachment blocking their march towards a white suburb of Vereeniging. Tear gas had to be used and a massive baton charge mounted. The commotion at this stage was such that the police commander requested headquarters in Johannesburg to arrange for Air Force Sabre jets to fly low over the township in a bid to distract the attention of the crowd–a tactic unprecedented in South African police history. At 10:20, the first police reinforcements arrived, by which time the demonstrators were thronging the streets around the fenced-off police post. Police officers endeavoured to negotiate with the local leaders of the PAC. They were told that the demonstration could be called off only by Sobukwe himself; and the PAC men demanded that they and their followers be arrested. This the police refused to do. By mid-day the crowd at the station was estimated at between 10,000 and 20,000. More reinforcements and senior officers arrived. Inside the police station enclosure, armoured cars were stationed. Taunts and threats were shouted at the police; and there were cries of "Cato Manor"–where, in the black township outside Durban less than two months before, nine policemen (five black and four white) had been done to death by a mob of rioters. An appeal made through loudspeakers had no effect, nor did the low-flying aircraft which had meantime arrived.

It is the tyrannical party machine which has kept Dr. Verwoerd in power, and unless the ordinary citizens of South Africa can reclaim their political individuality and initiative it may be that, far sooner than would have seemed possible a month or even a week ago, the South Africa of today may be only a memory: Rebecca West in the *Sunday Times*, London, 27.3.60.

Because of the suddenness with which the PAC had called the mass protest campaign, the authorities had had little opportunity to devise counter-measures. The reinforcements that were brought to Sharpeville were not trained riot squads but the personnel of ordinary police stations in various parts of the Witwatersrand: some of them had 20 years' service, one at least had one month's service. By 1 P.M. there were 130 white and 77 black policemen in the fenced-off area, and 29 white and 59 black policemen outside it. The mob was pressing against the fence, particularly against the double-gate entrance on the western side. Tension which had been building up for some 12 hours–since the demonstrators had first started gathering in the dark of night–was reaching break-point. The officer in command, Colonel Pienaar, ordered 70 of his men to line up in protection of the double gate. They were armed, variously, with revolvers, .303 rifles and sten-guns. There were cries again of "Cato Manor"; and Colonel Pienaar ordered his men to load their weapons but not to fire unless commanded. However the tumult by now was such that instructions could not be heard even a short distance away.

> Sharpeville was the nightmare that woke people up. When Mr. Macmillan made his speech in Cape Town, two people in five disclaimed any knowledge at all about it. After Sharpeville, 99 per cent of the public knew of events in South Africa. For foreign news this figure is unique: the *News Chronicle*, London, 7.4.60.

There is no reliable evidence that the police up to this stage had been needlessly aggressive. On the contrary, the evidence later adduced was that officers repeatedly warned the men against using firearms, and that time and again they tried to resolve successive confrontations by negotiation. However, by this time many of the police had been on duty in the township uninterruptedly for close on 24 hours, and added to physical exhaustion was the strain of ceaseless patrol activities and the several clashes in which they had been involved. Facing them in the huge crowd eight feet away were the young intimidators who had been ignominiously dispersed in the early hours that morning and thousands of others against whom tear gas and batons had had to be used.

It was at 1:40 that the final, fateful series of events occurred. An attempt was made to detain for questioning one of the leaders of the mob just outside the gate. He resisted and a scuffle ensued. The crowd in the

181

immediate vicinity reacted vehemently. Others further afield pressed forward. There was a crescendo of noise, a general surge, the gates burst open, a senior police officer was thrown to the ground, stones rained on the police, shots or sharp reports were heard from the crowd. There were two shots from the left flank of the line of 70 policemen, and then the rest of the line fired. The firing lasted some 20 seconds. One constable testified before the commission: "When they began to throw stones and a part of the crowd charged at us through the gate, at that moment I fired. I fired because my life and the others with me was in danger." Another constable testified that he fell as he was hit on the head with a stone. "As I got to my feet, I saw one of the natives with a stone in his right hand. He had his arm above his head and was aiming at me. That is when I fired at him."

Among the findings of the judicial commision were these: that there was no thought-out common intention on the part of the crowd to attack the police at any given time or in any given circumstances, but that under conditions such as those that prevailed that day the action of a crowd could be determined by the circumstances of the moment; that the commission accepted that the men who fired judged their lives to be in danger; that had they not fired when they did it was possible that there would have been no loss of life–but possible also that there would have been a worse bloodbath.

> Few would now doubt that the resignation of Dr. Verwoerd, and his replacement by a less brutally intransigent Prime Minister, is the only hope for averting bloody civil war in South Africa: the *Telegraph*, London, 8.4.60.

There is broad agreement among informed people with that judgment–indefinite though it was and, if it was to be fair, under such conditions had to be. The view of Mrs. Helen Suzman, of the Progressive Party, expressed in the Parliamentary debate on the commission's report was that no-one disputed that the young policemen that day judged their lives to be in danger, that they judged in good faith but that, untrained and inexperienced, they were not in a position to judge. Looking back six years after the event, Rudolf Gruber wrote for the journal, *Perspective:* "It is difficult to pin the blame on any single individual. The judicial commission, for one, did not try. Leaving aside the imponderables of long-term causes, however, it seems reasonably clear that the immediate spark was generated by a complex and interlocking combination of emotions and events in which the decisive ingredient was undoubtedly error in human judgment, and the real culprit, in all probability, the frailty of men under conditions of extreme tension and stress. What

182

every critic who seeks to sit in judgment on this incident must ask himself is what he would have done had he stood in the shoes of the people concerned. The answer, if the critic is honest with himself, might well be a humble and compassionate silence."

> There should be no argument about the duty of helping the opponents of South Africa's apartheid Government. If, despite all efforts, violence should break out, it is vital that the West should make it absolutely clear that it will not change sides–doubt about that would oblige the Africans to seek for consistent backers: the *Observer*, London, 28.5.61.

It might indeed. But there is one long-term cause that is neither imponderable nor can here be set aside. The prime agent of the tragedy was the PAC: had it not been for the incitement of the PAC there would have been no Sharpeville. As in so many other parts of Africa since that time a militant clique, in competition with another, exploited the people recklessly in its pursuit of power. The urban-based PAC and ANC were neither the chosen nor the traditional representatives of the great mass of the black people: according to their own membership figures they represented substantially less than one per cent of them. Nor can it be argued in favour of these movements that there were no constitutional avenues for the advancement of the black people: as has been pointed out, the PAC was formed at the very time that the Bill for the Promotion of Bantu Self-government was before Parliament, and eight years earlier the preparatory Bantu Authorities Act had been passed.

Brushing all objective considerations aside the world laid the blame exclusively at the door of Pretoria and its policies. In an outburst of vilification, unprecedented as it was unbridled, it presented Sharpeville as an atrocity committed by a totalitarian and reactionary state. While unprovoked brutality–involving not hundreds but often hundreds of thousands of victims–occurred in one country after another elsewhere, it made the word Sharpeville synonymous with vicious oppression. Nothing exposed more starkly the psychopathic prejudice–as irrational as anti-semitism–of the Western world towards Pretoria and its Afrikaner Government. Discussing the general Western attitude to Pretoria, Professor de Kiewiet was to write: "One cannot understand the depth of feeling against the policies of South Africa without taking into account an almost eschatological belief among liberals in an imminent and punishing end to such sin."

> In the few short days since scores of African demonstrators were shot down by police gunfire, South Africa has been

183

precipitated into a situation which many have been foretelling for a generation: Anthony Delius in the *Washington Post*, 27.3.60.

In the West's self-justifying condemnation of Pretoria immediately after Sharpeville there was also a note of exultation: how great the sin, how great the imminent punishment, and how great Pretoria's capitulation! Was it not already presaged, in the immediate aftermath of the shooting, in the suspension of the pass laws? The whole of the post-Sharpeville crusade was polluted by that nauseating emanation that issues from prophets of gloom and disaster, believing that they are about to be proven right.

How great the punishment! On April 9, less than three weeks after Sharpeville, Prime Minister Verwoerd travelled from the Parliamentary session in Cape Town to open the Rand Easter Show in Johannesburg. In the closing passage of his speech he declared: "Out of every crisis a new triumph is born. The future which lies ahead is greater than the past which lies behind us. We will not let ourselves be crushed. We will not be vanquished. We will fight for survival and we will conquer." There was tumultuous applause from the great congregation. Dr. Verwoerd left the platform to view the prize-winning cattle in the arena. He returned and was sitting back in his chair when a man approached from behind. He was well-dressed and was wearing in the lapel of his jacket the badge of the Witwatersrand Agricultural Society. "Dr. Verwoerd", he said quietly. The Prime Minister turned round. The stranger put his hand in his jacket pocket as though about to deliver a message. The Prime Minister smiled in anticipation. The stranger jerked a revolver from his pocket and shot the Prime Minister at point blank range in the face. Then as the Prime Minister, clutching his head in both hands, collapsed in his canvas chair, a second shot was fired.

> Dr. Verwoerd knows he is doomed and his arms are already around the pillars of the temple. Three years ago I would not have said that: James Cameron in the *News Chronicle*, London, 7.7.59.

That Dr. Verwoerd survived was, not figuratively but medically speaking, a miracle. The professor who headed the team of doctors attending him commented later: "It looks to me as if I'll have to take a refresher course in anatomy. According to everything I've learnt and everything I've seen and experienced in my practice, Dr. Verwoerd should have been dead within ten minutes." When it became known that he would recover, friends suggested a mass "welcome-back" reception

184

for him at the Voortrekker Monument: it was to be a token of the nation's thankfulness that he had been spared. The suggestion was conveyed to the Prime Minister in hospital by his private secretary. The Prime Minister asked that the idea should be abandoned forthwith and that it should be given no publicity. Although he was exhausted by the excruciating pain and his speech at that time was seriously impeded by the bullet wounds, he proceeded to issue instructions for the running of the country to his senior colleagues.

> Horror piles on horror in South Africa ... Now the shooting of the Prime Minister by a fellow white man. From apartheid to assassination, evil unleashes evil ... Since Dr. Verwoerd came to power, South Africa has seemed like the scene of a doom-laden tragedy; yet none of us awed spectators could have guessed that it was the man himself who was marching to his fate. The sense of dreadful destiny is heightened: the *Sunday Times,* London, 10.4.60.

The punishment South Africa was taking was great indeed: but the prophets of gloom had no cause for exultation. Not the British Prime Minister's blunt rejection of Pretoria's policy, nor Sharpeville, nor the attack on Dr. Verwoerd, caused the government to alter by one degree the course to its set objective. How could anyone have supposed it would who understood the calibre of the men involved and the meaning of their plans for the country? Sharpeville was the ultimate demonstration of the anarchy and violence inherent in unrepresentative organisations such as the PAC and the ANC competing for power within a single South African state. Sharpeville consolidated Pretoria's determination to pursue the path of separatism. Some argue that it was the determination of one man–of the man of granite, Dr. Verwoerd. But Dr. Verwoerd himself held the view that the national leader was no more than the apex of a pyramid, and that his authority and the height he reached depended on the strength of the pyramid's base. Had Dr. Verwoerd died in 1960 he would have been followed–as he was when he was killed in 1966–by another, his determination secured by the same foundation.

> When Dr. Verwoerd returned to office after the pistol attempt on his life last April, he said he had been spared by Divine Providence. He once told an interviewer who marvelled at his apparent freedom from the strains of office: "I never have the nagging doubt of wondering whether perhaps I am wrong": the *Observer,* 9.10.60.

In the days following Sharpeville and similar unrest in other parts of the country, the Government declared a state of emergency, introduced legislation for the banning of the ANC and PAC an illegal organisations, re-imposed influx control (and before the year was out extended its scope to include women). Meanwhile, in a bid to get into the act, the ANC under Luthuli had called on blacks to observe March 28 as a day of mourning and to stay away from work. The call went largely unheeded. By mid-April–and despite the temporary removal of Dr. Verwoerd from the scene–the life of the country was back to normal, and soon afterwards the state of emergency was ended.

> The present mistake of the Union Government, on a calm outside view, lies in the proscribing of both main African political bodies, the moderate African National Congress as well as the more extreme Pan-Africanists. Thereby it may hope to destroy African organisation, but it will certainly deprive Africans of public leadership; and in such situations it is less dangerous to deal with a party than with a mob, with overt leaders than with subterranean cells: the *Sunday Times*, London, 3.4.60.

But the virus of violence remained in the country's system. It had to be identified and isolated before it could be dealt with. In remote cells the banned PAC and ANC, still competing, spawned terrorist organisations called respectively Poqo and Umkonto we Sizwe (spear of the nation)– the latter with code initials MK. In December, 1961, Umkonto was responsible for an outbreak of acts of sabotage in various parts of the country. Towards the end of the following year a Poqo band went on the rampage in Paarl in the Western Cape, killing two white youths, attacking the local police station and destroying property. In the Transkei, Poqo fell upon two roadside caravans: in one a family of four whites were beaten and shot to death; in the other, a young white man was incinerated. Attempts were also made to murder traditional black leaders in the region. Early in 1963 the ANC distributed a pamphlet: "Listen white man! Five whites were murdered in the Transkei, another hacked to death in Langa. Sabotage erupts every other week throughout the country, now here, now there. The whites are turning vicious and panicky. At this rate within a year or two South Africa will be embroiled in the second, bloodier, more furious Algerian war. Sabotage and murders multiplied last year. Sabotage and murder will not cease." Some of these pamphlets were deposited in white mail-boxes.

> The back of the rebellion in South Africa may be broken, as
> it is claimed; but that does not affect the revulsion at the
> brutal way the Verwoerd Government has brought it
> "under control". Neither does it disguise the omens that
> there will be another day and another, and sooner or later
> the repressed coloured majority will have more than stones
> and defiance to fight with: the *Evening Star,* New Zealand,
> 9.4.60.

In July, 1964, the police in a surprise raid rounded up the occupants of
a house in Rivonia, Johannesburg–MK's headquarters. Documents seized
in the raid revealed the collection of large sums of momey for the
purchase of terrorist weapons. The list included 210,000 hand grenades,
48,000 anti-personnel mines, 1,500 timing devices for bombs and 144
tons of ammonium nitrate. At the Rivonia trial evidence disclosed a plan
to foment violent insurrection at home, to be followed by invasion from
across the country's borders. Eight of the men in the dock were convicted
and sentenced to life imprisonment. The ninth, though a self-confessed
communist, was acquitted.

Also in mid-1964 several white students were arrested for blasting
power pylons and train-signalling systems. They were members of an
organisation called the African Resistance Movement. Three weeks later
a man named John Harris, a teacher, left a suitcase beside a bench in the
concourse of the Johannesburg railway station. It was just after 4 P.M. and
the concourse was busy with commuters. At 4:33 the bomb in the
suitcase exploded. A woman was killed, 23 others maimed and injured.
Harris explained that he had been chosen by the African Resistance
Movement to do the job. He was tried, convicted, sentenced to death and
executed. A co-founder of the ARM, who escaped the police net, said
later in London: "The African Resistance Movement had enough
explosives and trained saboteurs to have brought South Africa to its knees.
But the South African freedom movement as a whole had the attitude that
if they made enough fuss and noise the world would do the job for them.
They wanted headlines. They were not equal to the demands of the
situation."

> South Africa's drift towards disaster is terrifying. Ac-
> customed as I am to the pace of change in Africa I find it
> almost unbelievable that the Union could have been so
> transformed in nine months since my last visit . . . This
> accounts for the violence of the present phase: it is the
> violence of a dying spasm: Laurens van der Post in the
> *Sunday Times,* London, 28.5.61.

187

Soon after it had come to power in 1948, the National Party banned the South African Communist Party and passed the Suppression of Communism Act. In the years that followed, the Communist Party continued its work through front organisations and through association with, or infiltration into, other subversive movements. In 1965 the communist master-mind in South Africa, Braam Fischer, was arrested. A well-known advocate and member of a prominent Orange Free State family, he had been counsel for the defence in the Rivonia trial. At his own trial there was evidence of his dealings with the Rivonia revolutionaries, of his links with communist headquarters abroad, of funds from London to support his activities, of orders he issued for the burning of sugar- and maize-fields, of his campaign to whip up sentiment at home and abroad against the country's security laws and to enlist the unwitting assistance of liberals and do-gooders. An instruction given by Fischer in 1965 was that the rebuilding of the Communist Party in the Republic was the primary task, and that to achieve this, flexibility and originality were called for: "We must not be hidebound or think only along old lines. All possibilities should be explored for enlisting, encouraging and helping new allies–even from among these who might appear to have given up any show of resistance. Progressive parties should be supported, and individuals in the non-white bodies which have been created by the Government. So, too, we must seek to pull into the struggle, to encourage students' and women's organisations, progressive churchmen, newspapers and journalists and even professional bodies–lawyers, doctors, teachers etc."

> These men on trial for treason are not scoundrels and
> eccentrics. Some at least of them are men who would be
> among the pillars of a just society. It is of the evil essence of
> the Afrikaner state that there is no place for them under its
> regime but in its prisons: the *Guardian,* 13.6.64.

At his trial Fischer did not deny his communist activities. He was found guilty and sentenced to life imprisonment. In 1966 he was awarded the Lenin Peace Prize: "the award will give this outstanding leader of Africa new strength and will encourage the fighters against neo-colonialism in their struggle for the freedom of Africa." Fischer died of cancer in May, 1975, after having been released from prison to spend his last days in the home of relatives.

The condemnation of Pretoria's security measures which Fischer sought was forthcoming abundantly. Each measure passed to protect the State, each police raid, each trial of revolutionaries, terrorists and saboteurs, each conviction and sentence raised an outcry of indignation abroad and often also at home–from the media, from churchmen, politicians, lawyers, the United Nations: oppressors, totalitarians, fascists!

188

When the Rivonia plotters of violence were sentenced, the *New York Times* commented that they were regarded as the George Washingtons and Benjamin Franklins of South Africa. After Fischer had been exposed, the Rev. Nelson Gray wrote in a British church magazine: "Thank God for such a man and pray for him. If he is a communist we could do with a lot more like him in the Christian Church." While in the Western world the growing menace of terrorism was being condemned as a threat to the survival of civilisation, millions of words were written, spoken and broadcast in defence of those who planned by terrorist means to overthrow the state in South Africa.

> In South Africa a heavily armed military regime, backed by
> a powerful economy, fanatically maintains its slave society
> by increasingly violent means: the *New Statesman*, 31.5.63.

The Covenant

The final act of violence in this fearful phase of South African history occurred on September 6, 1966: Dr. Verwoerd was stabbed to death at his bench in the House of Assembly by a white parliamentary messenger.

> *Pretoria, September, 1966:* Some speak of the futility of Dr. Verwoerd's death. They are bewildered by the seeming meaninglessness of a man murdered in the fullness of his power and authority. They point to the gross improbability of the Prime Minister of a democratic country being struck down in the midst of his fellow legislators at his bench in the sanctum of Parliament. The odds against were too great for reason. This was capricious, wanton waste.
> But there is another view.
> In those days between the assassination and the funeral, South Africans were given an intimation of the good society. The disputes of the nation were silenced and against her tribulations was set peace. Dimitri Tsafendas, the assassin, was but a shadow in the substance of the compassion that encompassed the people, for their country, for Dr. Verwoerd's family and for one another. In the good society of those days there was no place for vengeance . . .

> To say that there is no life left in the corpse of apartheid is
> to pay its champions an undeserved compliment. It never
> had a life to lose. A stuffed dummy substitute for a real
> contemporary policy is stretched across the public life of the
> Union with its sawdust gushing out for all to see: *The
> Times*, London, 31.5.61.

189

The Prime Minister's ambition had been to bring accord between the white people and those others whose destiny and right it equally is to find happiness and prosperity in our southern part of Africa. He died on a Tuesday: on the Friday before he had conferred for 3½ hours in the Union Buildings with Prime Minister Leabua Jonathan of Lesotho. For the first time on the Republic's soil a black national leader had met the South African Prime Minister. Through the length and breadth of the land the meeting was hailed as the opening of a new era in the country's history. The last photograph that South Africans saw of their Prime Minister was of him and Chief Leabua in friendly companionship. On the Tuesday morning the subject was still being headlined, and there was great expectancy about the statement which the Prime Minister was to make in the House that afternoon. It was commonly believed that he had waited for this meeting with Chief Leabua before outlining in detail to Parliament his plans for a commonwealth.

> The Afrikaner state, rooted in the cardinal doctrine of apartheid, is itself so gravely and irreparably wrong that there is no way to better it but by destroying it: the *Guardian,* London, 13.6.64.

The public galleries were crowded. Mrs. Verwoerd had accompanied her husband to the House for the important occasion, and the Prime Minister had just taken his seat when the blow was struck. Dr. Verwoerd had no notes and it may be that the detail of his plan will never be known. However his vision of a progressive, harmonious association of interdependent states was well-known: and suddenly in the last few days of his life it had taken flame. All at once it illuminated the future of the land; and by his death this flame in its golden beginning has been burnt on the mind of the people. This was his will and his vision and now, irrevocable, it is ours. The print on the drawing board may fade and the words grow cold in Hansard, but not so a vision branded on a nation's consciousness. At the funeral the wreaths of Chief Matanzima of the Transkei and of Chief Leabua had places of honour beside the coffin.

This has been no waste. In his broadcast address to the nation the acting Prime Minister spoke of the inscrutable ways of God. But may it not be that the Prime Minister died to sanctify this covenant of good neighbourliness between white and black, and that his blood was spilt in the heart of Parliament to be the ever present witness to future leaders of the pledge thus made? (26)

CHAPTER TWELVE / 1960 to 1970–
Civil Liberty

The Rule of Law

Pretoria has been condemned no less for its alleged violation of human rights, civil liberties and the rule of law than for apartheid itself. Taking into account the circumstances that have been outlined here, to what degree is the condemnation justified?

The general function of the law and the law enforcement officer has been radically broadened by conditions in the modern world, of which the Republic has the closest experience. In earlier times the main business of the law was to prescribe patterns of behaviour within society and to punish the individual wrong-doer who transgressed them: the murderer, the robber, the thief, the usurer. The duty of the policeman was to protect the law-abiding citizen of the State from the misdeeds of his fellow citizen. His duty was not the protection of the State itself from injury by others. That was the responsibility of the military establishment: and through the centuries it was soldiers, sailors and later airmen who in the field of battle settled the contest between nations. Three developments in particular in the past half century have drastically altered that state of affairs. Modern means of mass communication have made the printed page of the waves of the ether the new fields of conflict–of psychological conflict. Modern weapons of mass destruction have out-dated the conventional, declared wars of the past; and the modern communist ideology of mass revolution has harnessed these factors in the service of its own cause. Propaganda, infiltration, political and economic subversion, sabotage and terrorism are the means by which the commu-nists and those who imitate them seek today to overcome their enemies. It is the agents of these techniques with whom the authorities in the Republic have had to deal–and the fact that the agents may often be unwitting agents immensely complicates their task. Remember Braam

191

Fischer's instruction: "We must seek to pull into the struggle students' and women's organisations, progressive churchmen, newspapers and journalists and even professional bodies." The problems posed by such tactics and those posed by ordinary crime are of a totally different order, and so are the consequences of a failure to thwart them. Their respective dangers to society cannot be compared, nor can the measures needed to deal with them. Writing on the subject an authority as staid as the *Encyclopaedia Britannica* states: "The democrats found themselves in their struggle against communism often hindered because they were prisoners of their own methods of fairplay and civil liberty, and failed to understand the completely different nature of the communist doctrine and methods."

> Mr. Vorster, who now comes to the front as Minister of both Justice and Education, is known for his prominence in the Ossewa Brandwag, the underground organisation dedicated by its name to preserving the separatist spirit of the Great Trek, Germanophil in war and in peace resisting the reconciliation of Boer and Briton: the *Telegraph*, London, 3.8.61.

In recent years two of the world's leading democracies–Britain and Canada–have been obliged to protect their societies from anarchy by empowering their security police to detain suspects without trial. The taking of a similar measure by Pretoria is universally condemned as a violation of the rule of law: and yet the forces aligned against the Republic and the threat to the safety of the State and its people are incomparably greater here than ever they were in Britain or Canada. More than that: Pretoria has the awesome responsibility of avoiding a conflict that could engulf a continent.

> South Africa is perceptibly moving down the slippery slope towards becoming a police state: the *Observer*, London, 12.6.60.

Charges of violation of the rule of law and of setting the State above the individual are the pseudo-liberal weapons characteristically used to undo those who, despite whatever odds, are determined to maintain law and order. Referring to the pseudo-liberal clamour against "repressive justice" in his own country, Judge Lewis Powell of the United States Supreme Court has observed: "The charge of repression is a propaganda line designed to undermine confidence in our free institutions and ultimately to overthrow our democratic system." And this charge is the more difficult to turn aside because of the fuzziness of the concepts of "the rule of law" and "the State". To quote *Britannica* again, it observes that the rule of law often has emotional overtones, and that "appraisals of

192

its importance usually vary in direct proportion to the vagueness of the meaning the writer or speaker assigns to it."

> Ten days ago one of the greatest liberal leaders in South Africa said to me, "the rule of law is dead here from now onwards"; and it is some confirmation of what he said that I dare not give his name for fear he would get into trouble: John Dugdale, MP in the *Guardian,* London, 14.4.60.

In the course of the controversy in the Republic about "the rule of law" and "the State", their meanings have been spelt out as clearly as they can be by the highest judicial authorities. In 1969 Prime Minister Vorster appointed a commission to inquire into the country's total security needs; and the assignment was given to a judge of the Appeal Court, Mr. Justice Potgieter. The judge's point of departure in his investigation was his agreement with the view of Chalmers and Asquith (in their standard work, *Constitutional Law)* that a *State* is an independent political society "the members of which are united together for the purposes of resisting external force and the suppression of internal disorder." Points to note about this view are that it reconciles the conflict between State and individual, since the State *is* the individuals who compose it; that it consequently draws the clearest distinction between the State and the Government, and that it reveals security as the very essence of the concept of the State. Judge Potgieter went on to describe the threat to the State in the Republic of South Africa and the need for an intelligence service to combat it as "unique". Legislation which gave effect to the judge's view of the State and of the intelligence service needed to protect it was subsequently submitted to Parliament by the Government and supported by the Opposition.

> The Rule of Law can itself be infringed by a law. This is what the Verwoerd Government has done: it has passed a law which abolishes personal freedom and the rights of people, denying them the opportunity of defending them- selves in court: the *Montreal Star,* Canada, 1.11.63.

The meaning of the rule of law was the subject of a national debate towards the end of 1972, following a judgment by Mr. Justice Snyman in a case in which four Indians were charged with conspiring to overthrow the Government by force. The judge's remarks not only clarified the concept but warned against the manner in which it was abused. The rule of law, he said, was no more than a code: it was not itself a law and could not override the actual laws of the State. However the Republic's laws– and more particularly those regulating race relations and providing for its security–had been the target of attack by among others, legal academics. It was their entitlement and their duty, said the judge, to criticise the country's laws if they considered them bad or unjustified; but in the ardour with which some of them made use of the concept of the rule of law, they lost sight of the fact that it *was* only a code. The concept was employed to provoke contempt for the real laws, and to lead some to believe that they were morally justified in breaking them. Such critics should be more circumspect in their criticism: they owed both the public and their students a duty to point out that nobody had the right to break the law. The kind of legal teaching which one of the accused received (the judge found) might well have resulted in the behaviour which caused him to be brought before the Court.

This was the calm judicial voice of the State: it contrasts strangely with the shrill tones of those who, in the name of the rule of law, attack this State and its legislation.

> It is chilling to contemplate the lengths to which the present South African Government has gone to crush opposition to apartheid, a doctrine that seems in one way or another to poison everything and everyone it touches: the *New York Times*, 17.11.62.

Students and the Law

A main challenge to the authority, policies and laws of the State has come through the years from the National Union of South African Students–NUSAS. By placard, poster and demonstration–in the streets of Johannesburg, on the steps of the cathedral in Cape Town–they have championed a variety of anti-Pretoria causes. When the anniversary of Sharpeville has come round, they have planted crosses in the lawns of the Witwatersrand University: they have supported arms embargoes against the country and boycotts of its sportsmen: they have advocated a black-white polarisation of South African society: they have condemned violations of the rule of law, through several of their leaders have been convicted of acts of violence and sabotage. They were the darlings of revolutionary student movements in the outside world and of the pseudo-liberal media: Senator Robert Kennedy travelled to the Republic in 1967 to tell them how high they were holding the torch of freedom. They were praised abroad for representing and fearlessly expressing the conscience of enlightened people; and any action taken against them was cited as typifying the totalitarian nature of the State.

In March, 1973, following restrictions imposed on eight of their leaders, *The Times,* London, dealt with the subject in an editorial entitled *South Africa Tries to Tame Students.* Anyone could have told the South African Government, it declared, that it was inviting trouble by the move: no-one got away with that sort of thing in today's universities, least of all in the Republic. If the Government wanted to avoid trouble it would have to take a longer and deeper look at what was happening in the "English-speaking" universities. The leaders now placed under restriction were widely accepted as spokesmen for a genuine, questioning concern: that they were not isolated agitators was confirmed by the support they had earned among the students, the academic staff and in "responsible" newspapers. By using against them the Act designed for the suppression of communism, the Government exposed the weakness of its case and laid itself open to very serious criticism. The truth of the matter was that the Government was extremely nervous of the questions that these students were asking about the future of South African society. "It is thrown badly off balance when the future élite of the nation begins to question its policies. But it is these students who will inherit the problems accumulated by the present leadership."

> The civilisation which Dr. Verwoerd and his Ministers claim to be defending has ceased to exist because personal liberty is the vital part of it. All that is left now is fear and the animal instincts that go with it: the *Guardian,* London, 30.4.63.

These comments in what is perhaps the most famous of all newspapers characterise the arrogant and ignorant interference of the distant critics. It was not in 1973 that NUSAS began to question Government policies, but in 1948. Most of these rowdy campus apostles of reform are today men and women between the ages of thirty and fifty, and the contribution they have made as grown-up citizens to a solution of the accumulated problems which they inherited is (to coin a phrase) conspicuous by its absence. As for the academic staff and the "responsible" newspapers which backed them, these are the institutions which in season and out have backed virtually anybody and any cause calculated to bring the Government and its policies into disrepute. And as for these youths being "the élite of the nation", no comment could be more illuminating that of Mr. Alan Paton, revered author of *Cry the Beloved Country,* leader while it existed of the South African Liberal Party and honorary Vice President of NUSAS.

In the Johannesburg *Star* in December, 1975 he published a bitter attack on NUSAS. It was quite clear, he wrote, that some of the leading members of the Union had no conception of what it meant to be a member, and especially a high official, of an organisation. They had embarked on courses of action which were not known to their fellow members and sometimes not even to their fellow executives. In a president of an organisation that was unpardonable. Mr. Paton explained that in the circumstances he had considered resigning as honorary Vice President but had decided against. "Whether my resignation would or would not do harm to the Union in this crisis is not the main consideration. My big trouble is that I cannot get out of my mind those young men and women sitting among the ruins in Grahamstown (where Rhodes University is situated) trying to build something out of the dirt and rubble that is left." He described the departing President of NUSAS as the one who had left them the dirt and the rubble. It was his view, wrote Mr. Paton, that the leadership of NUSAS had set as its goal the radicalisation of the organisation. In the event, however, it had not been radicalised but nearly destroyed: the leadership did not radicalise NUSAS, it dichotomised it. "Let no-one suppose that I have criticised NUSAS for its activism. I have for most of my life been the enemy of pietism, the holding of great principles and doing nothing about them. My addresses to NUSAS (I haven't been asked to make one for years) always encouraged activism. But I am against the stupid kind of activism that demands everything NOW and that throws away years of life to achieve, in my view, exactly nothing." South African political life, declared Mr. Paton, was hard. It demanded not desperation but courage. "There is only one alternative and that is blood. I don't want to see our students, white or black, led to such a destination."

So much for the organisation which has figured so large in the charges against Pretoria of violation of the rule of law.

Influx Control

Influx control is said by some to be a violation of the rule of law. Influx control is provided for in the actual laws of the State. These laws may not be broken, and it was incitement to break them by black militants and others that was the immediate cause of the tragedy at Sharpeville. Influx control is provided for in the laws of the Republic of South Africa: it was provided for in the laws of the Union of South Africa before that, and in the laws of the colonies which constituted the Union when they were governed by Britain. Any government at all in South Africa had to, and has to, provide for influx control in its laws if it is to prevent unemployment, poverty, squalor, disease, crime, misery and degradation on a massive scale. Influx control is not a consequence of separatism or of any other political philosophy: it is concerned with a socio-economic problem.

196

> Let there be no mistake about it, the pass-laws constitute the
> very framework of apartheid as the Nationalist Goverment
> understands it . . . If the Union Government fails to resume
> enforcement of these laws, it will not be too much to say
> that the tide has turned in the country's history: the
> *Telegraph,* London, 28.3.60.

Commenting on uncontrolled urban inflow in emancipated Africa, historian de Kiewiet wrote in 1970: "Americans can best understand the tumescent growth in African cities of ghettoes of disappointment and frustration. On the ege of the privileged modern sector, and pressing up against it, is a far greater group of men who are a cause of the deepest concern. Lowly in their skills, close still to the rural peasantry, they seek a lodgement in the new world of cash and goods and employment. They wait with an incredible patience in a limbo of unemployment and under-employment. From Nairobi and Kinshasa to Lagos and Abidjan . . . everywhere have risen these great encampments of unorganised men with no greater power than their mute choice to escape from the confinement and the insufficiency of their lives. Each multitude is a petition laid before those in power to act in their behalf. The presentation is gentle. But its persistence is inevitable and grim. A radicalism from below, or a radicalism from above to contain it, can be prevented only if opportunity and satisfaction begin to flow from the modern sector into the hinterland and amongst its population."

Each multitude laid a petition before those in power to act in its behalf. Governments in South Africa, with its immeasurably greater urban attractions than anywhere else on the continent, must in the first place act in behalf of the potential multitudes of city slum-dwellers by keeping them away. It must act so not only in their behalf but in behalf of the established black communities in the city areas. They, not the whites, would be the first to suffer the consequences of free influx–wage-cutting, over-crowding, crime and general social retrogression. The white man in the long term would likewise be threatened by such a state of affairs, but in the short term he would stand to benefit from the cheapness of an over-abundant availability of labour. How, then, the world would cry "exploitation!" Influx control is designed primarily in the interest of an orderly society and in the interests of the black people themselves: of those who would come, not in thousands but in millions, to the metropolitan centres; and of those—some 4-million—already there. After the Anglo-Boer War, when he was British High Commissioner in South Africa, Lord Milner declared: "Alike for the protection of the natives and the protection of the whites, it is absolutely essential to have some reasonable arrangement by which the incoming native can be identified and his movements traced."

That the enforcement of the pass laws would sooner or later
lead to an explosion has been obvious to observers of the
African scene. It has now happened: the *Sunday Times*,
London, 27.3.60.

A reasonable arrangement! Through this century and before there has
been debate after debate, inquiry after inquiry, legislative measure after
legislative measure, amended laws and modified regulations in an
endeavour to devise a reasonable arrangement. If a man is to identify
himself as having employment and the entitlement to be in a city area, he
must possess a document to that effect: to ascertain whether or not he has
such document to that effect: to ascertain whether or not he has such
document he must be required to produce it: if he cannot produce it, and
respect for the law is to be maintained, he must bear the responsibility for
having broken it. Hardship is inevitable in this sequence–and humiliation
particularly for those who are required to identify themselves when they
are perfectly entitled to be where they are. As many as 2,000 people may
appear in Court in one day for contravening influx control. It is an
inordinately large number, and a stark account of the resentment which
the system breeds. However it is a measure at the same time of the
problem: 2,000 people a day is 700,000 in a year and 7,000,000 in ten
years. What would the social condition of this country be today if
7,000,000 people had been allowed to settle in the city areas in the past
ten years?

The plans to remove apparent irritations over the passbooks
which all Africans have to carry, and to set up centres to
help Africans in passbook trouble, are no liberalising
measures. The plans as a whole amount to no more than
another try at window-dressing for the outside world, and a
convenience for the white authorities. It does nothing for
the Africans: the *Guardian*, London, 9.6.71.

In 1952 the Government passed a measure to do away with the
separate, old-type documents–the "Passes"–and substituted instead a
single reference book. Critics scoffed at the idea: it didn't go to the heart
of the problem, they said. Of course it didn't, but it was at least an
attempt to lessen the inconvenience. The Government established aid
centres in the townships, closely associated with labour bureaux, to help
the influx control offender. The aid centre may arrange employment for
him and, only if this is not possible, send him back to where he came from
in his homeland. There are also rehabilitation centres in the homelands
for those who need to be rehabilitated. "The basic idea", said a

Government spokesman at the time, "is to assist those who are technical offenders and, if possible, to avoid their going to Court. The aid centres will do everything they can to help a man take up legal employment if there is a job for him to go to." The authorities tried to ease the burden by allowing people without their reference books on them time–several days–to produce them. "The experiment has not been a success", commented the responsible Minister. "In many cases the people concerned just did not turn up. The time of officials had to be wasted in looking for them, and in most cases the offenders gave a wrong address." Of course they did, if they were illegally in the city anyway. Time and again members of the Government and high police officials appeal to all concerned to implement influx control as sympathetically as they can. But to be approached in the street and to be asked to identify oneself is humiliating even if it is done politely–and often it is not done that way.

Within the city context it is impossible to eliminate the core of the problem. But the problem is not the making of this or any other government: it is the straightforward one of the attraction for rural people of employment opportunities (to which in even the most prosperous of industrial centres there is a strict limit) and of the bright city lights (deceptively bright, as Bambata those many years ago impressed on me). It is simple enough to define the problem, but that makes the solution no easier. Hardship and humiliation are built-in in the enforcement of influx control, but no responsible government could consider free influx since its consequences would be incomparably worse. In Lagos the great encampments of unorganised men, the ghettoes of despair and frustration, to which Professor de Kiewiet refers, led to crime on such a scale that General Gowon's Government was driven to try, unsuccessfully, to control it by the public execution of offenders.

The solution must be found, as the Professor suggests, outside the city context: life must be made more attractive and more rewarding for the rural people in their own areas. There is no government in Africa (and probably, in proportion to its resources, none in the world) that has done more than Pretoria has towards this end. It has spent immense effort and hundreds of millions of rands on developing the human and other resources of the black homelands. Twenty years ago it embarked, against heavy opposition, on a programme for establishing industries on the borders of the homelands: it has made the most generous incentives available to industrialists to operate there and in the homelands themselves, and it has set up development corporations to assist black entrepreneurs to start their own businesses. The emotional critics of influx control would do better for the people they champion by supporting this programme of industrial decentralisation than by rejecting it as "ideological" as so often in the past they have done.

199

The Press

Newspapers are in my blood. My paternal grandfather owned a clutch of them in New Zealand, and I discovered a few months after I joined the *Rand Daily Mail* as a reporter in 1935 that my news editor, Monty Williams, had been trained on one of them. Because a thing is in a man's blood it does not necessarily predispose him for or against it (any more than the relevant gene predisposes its host for or against red hair), but it does give him a built-in understanding of it. Environmentally also I know newspapers: daily during the past 40 years I have worked for, with or against them.

The newspaper is a most remarkable institution of modern society: it is more than a daily mail or a daily mirror, it is a daily miracle. Countless thousands of words flood into its offices each day from its own reporters, from overseas correspondents, from news agencies and specialist writers. They come type-written, hand-written, spoken: by telex machine, telephone, radio, satellite. Each 24 hours from this incoherent mass of material a choice of suitable copy must be made: it must be rewritten, sub-edited to fit available space left over by the advertisers, headlined, set in print, impressed on strips of paper for proof-reading, made up (together with photographs that have been rushed in from scenes of action around the world, and cartoons, maps, sketches and charts which have been drawn to illustrate the day's events) into page form, and then fed to the presses. Meantime, in selection and presentation, the editorial line of the newspaper has had to be taken into account, facts checked, possible libel and other contraventions of the law guarded against. Having been printed the newspaper must be delivered post-haste–and hastier–to subscribers, agents and distribution points. The citizen glances through it at breakfast or maybe in the bus on the way home, as likely as not remarks that there is nothing in it, and tosses it aside. At the newspaper office work has already begun on the next issue–and so it goes, day after day, year after year. Only in some quite extraordinary contingency–a power failure, a strike–is the appearance of a newspaper interrupted: and only then does the citizen, more particularly in a democratic country, come to realise how important a part it plays in his life.

A free press (and in this term I include the media as a whole) is indispensable to democracy–absolutely. When a man cannot say without fear: "I am going to write to the paper about this"–whatever it may be that is on his mind—then he does not belong in a free society. However, indispensability has potentially dangerous side-effects. For instance: the rays of the cobalt bomb may be indispensable to the killing of a cancerous growth, but they may also destroy the system as a whole. And again: since indispensability cannot be done without, it may cause the body possessing this attribute to act as a law unto itself, and to make judgments according to self-established norms.

This is very much so in the case of a newspaper. The daily miracle I have referred to is made possible only by teamwork of the highest order–from the editor-in-chief to the cub reporter. Inspiring it all is the newspaper's ethos, built through the years, decades and maybe generations. It is this that ultimately determines who joins the staff, who leaves, who writes the leaders, who draws the cartoons–and how they are written and drawn. It is not "public opinion" or the dictate of some distant board of directors that forms a newspaper's attitude but an in-built personality. There is no institution that demands of those who serve it a closer identification with it: in a peculiar way a newspaperman is an *Express*-man or a *Le Monde*-man or a *Monitor*-man, and he belongs in an *Express*- or a *Le Monde*- or a *Monitor*-world.

That is the background against which claims made by newspapers must be regarded. The newspaper claims to mirror the conditions of society: however the nature of the reflection is shaped by the criteria of this world of its own. It is a distorting mirror, moreover, because what makes the best story (and the good story is the lifeblood of all free newspapers) is, broadly speaking, what society conventionally deplores. A suicide is a better story than a death, a murder than a suicide. As the reporter speeds to the scene of a train derailment or a fire or a flood or an earthquake, he is hoping against hope for the sake of his story for a heavy casualty list, and that the dying will be dead by the time he goes to press. Good news can on occasion make a good story but bad news makes it better. It was good news and a big story when the Kariba Dam was opened: it would have been a better story had the dam burst. It is a good story when a Springbok XV has a resounding victory: it is a better story when they are involved in a punch-up and six jaws are broken. In national and international affairs the same general rule applies. Nations make headlines not when they live in peace but when they go to war: in the party political arena as on the sportsfield it is the quarrelling and the in-fighting that get the publicity: governments are reported less for their good works than for their bad. Newspapers in general do not depict society in the round but unrepresentative aspects of it that are newsworthy: and even these abstractions from the whole are processed by the introspective views of the particular newspaper. A *Time Magazine* correspondent remarked to me in Ottawa: "but of course we make the facts fit our views and not our views the facts." The bland admission was a cloak for the truth of the matter.

The newspaper in a democratic country claims freedom of speech as a right. However it is not a right which originates in the newspaper but a privilege conferred upon it by the body politic. The newspaper is the agent, not the principal: yet is is responsible neither to the State nor to

Parliament nor to the people. It is accountable to no outside authority; and should the legislators, the chosen representatives of the people, dare try to hold it accountable, there is hell to pay. Newspapers are wont to warn governors that power corrupts and that absolute power corrupts absolutely, but the indispensability which is theirs in a free society is itself a kind of absolute power.

Newspapers foster the impression that they are in some way more virtuous–more concerned with the public weal–than governments, parliaments, provincial councils, municipalities, civil services and most other (they tend to suggest that it is all other) institutions. The truth is that newspapers in a private enterprise society are straight profit-making businesses: they are as often as not involved in the worst of cut-throat competition, and survival (and dividends for the shareholders) just as often demand the exploitation of what is least virtuous in public and private behaviour. The sordid and the sensational are the headline-makers and the circulation-spinners: and when a newspaper runs an anti-crime, anti-drug, anti-prostitution, anti-poverty campaign, it is wrong to suppose that it is in fact standing in for social welfare organisations. The fact is that crime, drugs, prostitution and poverty make good stories. That is not to say that such campaigns have no value: in the course of producing a good story much good may often be done, but for the newspaper it is the story and the readership that count. The effect on society is a peripheral concern.

Their indispensability is less abused by some newspapers than by others: but the others are an alarmingly large proportion, and they have contributed much to the malaise of contemporary Western society: its preoccupation with the superficial and the sensational, its materialist outlook, its contempt for established values, its disrespect for authority, its lack of restraint, and its disregard for privacy. The newspapers have extended "the right of the people to know" to the disclosure to all and sundry of the details concerning the removal of the breast of the wife of the President of the United States and to the incidence of the President's rectal bleeding. It is grotesque. There is an acute paradox in all this: while a free press is indispensable to the survival of Western Christian culture, it persistently erodes the foundations on which the culture rests.

> For some time there have been suspicions that the National-
> ist Government has been imposing some sort of censorship
> on critical press messages leaving the Dominion: the *News
> Chronicle*, 30.11.49.

That is about newspapers in general. I am now going to discuss English-language newspapers in the Republic in particular. They account for some three of every four dailies that appear in the country; and in the general service they offer and in the quality of their presentation they are as good as any anywhere and much better than most. Their comprehensive and lively coverage of home and foreign events is a vital part of the country's life, and the country would be much the poorer without it. However this very real contribution is overshadowed by another consideration: namely that the English-language newspapers do not belong with the flux of Anglo-Afrikaner thought and sentiment: they too have created worlds of their own within the real South African world, and *Rand Daily Mail*–men or *Cape Argus*–men or *Natal Mercury*–men inhabit them. In Western countries, newspapers with a variety of political views came into being: one view was continually being set against another and there was the opportunity for people to come to a balanced judgment. In the worlds of the Republic's English-language newspapers this variety was, and is, in one essential respect absent: from their antecedents they have, characterising all of them, a dominant political gene. They were originally established by British money and initiative, and the editors who first gave them their form were British in outlook and most times by birth. They endeavoured to serve South Africa, but their views of what was best for the country did not spring from local experience and sentiment. Until a few years ago they had no doubt that peace and progress would best be secured by maintaining a close association with Britain. They consistently moved against the mainstream of South Africa's constitutional development–opposing the introduction of a national flag and anthem, the withdrawal from the Commonwealth and the establishment of a republic (and typically, in the economic field, the founding a generation ago of a local iron and steel industry). More recently they conceded that Britain no longer had a direct part to play in the nation's destiny. But the dominant gene was still there, and they continued to believe that the country's redemption was to be found in the application to its problems of the British "liberal" tradition. From the time this nation had its beginning, they have projected upon it ideas that had their origin elsewhere and in entirely different circumstances.

> The International Press Institute is particularly concerned at what has happened in South Africa. Papers may be prevented from reporting the news and journalists barred from their profession if the Government chooses: the *Guardian*, London, 14.1.56.

It was an attitude that could be afforded until the War: but it became positively dangerous for the nation when in the post-war years it aligned itself with the worldwide denigration of Pretoria's policies. Local press condemnation fuelled condemnation abroad: but worse than that, the English-language newspapers gave their Anglosan readers a hopelessly distorted interpretation of Government policy. This damaged national unity, and alienated Anglosan industrialists, financiers and businessmen whose co-operation was so necessary for the best implementation of separatism. There were three possible responses: one was to do nothing–to leave the field to the English-language newspapers and allow the harm they were doing to continue; the second was for the State to intervene–that is to impose some form of control; the third was to answer them–to meet charge with counter-charge, destructive fact with constructive fact, despondency with realistic optimism, loss of faith with the power of purpose.

The third, to my mind, was the only acceptable alternative: and I was fortunate in being offered the opportunity to do something about it. Towards the end of 1964 I was approached by the South African Broadcasting Corporation to edit a daily editorial commentary on national and international events. Called *Current Affairs*, it has been on the air each week-day since then. The commentary represents the corporate voice of the SABC: subject matter and approach are agreed upon each morning at a conference of some dozen senior officials of the Corporation. *Current Affairs* was never designed for audience appeal, it was never meant to be "popular" (though it now has a daily listenership of over a million) but simply to put into balance context the events of the day and to give expression on fundamental issues to the general sentiment–the broad will–of the Anglo-Afrikaner nation. This is something more substantial than "public opinion". The broad will of a people on fundamental issues is written clear in its record: in this nation's case, there are fundamental characteristics that stand out like braille from its history. One of the aims of *Current Affairs* is to ensure that by all and sundry they are read correctly. And in this the SABC has the advantage of being more constantly and widely in touch with all sections of the people than, perhaps, any other institution in the country.

> Broadcasting has been another victim of this determination on the part of the Nationalists to wield absolute power. Sound programmes are kept obediently to heel and, for the time being at least, there is to be no television for fear that it might open unwanted windows on the oustide world: *The Times*, London, 7.3.60.

During 1975 an official of the United States Senate Foreign Relations Committee was in the Republic to inquire into, among other things, the media. At a small meeting with local media-men at the United States Information Service's office in Johannesburg, he asked me how the SABC viewed its editorial function. I replied as above, including the bit about giving expression to the broad national sentiment. Our visitor then asked the representative of the Johannesburg *Star*, the Republic's premier daily, whether it sought to do the same thing. "Heavens no, good lord, I would hope not" was his answer in so many words. This is typical of advanced newspaper thinking: the thing is to be out ahead, to give a lead, to set the pace, and to be–at best–condescending towards established ideas and norms. The newspapers make no secret about it: the *Rand Daily Mail*, which is the darling of pseudo-liberals abroad, is proud of the fact that it speaks for something substantially less than ten per cent of the members of the Anglo-Afrikaner nation. And there is some reason for that pride, since it is necessary in a lively society that minority views should also be represented. However the operative word there is "also": the majority view, too, must be represented. It is quite essential if there is to be stability and orderly change: and a primary reason for the disorderliness and confusion of contemporary Western society is that the media have fallen so deeply into what former United States Secretary of Defence Schlesinger calls "the fashionable classes". Democracy cannot function if the majority is silent, and they are silent in so many democracies today for the simple reason that media through which they should be heard are not available to them. This is a problem requiring urgent attention by the nations of the West if free societies are to survive and prosper.

> South Africa has moved closer to its own peculiar version of Orwell's "1984" with the conviction of Laurence Gandar and Benjamin Pogrund of the *Rand Daily Mail* for violating the Prison Act of 1959. The law itself is barbarous, the trial, which the Government stretched out over eight months, was a farce: the *New York Times*, 11.7.69.

In the Republic, the unrepresentative nature of the English-language newspapers, the complex circumstances of the country, the composition of its population and the extraordinary threat to its security have resulted in certain limitations on the freedom of the press. The Native Administration Act of 1927 provides that "any person who utters any words or does any act or thing whatever with intent to promote hostility between Natives and Europeans shall be guilty of an offence." The Riotous Assemblies Act of 1956 prohibits the publication of information "calculated to engender feelings of hostility between the European inhabitants of the Republic on the one hand and any other section of the inhabitants of the Republic on the other." In 1950 the Suppression of Communism Act enabled the Government to take measures against newspapers which promoted the ends of communism, and to prohibit the publication of statements by individuals banned in terms of the Act. In 1953, following massive passive resistance campaigns designed to revolutionise South Africa's social structure, legislation was passed which made it an offence to incite the contravention of the law as a means of protest. Newspapers were left free to criticise and condemn any laws as they saw fit, but they were not permitted to advocate the breaking of them. The Prisons Act of 1959 made it an offence to publish information about prisons, knowing such information to be false or without taking reasonable steps to ensure its accuracy. In 1965 and 1967 amendments were made, respectively, to the Official Secrets and Defence Acts in order to tighten security against internal subversion and external attack. There are also laws against defamation, obscenity, contempt of court and contempt of the State President.

> In South Africa press freedom barely exists at all: the *Nation Review*, Australia, 22.6.74.

There is no limit at all to the advocacy by newspapers of political reform of whatever kind, provided only that it is to be achieved by constitutional means. The well-known British journalist, Douglas Brown, observed in the mid-1960s: "Throughout the whole of the African continent, there is only one country where an opposition press can mercilessly castigate the Government, and that country is the South African Republic." A decade later, in 1975, the African director of the International Press Institute wrote: "The unpalatable fact is–and this is something that sticks in the throat of every self-respecting African who will face it–that there is more press freedom in South Africa than in the rest of Africa put together." In the same year, Freedom House–a non-partisan national organisation in the United States–gave the Republic a higher rating for political and civil rights than any other African country except Botswana. In its global survey it rated 19.8 per cent of the world's population as living in freedom; 35.3 per cent as partly free, and 44.9 per cent as not free. The Republic was listed among the partly free: and in this category only the Republic, Swaziland and Nigeria were given a plus rating for a positive outlook on freedom.

> The Boer Parliament has added far-reaching refinements to its already extensive web of legalised tyranny: the *Globe and Mail*, Canada, 24.6.69.

During the War President Roosevelt proclaimed his Four Freedoms: they were freedom of speech, freedom of worship, freedom from want and freedom from fear. In no country in the world in the past 28 years has any Government been more persistently or more widely criticised by its own press than the Government in Pretoria. The church, the synagogue, the temple, the mosque standing serene and undisturbed in

206

city, town and village testify to the unimpeded right of all to worship as they please. There is less want among the people of South Africa at large than in any underdeveloped country, and less also than in the poor European countries. The incidence of malnutrition among the black people is altogether too high, but this is largely due to bad dietary habits: famine and starvation are unknown, and it is inconceivable that they would be allowed by the State. And, so far as the State is concerned, only those who seek to destroy it by unconstitutional, subversive, revolutionary and violent means have cause to fear. No man or woman has ever been arrested or detained in the Republic for his criticism or condemnation of Government policy. Taking into account the external and internal threats which have been directed remorselessly and without respite at the heart of the Anglo-Afrikaner nation since the War, the degree to which fundamental rights and civil liberties have been maintained is remarkable.

> Such is the philosophy of totalitarianism—whether it be Communist or Fascist. The chilling effects, in Czechoslovákia or South Africa, ought to be an object lesson to anyone, anywhere: the *Vancouver Sun,* Canada, 6.7.69.

The man who was responsible primarily for safeguarding the State during those critical years of the 1960s was the then Minister of Justice, Mr. John Vorster: and if there is any modern statesman who has proved his *bona fides* as a man of peace, good-neighbourliness, tolerance and humility it is surely he.

> Apartheid–just like Communism–is tainted not so much by the abstract theory behind it as by the injustice, force and torture that have to be applied by the authorities to implement it: the *Ashburton Guardian,* New Zealand, 13.11.71.

CHAPTER THIRTEEN / 1960 to 1970–
The Achievement

Portrait of the Afrikaner

Mr. Vorster, who became Prime Minister after the assassination of Dr. Verwoerd, is known today for his tireless efforts to reconcile black men and white in Africa. But his first historic contribution was made earlier, among his own Afrikaners. He sensed that a crucial requirement for South Africa was a clear understanding at home and abroad of the true political nature and aspirations of the Afrikaner. It was urgent that these should be precipitated out of the misrepresentation and controversy which had for so long obscured the character of the Afrikaner *volk*, and that they should be harnessed in the cause of understanding among the people of South Africa and with the rest of the continent. A dispute within the ranks of the National Party and the subsequent formation by the breakaway wing of a new party provided the opportunity.

> The Afrikaners, worshipping the myth of race superiority with a fervour equalled in modern times only by Adolf Hitler . . .: Frank Barber in the *News Chronicle*, 11.8.59.

The name of the new party was the Herstigte Nasionale Party (the Re-established National Party) and it was led by Dr. Albert Hertzog, son of the former Prime Minister J. B. M. Hertzog. The overriding issue of the 1970 general election was the contest between these two factions of the *volk* . . . and the outcome erased at one sweep the caricature of the Afrikaner which had distorted understanding of South Africa from the beginning.

For the world at large, the basic outlines of the caricature were drawn during the Anglo-Boer War at the turn of the century. The international spotlight was directed on the handful of men and women then standing

208

up to the military might of the British Empire. In its crude light the character of these people–the Boers–was given its first outside definition. They were shown as brave and persistent–but rough-hewn and pig-headed; arrogant in their mastery of a distant, isolated land; contemptuous of the ways of others–of black men nearby and of white men far away; and reliant only upon themselves and a Christian faith expediently interpreted. As the century progressed the behaviour of the Afrikaner appeared to others to etch ever more deeply these basic outlines: his refusal before and after the creation of Union in 1910 to merge into a wider South African community; the establishment of the National Party to further his own exclusive ideals; the struggle for his language, flag and anthem; his reluctance to support Britain in two world wars: his dedication to Christian Nationalism; the coming to power of his party in 1948 on the basis of apartheid; his adamant resistance to the trends of post-war thought in the world community and at the United Nations, and finally the establishment in 1961 of a sovereign independent Republic, and withdrawal from the Commonwealth. All these developments contributed to the completion of the caricature–and finished, fixed and framed, it was put on view around the world. This was done in the name of enlightenment: though in fact the picture of the Afrikaner as obstinate, non-co-operative, isolationist, racially-proud, archaic and reactionary served as a purgative for the post-war conscience of the Western world. Viewing it, men wondered in comparison at their own tolerance, co-operativeness, cosmopolitanism and racial humility. The picture was touted from country to country, put on public exhibition and hung on the walls of Presidents, Prime Ministers, Bishops, Trade Union Leaders, Women's Leagues, Newspaper Editors and Television Producers.

> As a Cape Town journalist wrote last week: "Our country
> is probably the most unpopular in the whole circumference
> of the globe." The sad fact is that Hendrik Verwoerd and
> the Afrikaners will glory in their unpopularity: the *New
> York Times*, 31.5.61.

It was hanging during the Republic's 1970 election campaign on the wall of the producer for the Thames Television Company of Britain: and seeing its embodiment in the newly-formed *Herstigte Nasional Party*, he sent a team out to capture it in living sound and motion picutre. The necessary arrangements were negotiated with South Africa House in London, and an undertaking was given that the film to be made would present the Afrikaner objectively and in true perspective. Back in London in the days before the polling the programme was put together. Entitled *Whiter than Thou*, it concentrated on the policies, statements and attitudes of the HNP. But in approaching his subject in this way, the producer might well have believed that he was keeping to his undertaking, since the features of the HNP–those claimed for it by itself and attributed to it by others–corresponded precisely with the picture on the wall. He would have had no doubt that it was this that represented the truth about the Afrikaner, and that it was the presentation of him by South Africa House as a reasonable man that was false. There was excuse enough for his attitude: the basic claim of the HNP was that it was the faithful standard-bearer of Afrikanerdom, and that it was the ruling National Party who were the deviationists.

Often the Afrikaner Nationalist acts as though he not only lacks a friend in the world but does not even want one: the *Telegraph,* London, 31.8.63.

Before the polling all were agreed that the essential issue was the conflict between the National Party and the HNP–and, indeed, it was. For the first time in history the political character of the Afrikaner was being put to the acid test. Through the previous decades judgment had been held in abeyance: from 1910 to 1961 the verdict of Afrikanerdom upon itself had been obscured and postponed by the overriding common purpose of independence from Britain and the achievement of a Republic. The 1966 election had been overshadowed by Rhodesia's unilateral declaration of independence and the ensuing threat to the security of Southern Africa as a whole. But the Republic having been achieved and the threat moved, the scene was now set for this historic verdict.

Mr. Vorster had already moved even farther to the Right to counter the threat of the HNP. If they do well in the elections, he (or his successor, since he has staked his position on smashing them now and may be forced to resign) will stay on the extreme Right: the *Guardian,* London, 20.4.70.

As the Thames Television Company projected to millions of viewers its *Whiter than Thou,* the final votes were being counted in the Republic. The previous day the HNP had presented in predominantly Afrikaner communities 78 candidates for the House of Assembly. The TV "documentary" had scarcely stopped running when the final results were know. All 78 HNP candidates had been defeated: all but three had lost their deposits of R400 each–that is, they had polled less than one-fifth of the votes of the winning candidate. The National Party under the leadership of Mr. Vorster had stood unequivocally for: the separate developmen⸱ of the Bantu nations in the Republic towards their own parallel independence with the Anglo-Afrikaner nation; absolute equality in the white nation between Anglosan and Afrikaner; co-operation and diplomatic relations with the black states of Africa: friendly ties with all nations prepared to accept the Republic as she is; respect for the sovereignty of the smallest of states and non-interference in their affairs; and a vigorous immigration policy. The National Party's share of the total vote was 54.43 per cent; the HNP's, 3.56 per cent. Was there ever in any election so clear-cut an issue, so decisive an outcome? And it was given by all of Afrikanerdom–by the country Afrikaners no less than the city Afrikaners. The leader of the HNP, Dr. Albert Hertzog, stood in the constituency of Ermelo which spreads out to distant horizons through the rolling veld and the maizefields of the Eastern Transvaal. He bore one of the most famous of all Afrikaner names, and he is personally a man of great charm and distinction. He came bottom of the poll–after both the National Party and the United Party–and forfeited his deposit. The deputy-leader of the HNP, Mr. Jaap Marais, stood in the dense, drab, lower-middle-class constituency of Innesdale in Pretoria. There are few men in the country's political life more determined, courageous or articulate than Mr. Marais. He came bottom of the poll–after both the National Party and the United Party–and forfeited his deposit.

That was the scope of the verdict, and it was an immense victory for Mr. Vorster. Against weighty evidence but with his own certain faith in the good sense of his *volk*, he accepted the challenge, and in doing so he rendered a service of inestimable value to the country. The central significance of the election was that the Afrikaners had revealed in this conclusive fashion the kind of political beings they are. Those who are prepared to set prejudice aside will discern three strands running unbroken back through the Afrikaner's history–from 1970 through 1961 and 1910 to 1836 and beyond: his determination for freedom, the power of his purpose in preserving his culture, and his readiness to grant to others what he demands for himself. These are the true outlines of the Afrikaner's political nature. On April 22, 1970, the real-life portrait was drawn . . . and if the Presidents, Prime Ministers, Bishops, Trade Union Leaders, Women's Leagues, Newspaper Editors and Television Producers were honest they would have taken down the caricature. I believe some of them did.

> Cut off by geography and an intellectual isolation that stimulated strange theories of democracy and race relations, the stolid Boers push against history's currents . . . They are, I fear, as anomalous as the whooping crane: C. L. Sulzberger, *New York Times News Service*, December, 1967.

211

Verlig and *Verkramp*

The election was fought to the accompaniment of two new terms in the country's political vocabulary– *verlig* and *verkramp*–which had gone into circulation three or four years before. Dr. Hertzog and his followers were presented as the "cramped" ones; Mr. Vorster and his, as the "enlightened" ones. However it is important that a wrong conclusion should not be drawn from these generalisations and the election outcome.

Pretoria, 1968: Verlig and *Verkramp* are today the stock slogans of politicians, leader-writers, cartoonists. Each week the Sunday papers are ablaze with them, and they are having an odd and widening impact on the public at large. Many a person when he enters for the first time the home of another these days inclines to ask himself, not whether the man is rich or poor, fond of dogs or gardening, but whether he is *verkramp* or *verlig*. The fact that he may not be quite sure which of the two he is himself adds to the fascination of the speculation.

Perhaps after all there is a chink in the Afrikaners' psychological armour. Their ruthlessness, terrible as it seems, may yet prove less than that of their African enemies: the *Sunday Telegraph,* London, November, 1963.

However it must be conceded that the speculation is not objective but, by definition, weighted. *Verkramp* means literally "cramped"; *verlig*, "enlightened". Thus mere terminology–the arbitrary choice it was of a single individual–imports immediately into the situation a heavy bias (since, while no man likes the cramps, all men are eternally groping for the light switch). There is a *prima facie* case of prejudice here: not attributed but built-in–and this is surely inequitable. At the same time it should be said that the degeneration of the terms into uncomplicated cuss-words has somewhat mitigated the bias: each of them is now approximately as closely related to dictionary meaning as, for instance, bloody swine. Cussing, the psychologist will say, has its value as an emotional outlet. Nevertheless it tends to disturb tranquillity, engender ill-feeling and provoke unthinking reaction. More important, it is–though expressive–seldom definitive. The best-organised counter-cussing is a poor substitute for intelligent debate . . . and underlying the *verkrampte-verligte* feud–beneath the superficial name-calling–is a deep and broad issue which demands the clearest and calmest application of intelligence. Anglosans are led to suppose that this is peculiarly an Afrikaner domestic affair: but in reality they are also closely involved and so is Western civilisation and mankind. This is, in the truest sense, an historic issue.

212

There is a battle of ideas going on around the world in which all of us are concerned. Are reason, science, technology to be the sole architects and arbiters of our destiny, or is it to be guided by intuitive things like the accumulated experience of the generations, tradition, prescription, faith? Is the ultimate criterion the freedom of the individual or the welfare of society? Is patriotism archaic, or is it relevant to the modern age and inspiring? Should there be world government, or should separate states retain their sovereignty? Should we move towards a common kind of humanity, or should we protect diversity?

> The split in the Nationalist Party between so-called Verkramptes (hardliners) and Verligtes (enlightened ones) is really a division of opinion between Ancient and Modern, between fundamentalists and pragmatists. But the basic philosophy remains the same: the *Guardian*, London, 28.10.69.

Such are the broad battle-lines; and because it is in the nature of the great majority of Afrikaners and Anglosans to be conservative, the desire to defend the position suggested in the second part of each of these questions is general. The real dispute concerns the nature of the defence. How fixed or mobile is it to be? In the present condition of the outside world–egalitarian, rationalist, permissive–is there not the danger that communication with it will be the beginning of capitulation? That danger must be taken into account and guarded against. But like the sentiment of nationality (that is, the self-regarding sentiment), the sentiment towards communication and co-operation with others is also deep-rooted in the human psyche. In South Africa at the present time, the degeneration of this debate has brought the sentiments into headlong opposition: but they are not necessarily opposed: on the contrary, if a society is to prosper each must be given its due weight and the two must be reconciled.

The effects of localising and universalising forces, the ability or inability to hold them in balance, has all along marked the lot of Western civilsations. The pride of the ancient Greek citizen in his city state, his intimate association with the local environment, the personality which he gave to and drew from his circumscribed society, his determination to contribute to the glory of the known and shared fatherland–all this led to accomplishments in art, thought and design that have yet to be surpassed. Nevertheless, the intensity of the self-regarding sentiment of the Greek city state bred a parochialism and indifference towards others that brought the downfall of this venerable civilisation. Rome, on the other hand, was at her greatest when, as the supreme member of an expansive common-wealth, she retained her own ways while freely allowing others to retain

213

theirs. Rome fell when, through military extravagance, rapacity and the importation of exotic ways, she lost her own sober and hard-working nature.

> There are people in this country who would be genuinely angry if the Afrikaner changed radically: needing him as a scapegoat, they long for him to persist in error till he meets his just, inevitable and psychologically satisfying retribution: the *Telegraph*, London, 10.5.61.

Throughout history the greatest of societies have disintegrated at the point where localising and universalising forces have got themselves out of gear. The opposing instead of synthesising of them has had cataclysmic consequences. The thought of Jean Jacques Rousseau step-fathered the horrors of France's egalitarian revolution, and yet the essence of his teaching was nationalistic and patriotic. In producing the theory of a common ancestor of all mankind, Darwin gave the universalists a potent shot in the arm, but his companion idea of the survival of the fittest contributed largely to the aggressiveness of the nation-state. The aggressive nation-state led in turn to the disasters of 1914 and 1939. The reaction was the rejection of nationalism and the wave of cosmopolitanism that swept across the world after World War II.

This is the sweeping context of the *verligte-verkrampte* dispute–and it deserves something better than bickering. In the world today the localising and universalising forces are grossly out of gear, and personality is in peril of submergence in the mechanistic patterns and rationalist thinking of modern life. South Africa, with its widely divergent but interdependent populations, is uniquely positioned to set the example of a new equilibrium. The spirit of the Afrikaner people is permeated with the determination to preserve their identity, and their achievements are stirring vindication of the abiding worth of the sentiment of nationality. At the same time history prescribes that the Afrikaners must communicate and co-operate with others–fellow members of the white nation, fellow black nations–in this sub-continent. It is their conviction, entrenched in 300 years of experience and in the policy to which they are committed, that this can be done–but only if the various peoples are left free to pursue their own kind of life and their own course to happiness.

> The ruthlessness of the fight between Dr. Hertzog and Mr. Vorster for the soul, and the votes, of the Afrikaner people has now boiled over: *The Times*, London, 24.2.70.

The conditions are splendidly there for reconciliation. The *verkramptes* emphasise the virtue of cultural integrity and the self-regarding sentiment:

the *verligtes* emphasise the need for communication and mutual participation. Together they provide the means towards a dynamic synthesis. And we owe it to history and humanity–the Afrikaner owes it to himself–to go out with it. Unless it can be demonstrated in this atomic age that the recognition of diversity is the basis for organic harmony, the death-hand of egalitarianism and uniformity will prevail–here also. We dare not stay at home. Athens in all her glory did and died.

The Black Man's View of Separatism

The more reasonable critics of Pretoria for many years held the view that separatism would be acceptable provided that it was the result of consultation with the blacks and was not imposed on them. It was as long ago as 1958 that Archbishop de Blank of Cape Town spoke of the importance of the different race groups "sitting round a conference table and, through their representatives, deciding that they would like to develop their country, with all its potentiality, more or less in segregated groups." But how reliable is such consultation, how representative in fact? In the decolonising years the intelligentsia of the emerging black states, in consultation after consultation, declared themselves unequivocally for parliamentary democracy. Within a decade, though, it had been shown and universally conceded that their choice was radically wrong for their people. For years, consultation with the black people in the United States suggested an overwhelming preference for integration with white Americans. The triumph of the civil rights movement followed: but can it be said today that the majority of America's blacks want integration? Many of their present spokesmen are uncertain, and I am not referring to the extremists among them. Soon after all discrimination and differentiated treatment had been legislated away, Mr. James Farmer, previously head of the Congress of Racial Equality, published his book, *Freedom— When?* In it he asked specifically for the recognition of his black people as an ethnic group of their own. He expressed the view that the law itself should recognise a distinction between black and white, and he foresaw "a kind of separation" between them. And in 1946, when the non-white population of South West Africa expressed an overwhelming preference for incorporation with South Africa, the United Nations rejected their verdict, saying that they were insufficiently advanced to know what was good for them. Edmund Burke in this day pointed to the danger of the choice "of one day, of one set of poeple, a tumultuary and giddy choice," and recommended instead a constitution máde by "what is ten thousand times better than choice: by the peculiar circumstances, occasions, tempers, dispositions, and moral, civil and social habitudes of the people . . ."

215

The Government in Pretoria in 1948 was responsible for the welfare of all its peoples and for the kind of future they were to have. It was the custodian of the black man's heritage: and what would the verdict of history have been had it abandoned its role as custodian and put that heritage to risk upon the *ad hoc* judgment of an urbanised, Western-orientated "representative" of the black people such as the African National Congress? The Congress would without doubt have recommended integration, which would have meant the submergence of black culture–of all those attributes Burke wrote about–in a polyglot, Western-dominated South Africanism. Pretoria had no intention of taking that course. It worked out in rough outline its programme for separatism, while understanding full well that it could never succeed without the co-operation of the black people.

> The lack of contact and constitutional channels between white government and black governed is almost complete. Only bullets and stones pass across the gulf: the *Washington Post*, 27.3.60.

In the early 1950s, as Minister of Native Affairs, Dr. Verwoerd moved regularly and widely about the *Reserves*, discussing at *indabas* his ideas–informally, in the shade of a tree or beside a mountain stream: "You see that bird in the reeds there. It calls, who answers? It is birds of the same kind who answer, who have the same way of building their nests and rearing their young and bringing in food for them. They come together and·build their homes together." The Bantu Authorities Act of 1951, like the Bantu Self-government Act eight years later, was not mandatory: it was left to the individual black nations and their authentic representatives to consider it and to accept or reject it as they chose. The Xhosas of the Transkei (who number today over 4-million) set the pace in acceptance. By 1963 they were ready for self-government, and the constitution provided for 64 traditional chiefs in the Legislative Assembly and for 45 popularly-elected members. The critics of separatism were not impressed: this was merely the perpetuation of the old tribalism; and their scepticism increased when, at the first general election, only 14 of the 45 elective seats were won by supporters of the pro-separatist Government Party of the Paramount Chief Kaiser Matanzima. But in 1968, after five years' experience of self-government under separatism, the ruling party doubled the number of its elected representatives–from 14 to 28. This was the freely given verdict of Xhosas living within the borders of the Transkei and across them in the Republic Proper.

> The policy of apartheid is based on a total and unqualified white distrust of the blacks. As such it must poison the fount

216

of white authority at source, tainting every social measure with the bitterness of political exploitation: the *Telegraph*, London, 22.6.59.

The Zulus, also with a population of 4-million plus, are perhaps the most famous of all black nations. Under Shaka at the beginning of the last century they built a formidable empire. Their military feats, advanced social organisation and colourful customs caught the imagination of historians and novelists, and they were known around the world. The empire of the Zulus endured until 1879 when they were finally defeated in battle by Britain. Their power was broken, their territory annexed, and they lost the right to decide their own destiny. However there are no Bantu people prouder of their heritage, and through the decades of uncertainty that followed, the Zulu spirit survived. But how was it to find expression in the radically changing conditions of South Africa? That was the dilemma that reached a climax in the 1960s. By that time there were many blacks, Zulus among them, who had come to doubt the worth of their nationhood and culture in the modern world. They dismissed them as outdated: they were persuaded that they should trade them in for the white man's model; and that action, militant if necessary, within the white political structure was the only means for achieving progress. Meanwhile, though, in many parts of the world the sense of identity of a people was being stressed as the mainspring for their advancement. Among the Zulu leadership the two ideas were in sharp conflict and for many years the issue remained unresolved. Then as the 1960s ended it was decided in favour of the second, of consolidating the Zulu identity. Soon before he died in 1968 Paramount Chief Cyprian Bhekuzulu asked for the inclusion of his people in the system provided for by the 1959 Act. The Zulu College of Chiefs thereupon proceeded to choose a leader for their Territorial Authority. Their choice fell on Gatsha Buthelezi, a great-grandson of Chief Cetewayo who in his day caused Queen Victoria no end of trouble. Chief Buthelezi had studied history at Fort Hare University in the Cape and had travelled in Europe and America. He was an active member of the Anglican Church (which is sharply opposed to separatism), and counted among his friends Alan Paton, the author and leader of the radical Liberal Party while it was in existence. It was known that through the years Buthelezi had been a key figure in the Zulus' opposition to the acceptance of the 1959 Act. In these circumstances the question was: what was Pretoria's reasction going to be to his choice by the College of Chiefs? Its reaction was to install him as principal minister of the new Zulu Government.

It is impossible to believe that the Afrikaner, whose basic article of faith is white supremacy, intends to allow the

217

> black areas to be anything other than exploited satellites. It
> is highly illogical for a regime which, within its own
> borders, divides its population into supermen and submen to
> declare that the submen can have a national home just
> outside. The submen just won't believe it: the *Telegraph*,
> 3.7.59.

The 1968 Xhosa vote was *prima facie* evidence of the support of the black people for separatism: the 1970 appointment of Buthelezi was *prima facie* evidence that South Africa's black leaders are not puppets. The fact is that Matanzima and Buthelezi speak straight from the shoulder. Matanzima says: "It is our right as a fully-fledged nation to plan our own future. I do not want to interfere with the white man's freedom, and they must not interfere with ours." It is in this context that he says: "Separate development is the saviour of my people, because in a multi-racial free-for-all our land and our people would be lost within a decade." Buthelezi says that he works within the system of separatism because his people are allowed no alternative. At the same time, he has stated: "I believe in the honesty of the Vorster Government's intention to grant the Zulus independence, and have therefore put my cards on the table right from the start. Top of the priority list is the granting of more land to the Zulu nation. Pretoria's policy is not wrong in principle, but in partitioning South Africa the black people will have to have some of the fat and not just the lean meat."

> The repressed Africans in South Africa itself have no faith
> whatever in the Bantustan policy, the policy of returning
> Africans to states of their own within South Africa, or even
> in the Government's good intentions with regard to it: the
> *Montreal Star*, Canada, 7.8.63.

The third-largest of South Africa's eight Bantu nations (each of which had meantime opted for separatism and was progressing to self-government) are the 2-million strong Tswanas of BophuthaTswana. Their leader, Chief Lucas Mangope, says: "I believe the concept of separate development has the potential to provide the golden key for safeguarding the existential security of all groups, if implemented with the utmost integrity both in purpose and method. The moment the policy of any government threatens the security and existence of another group beyond tolerance, it threatens the welfare of the whole state . . . I want to make it quite plain that I consider various alternative policies put forward by various white Parties as just not acceptable."

As the 1970s began some commentators abroad were beginning to take note of these developments. In September, 1970, the highly respected

Swiss Review of World Affairs carried a three-page article on the subject. It said that internal relations in South Africa were clearly approaching a new phase. The white monologue on the separate evolution of the racial groups was turning into a dialogue between black and white as to how the policy should be executed. "Knowledgeable observers", wrote the *Swiss Review*, "have long been pointing out that the image of the African National Congress and the Pan Africanist Congress–both banned for ten years now–has paled, and that the relatively extended autonomy of the Transkei under Chief Matanzima has made an impression on the blacks. Africans hitherto bitterly opposed to apartheid have come round to the policies of the Verwoerd and Vorster Governments. They have ceased to object to separate development as such, only to its slow pace of realisation . . . Pretoria has recognised that blacks who are puppets are no help to the whites: only the approval and collaboration of independent Bantu leaders can make it possible to get the policy accepted by the blacks." There was an article on the same subject in London's *Spectator* in November, 1970. It described Matanzima as "an uncompromising African nationalist"; said that Buthelezi, "the great and respected Chief of the Zulu people", had accepted the concept of a Zulustan, and had demanded that the white man of South Africa should aid him with technical skill and finance to build a self-governing and educated nation at speed. The *Spectator* article concluded: "Even if the Bantustans never prove completely viable or capable of containing all their peoples, this is not the issue. Ireland and Israel have taught us that even if a majority of their people live abroad, it is vital for a nation to have a local habitation and a home. American Negroes, after 300 years, are seeking their African not their Anglo-Saxon heritage, and Black Power has demanded its own Bantustan in the Southern States of the USA. In furthering her Bantu homelands South Africa, not our left-wing multi-racialists, is carrying out the terms of the UN Charter: to promote to the utmost the self-determination of her people."

> Even if the black man were still in a mood to accept it, the South African Government has ruled out gradualism. It has denied the Negro not merely dignity and justice but the hope even of a slow change for the better: the *Washington Post*, 3.4.60.

Back home, in November, 1973, leaders of five of the homelands met at their first "summit"–in Umtata, capital of the Transkei–to discuss among other things the future relations between their countries. There they agreed to propagate, as a long term objective, the idea of federation. But immediately after the meeting, Chief Mangope of BophuthaTswana expressed the view that it would be more in the interests of his people to link up with ethnically-identical but politically independent Botswana, than with ethnically-different nations at present within the Republic's borders. A few days later Chief Buthelezi advocated a Federal Union of Autonomous States of Southern Africa. He dealt in detail with the necessity for co-operation if this part of the world was to realise its great potential. But at the same time he spoke of "our new sense of nationhood in the various black states." He stressed the need "to guarantee the identities and cultural autonomy of every racial, ethnic and cultural group"; and he declared the right of "the black man, the white man and the brown man to translate the great principles handed down to each one of them by their ancestors into satisfying social, economic and cultural action."

One of the resolutions of the black "summit" was a request for a joint meeting with the Prime Minister: and in early 1974 members of the Pretoria Government, headed by Mr. Vorster, conferred with the leaders of the eight black nations. There had never before been a conference of this kind, and no less significant than the occasion itself was the nature of the deliberations. There was no attempt to duck controversial issues. All of them–land, wages, influx control, discrimination, the urban Bantu– were on the agenda, and they were discussed on both sides frankly and vigorously. The political correspondent of the Johannesburg *Star* commented that the conference had confirmed the view of the homeland leaders that Prime Minister Vorster was a man they could talk to and get through to despite wide divergence on many essential matters. It has also shown the homeland leaders to be men capable of statesmanlike dialogue . . . From those informal meetings under a tree a couple of decades before to the "summit" in the Union Buildings in Pretoria: it was, indeed, notable progress.

> South Africa's three million whites were determined to maintain themselves as the master race, relegating more than three times their number of Negroes and "coloreds" to second class citizenship. Racism has not been enforced so relentlessly since the days of Nazi Germany: *The Age,* Australia, 17.3.61.

That is an indication of the attitude of black leaders. But what does the ordinary black man think about Pretoria's policies and the way they are being administered: or rather the "detribalised African" who is said by some to be opposed to the whole concept of separatism and to be the insurmountable obstacle to its implementation? A clue was provided by a reader letter competition organised in January, 1976 by *The World. The World* is a black newspaper circulating mainly in Soweto, the black town near Johannesburg with a population upward of 750,000, and other urban areas of the Transvaal. The newspaper simply asked its readers: "What do you think of Mr. Vorster? Is he a good or bad Prime Minister?" Fifty-three per cent of those who responded thought he was a "good" or "excellent" Prime Minister; something under 47 per cent that he was a "bad" Prime Minister, while a number said he had some good and some bad points. Reasons given for supporting the Prime Minister were: his detente policy, his opening of "white" jobs to blacks, his leading of the homelands to independence without bloodshed and his allowing all nationalities to practise their traditional customs. Main criticisms concerned influx control, the regulations governing the purchase by blacks of houses in the urban areas, the wage gap between whites and blacks, and "token concessions" made to "fool foreigners".

It was a lively response to the editor's question and evidence of how, together with whites, blacks at a variety of levels participate today in discussion of the country's affairs.

> There is real danger that, in its impossibly rigid and cruel effort to compartmentalise the Africans upon whose labour the country depends, the government may set off the race war it dreads: the *Washington Post*, 30.3.60.

Ingenuity, Enterprise, Prosperity

Following Mr. Macmillan's Cape Town speech, Sharpeville, the attack on Dr. Verwoerd and the Republic's withdrawal from the Commonwealth, prophecies of economic doom proliferated. For a dozen years Pretoria had withstood the political onslaught. But universally ostracised and alienated now even from Britain, could it possibly meet the economic consequences of isolation: the threat to established markets; the shock to investors and the drying-up of capital inflow; the "brain-drain" of academics, scientists and professional men leaving the country, and the abandoning by all those others of what they thought was a sinking ship?

> When order has been restored and normal economic life returns–what then? It is here that the walls of the dead-end close in with such nightmare terror: the *Sunday Times*, London, 3.4.60.

The answer of the pessimists was *no:* but the faint of heart should have taken account rather of the long record. Since the turn of the century the country had faced many crises: the devastation of the Anglo-Boer War: participation in two world wars with, on each occasion, traumatic political repercussions at home: the gold-standard confusion of the early 1930s: the international assault on apartheid: boycotts, and the shockwaves of decolonisation. But during all this time, for half a century and more, the country succeeded in maintaining an average real growth rate of close on 5 per cent per annum and an increase of some 2.2 per cent a year in the real living standards of the people as a whole–despite a high population growth of 2.4 per cent a year.

This enviable performance has continued; and the decade that followed Sharpeville and the withdrawal from the Commonwealth proved in the event to be one of unprecedented expansion. In the 12 years after 1962 the gross domestic product in market price terms more than trebled from R6,000-million to R22,000-million; and in the last of these years–1974– the real growth rate of 7.4 per cent was the highest among the free world's industrial nations. By the mid-1960s overseas confidence in the Republic was burgeoning: between 1966 and 1972 foreign investment in private enterprise increased at some 11 per cent a year–from R2,286- million to R4,700-million; and the total historic value of all foreign investment in the country–in both private and public sectors–by then exceeded R9,000-million. Capital inflow in 1975 was an all-time record; and in that year the best estimates were that new fixed investment in infrastructure and other sectors of the economy would be some R50,000- million during the ensuing decade.

> The major tragedy is that South Africa will pursue its present policies. Today it is almost a garrison state. The economy is suffering through the expense of keeping a large armed force in a continual state of emergency against a foe of its own making: the *Evening Star*, New Zealand, 23.10.61.

This is the answer in figures to the prophets of doom. In several areas of industrial activity there was also evidence of much ingenuity and enterprise–often the direct result of world hostility. Thus, in the early 1960s following the imposition of the United Nations arms embargo, Pretoria began the establishment of its own sophisticated armaments industry. It was highly successful. Weapons ranging from ammunition through rockets and armoured cars to jet aircraft were within the decade being produced–and some of them, exported. Pretoria's scientists, together with colleagues in France, developed the Cactus missile for defence against high-speed, low-level air attack, and soon it came to be regarded by many experts abroad as the most effective system of its kind. In other areas during the 1960s local corporations won, against interna- tional competition, contracts to build: near Cape Town, the most advanced maritime communications centre outside North America; in

South America, a major irrigation project; in Mocambique, a dam and hydro-electric scheme greater than Egypt's Aswan; in Australia, an underground railway system. Such activities were accompanied by the development of a network of financial institutions for the highest sophistication. The Council for Scientific and Industrial Research and the Bureau of Standards in Pretoria City provided models of efficiency which engaged world attention. In particular branches of science, the Republic's specialists led the way in revolutionary techniques in surgery ... and in a department that was soon to be of critical world significance–fuel–did pioneering work:

> If the Nationalist citadel survives the next few weeks without a crack, then South Africa is in for a long siege, from which South African industry may take years to recover–a self-inflicted wound that may not heal for generations: the *Guardian,* 7.4.60.

In the 1950s the chemists of the South African Coal, Oil and Gas Corporation (Sasol) had set themselves the task of converting coal, of which the country has abundant supplies, into petrol. In 1954 a Sasol executive, Mr. D. P. de Villiers, explained the reason for the daring undertaking–and daring it was since nowhere before had it proved possible to operate a petrol-from-coal plant profitably. The world's known oil reserves, said Mr. de Villiers, would last another 20 years (that is, until the mid-1970s). New fields would certainly meantime be discovered: but since the developed countries had been intensively prospected, "it must be accepted that the greater proportion of the undiscovered oil will be situated in areas which, from the political angle, cannot be considered as very secure for the West. The West would thus have to take effective steps to safeguard its fuel position, and the answer lay in coal ... The year after that prophetic statement Sasol put its petrol on the market. Almost exactly 20 years after the statement the fuel crisis hit the world–and the most advanced nations, including West Germany and the United States, began queueing up at Sasol for technical assistance. In 1975 in the Transvaal work began on building Sasol 2: a multi-billion rand project, it will produce ten times as much petrol as Sasol 1 and provide the country with close on half its total requirements.

The triumph of the Republic's physicists in this same energy field began in 1961–the year after Sharpeville. At an undisclosed address in Du Toit Street, Pretoria City, four of them met to tackle a problem which for a generation had defied the ceaseless efforts of leading scientists in the major countries of the world: it was to devise a technique for producing enriched uranium (the essential fuel for modern nuclear power stations) cheaper than the prohibitively expensive one developed by the United

223

States. In July, 1970 Prime Minister Vorster informed Parliament that the technique had been devised; in April, 1975, that the pilot plant had come on stream and that theoretical forecasts had been confirmed in all respects. This meant that the Republic was one of five countries in the free world capable of producing the precious fuel (the others being the United States, Britain, France and West Germany), and one of only two countries in the free world capable of producing it commercially (the other being the United States). Immediately after the Prime Minister's 1975 announcement, plans were put in hand for the construction (perhaps with foreign partners) of a large-scale manufacturing plant. Estimates were that it would come into operation in the mid-1980s, and that it would earn some R250-million annually in foreign exchange.

> *South Africa's siege economy:* Further ahead there are the effects of the Commonwealth break to be absorbed ... Still more significant is the formidable number of able scientists and technicians who have left the country recently ... How long can this kind of battering be sustained? How long can an economy in the full flush of industrial growth go on losing money and men?: David Howell in the *Telegraph*, London, 19.5.61.

It is stranger surely than fiction–and more romantic–that a country cut off by the world, written off as the 1960s began economically and scientifically, and "brain-drained", should within the decade have led the world in two such vital technological developments.

More generally, the fuel crisis which blew the world such ill blew the Republic much good. It was as though a Balancing Force were making amends. The rocketing oil price played havoc with an out-dated and politically-manipulated international monetary system: and one of the consequences was the release of the price of gold from the absurdly low level at which it had been pegged since the mid-1930s. Within a couple of years the value of the Republic's main export shot up from R800-million to R2,500-million a year. The oil shortage, moreover, placed the Republic at an advantage as against other industrial countries, since it depends to the extent of only some 20 per cent on oil for its total energy requirements (compared with 68 per cent in Europe and 80 per cent in Japan). And as the industrial nations suddenly realised that they were threatened not only with a shortage of oil but with a general shortage of basic materials, the importance of the Republic's mineral resources was dramatised. It is among the richest of all mineral-rich nations: its deposits of several essential ores are the largest in the world, and of many others it has vast reserves. Its underground treasures range literally from A to Z of the mineral alphabet: antimony, asbestos, chrome, coal, copper, diamonds, fluorspar, gold, iron, manganese, nickel, platinum, titanium, uranium, vanadium and zinc. Professor Alastair Buchan, Professor of International Relations at Oxford, dealt with the political implications in a BBC Reith lecture in November, 1973. He said that the Republic's vast raw material deposits would, like oil, become a political factor. He pointed out that most of the reserves of such key minerals as nickel, chrome, platinum and manganese were either in the Soviet Union or South Africa or in politically unstable states. That fact, he said, necessitated a decision on "our political priorities."

> Exclusion from world trade by economic sanctions must fol-
> low if the Nationalist Government persists with apartheid.
> This is the logic of the growing weight of world opinion.
> The latest moves in the United Nations are steps along this
> road: the *Guardian*, London, 6.12.63.

The Professor's observation would seem to be well-founded. Important though it has always been in the past, the possession of minerals has acquired an altogether new meaning in recent years. Since the beginning of the industrial revolution a couple of centuries ago, the acquisition of raw materials to feed fast-proliferating factories and furnaces has been a prime mover of history. It was a main cause of the extension of European influence to the most distant reaches of the globe, of the establishing of empires and of the waging of wars. Later there was the burgeoning of industrial activity in North America and then Japan. Coupled with high-powered advertising and other techniques to stimulate the consumption–and waste–of manufactured goods, this has multiplied again and again the demand for raw materials. Meanwhile, empires have been dissolved; many of the ex-colonies are no longer reliable suppliers, and leading industrial nations have been depleting recklessly the reserves within their own borders. The dependence on others of Japan (never richly-endowed by Nature) is virtually complete: Europe's is growing alarmingly, and even the bountifully-endowed United States is beginning to feel the pinch. In the past 30 years that country has consumed more minerals than has the entire world since the beginning of recorded statistics. Today it imports some 15 per cent of its basic industrial requirements: estimates are that the figure could be 50 per cent by the end of the century.

> But from now on South Africa must be, for the investor, a
> suspect country. South Africa seems set for a steady decline
> in business and activity, with all the likelihood of unrest and
> discontent which that implies: the *Telegraph*, London,
> 20.6.61.

This helps to explain Professor Buchan's call for a review of priorities: the Republic has a vital role to play in the world economy, and she is making unprecedented efforts to play it with maximum efficiency. Prospecting techniques–undreamt of when gold and diamonds were first discovered, and including photography from space–are now being used. One result has been the recent locating in the north-western Cape Province of a variety of deposits so rich that they may well yield more wealth in the years to come than the gold of the Witwatersrand. Giant overseas as well as local corporations are at work in the region, and some ten to twelve mines will be opened there in the near future. Sales today of the Republic's non-precious minerals are worth some R700-million a year: the consulting engineer of General Mining believes they will yield close on ten times as much by the end of the century; and great new harbours have been built at Richards Bay on the north coast of Natal and at Saldanha Bay on the west coast of the Cape Province to carry them abroad. The Republic's mining industry is poised to make a massive contribution to the country's economic growth, and to provide substantially in the raw material needs of the industrialised world.

The period that began so ominously in 1960 proved in the event to be one of great expansion and excitement–politically and economically. In 1975 Dr. Ray Cline, former chief of intelligence at the US State Department and deputy chief of the Central Intelligence Agency, published a list giving his assessment of the relative power of the world's 152 states. In making his assessment he assigned weighted values to various factors: population, land area, national product, raw materials, strategic location, military strength, national cohesion, strategy and will. South Africa's population of 25-million (28th in the world) put it among medium-sized countries which have between 20- and 40-million people. Its land area (21st in the world) again put it in the middle ranks. In energy production it was ahead of leading European countries: in the category of non-fuel mineral supplies it ranked seventh: and in that all-important factor–surplus food production–it ranked sixth. A characteristic of the analysis was the even and wide spread of South Africa's sinews of power; and according to Dr. Cline's reckoning there are in the world today only 14 more powerful countries.

> But external criticism especially from the liberal angle, probably does more to confirm them in their illusion than it moves them to question it . . . Is there any body of influence which can shake their self-confidence before it is shivered into fragments by a revolutionary movement, coming sooner or later, which would sweep away the whole structure of the Union, the good with the bad?–the *Guardian*, London, 7.4.60.

This is the result, despite the worst that the world since 1948 has been able to do. How has it been possible? Well, in many ways South Africa is a lucky country. It is not the determination of the Afrikaner that placed it astride the Indian and Atlantic Oceans, and it is not the ingenuity of the Anglosan that put its minerals in the earth. That is so: but over and above its natural, god-given advantages, and in addition to determination and ingenuity there was another quality of mind: through all these years it was the Western critic, not the Anglo-Afrikaner, who was burdened with a guilt complex.

> South Africa has to live with the rest of the world and her
> people have to live with their own consciences: the *New
> York Times*, 26.3.60.

Part three: / Section one
Now

The World Context:
Balance

There was in the West following the War a radical reaction against authority and in favour of individual freedom: against distinctions between people and in favour of equalitarianism. There was the period of obsession with the threat of communism and the period of complacency towards it: the period of patronising the emergent states and the period of pandering to them: and, over all, the period of idealism and the period of disillusionment–the substitution, as the danger of nuclear war and inflation loomed, for the hope of utopia of the fear of hell. Between these extremes is there the possibility, within and among nations, of a balance being struck?

CHAPTER FOURTEEN / NOW
United States, United Kingdom, United Nations

(1) THE UNITED STATES

Leadership at Stake

This part of the picture so far: America's post-war revolution was a revolution of expectations more intense and widely-shared than any experienced by the emergent countries. There was the sense that America's historic destiny was about to be achieved: the American Government and people confidently expected the coming of the Great Society at home, and elsewhere "a worldwide democracy, victory for all mankind, a worldwide victory for freedom." American means for achieving these goals ignored the complexity of the world and of human nature–and failed. Totalitarian governments tightened their control, emancipated countries rejected democracy. The immense expenditure of effort and resources by America was repaid on all sides by ingratitude and insult. The protracted war in Vietnam compounded the disillusionment: and with national purpose everywhere frustrated and with theologians and churches striking at the roots of Christianity, individual freedom degenerated into moral anarchy–"a Babylonian society, a late sensate period in which all the codes have been broken down." Richard Nixon, assuming the Presidency in 1969, led a counter-revolution. He restored respect for America abroad and, at home, respect for order in the streets, on the campuses and in the ghettoes. These were substantial successes but they were vitiated by Watergate. Now read on:

The fall of Mr. Nixon from power and in the esteem of the people accelerated the draining away of public confidence in the honesty and competence of the Presidency and Congress. There was impatience at the apparent inability of democracy to deal with both international and national problems. The pseudo-liberals, who had launched the post-war revolution of expectations, asked now whether the values of American society were any longer worth defending and suggested, in any case, that the use of force was immoral. As Gerald Ford entered the White House, with no mandate from the electorate, there was a general mood in the nation of despondency and defeatism: an inclination to have done with involvement in the problems of the world; and signs of a resort to authoritarianism to cut through the intractable complexities at home. Abraham Lincoln's promise to the nation of a new birth of freedom was in peril.

Then came the disaster of the communist victory in South Vietnam. Through a decade and more Vietnam had been a running wound through which the morale of America had seeped and consequently, also, decisive leadership in the free world. The peace in Vietnam which Mr. Nixon engineered in 1972 was not the end of the affair: people feared that: that the communists, as soon as the time was opportune, would press on despite the Paris Peace Accords; and that the United States, despite its undertakings, would not and could not return. Now, in April, 1975 the communist flag flew over Saigon. The United States did not return: the undertakings it gave in Paris were not honoured–its role was reduced to evacuating refugees. There was a sense of impotence and frustration–if not shame–among the Americans: of despondency and gloom–if not despair–in the Western alliance: and everywhere, among friends and foes, murmurings of the decline of Washington's credibility and authority.

In 1968 when he was campaigning for the White House, Mr. Nixon had said: "Each incident reduced respect for the United States until the ultimate insult inevitably occurred: when respect for the United States of American falls so low that a fourth-rate military power like North Korea will seize an American naval vessel on the high seas, it is time for a new leadership to restore respect for the United States." In mid-May, 1975 an unarmed American merchantman, the *Mayaguez*, was seized by the gunboats of a fourth-rate military power, Cambodia, in the Gulf of Thailand. Through Watergate and Vietnam the wheel had turned full circle: what now would the reaction of the new American leadership be? It was immediate and decisive: President Ford sent in his military forces and freed the *Mayaguez*. This dramatic demonstration that America, despite the bleatings of the pseudo-liberals, still had the capacity to *act* was a tonic for the nation. The American capital (one correspondent reported) was aglow with satisfaction. Mr. Ford's response to his first test of its kind boosted his reputation: and his Administration began immediately to conduct itself with a restored sense of purpose. Defence Secretary Schlesinger warned North Korea that if it invaded the South,

232

the United States would not limit itself to Vietnam-type counter-action. He said one of the lessons learnt in Vietnam was that "rather than simply counter your opponent's thrusts, it is necessary to go to the heart of your opponent's power: destroy his military forces rather than simply involve yourself in ancillary military operations." In the same statement he said that the United States would be less likely than in the past to be as tolerant of any new Arab oil embargo: economic, political and conceivably military measures could be taken in response. Uncle Sam was giving notice that he no longer intended to be pushed around by minor military powers–or by Super Powers either.

Relations with Russia

Before the communist victory in Vietnam, Eugene Rostow–one-time adviser to Lyndon Johnson–had observed that the United States and the free world were walking in their sleep as they had done in the 1930s. Part of the sleep-walk was Vietnam. For the Americans it was a nightmare: but hard though the awakening was, with the fall of Saigon it had finally ended. Another part of the sleep-walk was detente with Russia: the illusion in the West that the guard against Russia could as a result be lowered.

But those who wish to see will perceive no change in Russia's motivation–back to the revolution in 1917 and beyond. Communism itself is a means towards another end: the men in the Kremlin are not concerned with the supremacy of the international proletariat but with the supremacy of Mother Russia. The sympathy of Russia's leaders with other communist peoples is a concern of expediency. At the dictate of Russian interests they supported and rejected Mao Tse Tung. When their European empire was threatened from within they crushed Hungary and Czechoslovakia. After the Czech operation Leonid Brezhnev declared the Kremlin's intention to maintain its hegemony over its satellite states by force if need be–and Russian hegemony in Eastern Europe is the base for Russian expansion around the world.

Modern Russia is an imperialist power with ambitions closer to the Romanoffs than Mr. Marx. During the First World War President Woodrow Wilson had said that the Tsarist autocracy was not in fact Russian in origin, character or purpose and that the great Russian people had now been freed to add their might to the fight for freedom: during the Second World War President Roosevelt looked forward to the inclusion of Russia as a senior partner in the company of democratic nations; and when, despite all that had happened in the intervening years, Mr. Nixon travelled to Moscow in 1972, the myth was revived. But Mr.

233

Nixon's mission was based on his clear understanding of the unbridgeable ideological differences between Moscow and Washington: its purpose was to relax tension between the Super Powers in the overriding interest of safeguarding humanity from nuclear disaster. Mr. Nixon knew and stated that detente depended on a balancing of Soviet power with the power of the non-communist world pulling together: otherwise it would be appeasement. The West at large chose to view the situation differently. Detente was seen as an acknowledgement of the respectability of communism: and many Europeans began to wonder whether their future would not be better secured in an alliance with Russia rather than the United States. Western electorates were reluctant to make sufficient funds available to maintain effective military establishments: the indignation of Western media was directed not at communist countries but at anti-communist countries whose form of government they disapproved; and when in April, 1974 the Caetano Government was overthrown in Portugal they were jubilant.

A first priority of the Ford Administration, in its requests for heavy defense allocations and in its public statements, was to correct this illusion. "The Soviets," stated Defence Secretary Schlesinger, "look primarily at the realities of power–what they refer to as 'the correlation of forces.' They regard detente as a consequence of a shift of forces to their advantage. Their view is that the West is making accommodation to the expansion of Soviet military power. The Soviets see detente as a way to avoid the risk of war and to expand their power." The issue was clearly stated; and when it became apparent that the Portuguese revolution was a Kremlin plot to extend Russian power into the heart of Western Europe, reaction was sharp. Secretary of State Kissinger addressed himself to the Soviet Union in terms more forthright than any that had been used since the dawn of detente. The will of 80 per cent of the Portuguese people was, he said, being subverted, and the United States would not tolerate the intervention of the Soviet Union on behalf of the minority.

Direction, it seemed, was being restored to Washington's approach to world affairs: and events during the first year of Mr. Ford's Presidency moved impressively in favour of the United States, with the Soviet Union suffering a series of setbacks. As 1975 opened, the United States and Europe were grappling with grave economic problems: by contrast Russia, with no fuel crisis to cope with, appeared to be prospering. But soon there was the disastrous crop failure. The weakness in a key area of the Soviet economy was again exposed, and Moscow was forced into the position of having to rely on American wheat to feed its people. Meanwhile, as 1975 ended, the United States was coming out of recession and making good progress against inflation. There were reversals for the Kremlin also on foreign fronts. By April, 1975 America had experienced in South Vietnam the most humiliating defeat in its

234

history, and within weeks the whole of Indo-China was under communist control: but it was to transpire that the main winners there were not the Russians but their hated rivals, the Chinese. In Cambodia, for instance, the Russian Ambassador was not welcome: and in nearby Bangladesh the pro-Soviet Government was overthrown. In the Middle East in early 1975 everything seemed to be going Russia's way. Dr. Kissinger's mission had failed ... but before the year was out America had firmly regained the initiative. Egypt was aligned with the West, and President Sadat had established cordial relations with the United States, Britain and France. In early 1975 it seemed that the communists–Russia's agents– were entrenching themselves as the rulers of Portugal in the heart of Western Europe: before the year was out they were dislodged, discredited and fighting for their political survival.

Within six months of the humiliation of Vietnam, America's self-confidence and its reputation in the world had been substantially restored ... and then came Angola. Compensation for the reverses it had suffered could have been a reason for Russia's decision to embark on the Angolan adventure: however that may be, the effect was to swing the balance spectacularly again in the Kremlin's favour, and to expose weakness in America's leadership.

Angola

Angola confirmed more vividly than any single event since 1917 the continuing ambitions, under the Marxists, of Russian imperialism. The invasion of Angola (for, with 15,000 and more Cuban troops dispatched to the country, that is what it was) was in a different category from the invasions of Hungary and Czechoslovakia. It could be argued that it was more compelling evidence of the Kremlin's imperialist designs even than the recent massive build-up of the Soviet Navy: Russia could contend with some justification that as a Super Power it was entitled to a presence in the oceans equal to that of the United States. No such considerations applied in the case of Angola. It was altogether beyond any recognised sphere of Russian influence: unlike Hungary, Czechoslovakia or any member of the Warsaw Pact, Angola could in no way threaten Russian security; and the acquisition of naval facilities in Angola, together with others on Africa's eastern littoral, could not be seen except as a threat to vital communications between the Persian Gulf and the West. This is precisely how it was seen in Peking: in December, 1975 the official newspaper, *The People's Daily,* declared that the Russians proposed to have the use for their fleets of the "excellent" ports along Angola's coastline of more than 1,000 km; that Russian control of Angola would threaten the safety of the Cape sea route and, in particular, the supply of oil to Europe; that it would reinforce the Soviet position as against the United States in the South Atlantic; and that "the activities of the Russians in Angola are related to their expansionism in Europe." However it was not necessary to look to Peking for an explanation of Russia's intervention in a distant part of the globe: through the years their intentions had been described with great clarity by the men in the Kremlin themselves. It was Lenin who wrote that "we must blow every spark of discontent and agitate every cause because we cannot tell which spark will touch off the final conflagration."

What now would the reaction of the United States be to blowing the spark of discontent in remote Angola? There was much apprehension abroad–in the aftermath of Vietnam and more particularly of the dismissal in November of the strong Secretary of Defence, James Schlesinger–that it would not be sufficiently firm. What Dr. Kissinger immediately did was to warn that the action was a threat to detente . . . but the Kremlin brushed the warning aside. Detente, it said, in no way precluded Soviet support for "national liberation struggles" elsewhere in the world; nor did it mean the freezing of the socio-political status quo in the world, or the cessation of the anti-imperialist struggle of the people for a just fate against foreign interference and oppression. It was an explicit extension of the Brezhnev doctrine of justifiable intervention. It was now a matter of stated policy that Russia saw it as her right to intervene in the affairs of a country where socialism was threatened by capitalism or where, in the view of the Kremlin, a struggle for national liberation was in progress, or where the socio-political status quo was unjust, or where the forces of imperialism or foreign oppression were operating. What country, then, was beyond the reach of what Russia regarded as justifiable intervention?

Dr. Kissinger repeated his warning that Washington's relations with Moscow were being jeopardised: the American Ambassador at the Untied Nations, Daniel Patrick Moynihan, accused Russia of re-colonising Africa. The Kremlin went on pumping men–Cuban men–and arms of ever increasing sophistication into the conflict to support its agent, the MPLA. President Ford declared that the Kremlin's intervention could not go unchallenged, and that the United States would provide weapons to the pro-Western factions, UNITA and the FNLA. The American arms started coming through: but as the Senate rose for the Christmas recess it cut off funds for their further supply. The President described this deliberate undermining of his policy as an abdication of responsibility which could have the gravest long-term consequences for the United States. The Congressmen were not impressed: but Dr. Kissinger stated that he would confront the Russian leadership over Angola during his visit to Moscow in late January, which had previously been scheduled to discuss the Strategic Arms Limitation Talks.

However this visit did no more than dramatize the arrogant self-confidence which throughout had characterized the Russian attitude. As reporters witnessed the Super-Power handshakes in the Kremlin (Brezhnev and Gromyko on the one hand, Kissinger on the other) the question of Angola was raised. "Angola is not my country," Brezhnev (reportedly in a jovial mood) observed. "It will be discussed," retorted Kissinger. Gromyko (reportedly with a thin smile) put in: "The agenda is always adopted by mutual agreement." Kissinger repeated: "I will discuss it." Brezhnev applied the *coup de grace:* "You will discuss it with Sonnenfield", he said, referring to a senior member of the American team. "That will ensure complete agreement. I have never seen Kissinger have a disagreement with Sonnenfeld."

Banter–yes: but was international banter ever more revealing? This public baiting of the Secretary of State of the United States typified the psychological ascendancey at this time of Moscow over Washington. As the talks in the Kremlin were beginning, there had been reports from Washington that the American Administration had a strategy to force Russia to withdraw from Angola. Brezhnev and Gromyko were calling what they clearly regarded as America's bluff; and they no doubt felt free to do so because of the impasse between the White House and Congress. The President had stated that the Senate's refusal to grant funds to support the allied forces would destroy the credibility of Washington's foreign policy–and here was the brutal evidence. The world's faith in American leadership again plummeted: and Aleksandr Solzhenitsyn commented: "The very process of surrender of world positions has the character of an avalanche. At every successive stage it becomes more difficult to hold out and one must yield more and more. This is evident in the new conditions across entire continents and in the unprecedented encroachments by the Soviet Union in south-western Africa."

The Twilight of Authority?

In a Presidential election year Angola, though of no interest to the ordinary American, nevertheless precipitated the crucial issues confronting the electorate: the powers of the Presidency, the challenge of Congress, the merits of detente, the reality of Russian imperialism, and the role of the United States–its continued active participation in world affairs or its retreat into isolation and thus from greatness. In the titanic struggle under way for the mind and spirit of America, who was it that truly represented the people? The Congressmen were the chosen representatives of the people, but whether in fact they spoke for them was another question. A Gallup Poll in late 1975 reported that Congress was experiencing a serious decline in public esteem: only 29 per cent of Americans said they were satisfied with the way the legislators were doing their job. The strictures of Congressmen themselves were cynical and harsh. Republican Representative James Cleveland of New Hampshire, commenting on the poll, declared: "There is no question that the American people are coming to the conclusion that the Government couldn't run a two-car funeral without fouling up the arrangements." Democratic Senator Richard Stone of Florida described as alarming the frequent disillusionment and hostility expressed by citizens toward Congress.

It was this Congress that was challenging the Presidency, but many held the Presidency no less culpable for the failure of the System. One of them was Professor Robert Nisbet of Columbia University. In 1975 he wrote in *The Twilight of Authority* that it was not principles and convictions but the amassing of power and all that went with it that had become the foremost interest to American Presidents: the art of government had gradually but surely been transformed into that of outright lying or the management of truth. President Ford and members of his Administration themselves were aware of the urgent need for a return to integrity and strength of purpose to the political and general life of the nation. James Schlesinger stated while still Secretary of Defence: "I think our basic problem as a nation is not our physical strength or stance: it is a question of reviving the underlying moral stamina and the internal fibre of the nation."

An equilibrium of power in the world necessitated not only an equilibrium of military power but an equilibrium also of will power: there must be a faith in the American way of life which matched Russia's in hers, and a determination that it should prevail. Of all men in Mr. Ford's Administration–and, indeed, of all men in contemporary American history–it was Patrick Moynihan who represented and personified this sentiment. It was he who proclaimed that America should stop apologising for her role in international affairs: that she should answer firmly the charged habitually brought against her: that she should challenge the Third World–communist coalition: that she should speak out proudly for liberty against egalitarian socialism; and that American spokesmen should be feared in future for the truths they might tell.

Fearlessly, in the eight months he held his United Nations appointment, Mr. Moynihan told them. Cutting through humbug and hypocrisy whereever he encountered them, he startled many and inspired millions in his own country and abroad. He also made many enemies in the Third World (for reasons which will appear later, in the communist world, in the Western world (British Ambassador Ivor Richard alluded to him as a Wyatt Earp looking for a shoot-out in the OK Corral), and in his own State Department. But as for his own people, an observer as reliable as

238

London's *Economist* expressed the view that his stand indicated a new post-Vietnam mood in America towards a more assertive defence of Western values and that American public opinion was moving more and more solidly behind him. As he resigned in early 1976 a poll conducted by the North American Newspaper Alliance showed that he had overwhelming support, among men and women and in all regions and classes of American society.

In politics had the authentic voice of America suddenly been heard?

As for the general condition of American society, a penetrating analysis written by William Shannon appeared in the *New York Times* towards the end of 1975. In trying to foresee the shape of the near future it was possible (in Mr. Shannon's view) to begin with either an optimistic or a pessimistic reading of recent events. A main ground for pessimism was the condition of American culture. A culture in which *Playboy* was a widely-read magazine, in which *Portnoy's Complaint* was a widely-accepted novel, and in which *Last Tango in Paris* won an award from the movie industry was a culture in moral anarchy. Any recognition of the importance of privacy or of the need for self-discipline had almost vanished. Exhibitionism and voyeurism were mistakenly identified as civil liberties: pornographers, publicity freaks and manufactured "personalities" paraded across the cultural scene, popped up on television and haunted the fringes of politics. Could democracy survive if common moral values were leached away by a popular culture that endorsed violence and self-indulgence? Could there be political heroes if there were no cultural heroes? If old institutions continued to lose their legitimacy and failed to be renewed, could society find sufficient cohesion and authority in national advertising and television talk shows? Was the fact that all Americans drank the same beer and watched the same programmes enough to keep them moving together as one people?

There were these reasons for pessimism, but there were also reason for optimism. Looking back on a dozen years of assassination, an unpopular and unsuccessful war, racial and generational turmoil, inflation and grave political scandal, it could be confidently concluded that America's social and political institutions must be remarkably strong and its traditions of freedom wonderfully alive to have withstood so much stress. Here is cause for hope, discerned by Mr. Shannon; and in the area of Christian morality, disheartening appearances are perhaps deceptive. Professor Nisbet notes that the authority of the great organised religions has declined alarmingly. Roman Catholicism is undergoing a crisis of faith it has not known since the 16th century. So too is each of the major Protestant Churches. In them, writ, symbol and membership have become so secularised, so loosely textured, so infiltrated by the idols of the theatre and the market place, that the sense of the sacred community has atrophied. However that is not the whole story: religion has not lost its

239

authority for modern man. There is a growth of membership in those Churches where no possible confusion can exist between what is religious and what is secular, and where sermons do not represent watered-down versions of sociology or socialism. Such churches are prospering and so is the whole evangelical movement–in America but also in other parts of the world.

Those are Professor Nisbet's views; and in early 1973 *Time* magazine published the result of a national survey in an article entitled *In Search of the Sacred*. Noting the disillusion that had set in at man's inability to transform the world and himself, it wrote that life had again begun to be a matter of basic questions: Who am I? Why was I born? Why must I die? Few were finding the answers in liberal Churches, and increasing numbers of Americans were turning to the conservative denominations. What was called *The Small Group Movement* had come into being around the nation and concentrated on Bible and prayer meetings in private homes. The inspiration of the *Campus Crusade* was the passage from St. John: *I am the way and the truth and the light.* Bishop Kilmer Myers of California was reported as describing this as "the response to the hunger of all people for the mysterious." And the *Time* essayist concluded that the problem for Americans and others caught up in the West's renewed search for the sacred was just how and where to strike a fruitful balance: between reason and imagination, between discipline and intuition, between a creative awe of the worlds men can only contemplate and a creative concern for the world they live in.

This is the critical balance.

(2) THE UNITED KINGDOM

A Place at Last

This part of the picture so far: Britain's brave effort in World War II stripped her of her strength and resources which through the generations had made her the greatest among the nations. She was obliged to liquidate her mighty empire. In doing so, like an old pod bursting, she scattered the seed of Fabian socialism far and wide across the globe–into alien soil. The cohesion hoped for with her former dependencies withered away, and the vision of Britain as the open heart of a worldwide multi-racial community of nations died. Even in its home soil the Fabian seed, come to maturity in the welfare state, bore bitter fruit. With her people set one against the other in pursuit of their own national interest, without international role or national purpose,

240

Britain's ancient heritage and illustrious institutions–even her Parliament–were in jeopardy . . . Now read on:

As in America so in Britain the unreachable goals set in the post-war years have been abandoned: America will not reform the world: Britain will not maintain a separate role as leader of a worldwide association of nations. And while America, in pursuance of her goals, was torn apart by the Vietnam War, Britain, in pursuance of hers, was confused and debilitated by indecision over membership in the Common Market. The referendum in June, 1975–the first ever held in Britain–finally ended the indecision. Britain's future role in the world as a member of the European Community was thereby fixed, and the prospect of European solidarity was substantially strengthened.

Through the centuries the continental Europeans had noted the insularity of the Briton, and had wondered all along whether he really wanted to be one of them. Their doubt continued even after Britain, under a Conservative Government, joined the Common Market at the beginning of 1973: and their suspicion that this was a move which did not reflect a national sentiment was reinforced as Mr. Wilson–returned to power–pressed for renegotiation of Britain's terms of entry, and as the resistance of workers and trade unions to membership steadily increased. However, after the overwhelming vote in favor of Europe, membership could no longer be seen as the wish only of a Government or of a Parliament: it was the unequivocally declared choice of the people.

Britain's decision for Europe ended the long and distracting aspiration for an independent role in the world. That was important progress. But by the mid-1970s there were still no signs of a return of national purpose: on the contrary there was widespread cynicism concerning the ability of traditional institutions and even the Parliament at Westminster to cure the nation's ills . . . and the very heart of Fabian socialism was under attack–that is, "social justice", or the organised sharing among its members of the community's material wealth. The argument advanced against it (by men like Peregrine Worsthorne) is of cardinal importance, since the achieving of social justice has been the mainspring of political thought and action in the past generation in Britain and innumerable other countries. The argument goes like this:

Social Justice

In a politically competitive system the elevation of the concept of social justice to a position of overriding priority cannot produce contentment and co-operation but only resentment and conflict. This is demonstrated by Britain's experience. Despite the remarkable advance of social justice in Britain in the past half-century, the rhetoric of contempt at the abuses of capitalism is no less passionate than it was in the bad old days, while trade union militancy has not been mitigated but aggravated. The explanation (it is said by critics such as Mr. Worsthorne) is to be found in human nature: the more people get, the more they want; and as the gap between what working people can earn and what the bosses can earn is narrowed, this must be expected to increase rather than decrease the incidence of envy and resentment felt by the former for the latter. Envy grows greater the nearer it approaches its target: relatively few envy the Queen in her Palace nearly so much as they envy the family next door with just that bit extra.

Also, the aim of democratic socialism was, is and always must be to draw attention to existing grievances–since only by doing that can it hope to win. In party political competition for power the most effective means of achieving it today is to suggest that social justice, far from having been achieved, is being flagrantly flouted. Opposition parties have a vested interest in propagating discontent; and this is the manner in which a free political system inevitably operates in societies where the ideal of social justice has taken hold of the popular imagination. Thus, whatever advantages may flow from elevating the ideal of social justice to the main political value, increased social contentment is not likely to be among them.

This diagnosis is relevant to any country where today a party political system operates: and the fact is that the justice of the socialists is a Marxist proposition. Marx expounded the idea that the material environment is the ultimate determinant of all else, and that the real world is the one governed by the necessity to eat, drink, have clothes and shelter–an idea which more recently has been given Christian sanction by the Social Gospel. It is simply not true: however important a decent material environment may be–and is–the real satisfactions in life lie elsewhere. Britain's present experience is proved, conversely as it were, by South Africa's experience. The Afrikaners achieved their fulfillment as a community and their satisfaction as individuals by contributing in the first place–each and virtually every one of them–to the realisation of their national aspirations. In the process many of them in those days eschewed material advantage. The inspiration and excitement of establishing and enriching their language and culture mitigated personal grievance and evoked a remarkable sense of community and *esprit de corps,* often among individuals widely disparate in status, influence, and wealth. The truth surely is that the satisfaction to be had from acquiring the means for purchasing food, drink, clothes and shelter is, at best, second-best: in societies.which have advanced beyond the most primitive state this is the residue, the tawdry remnant, that remains to the individual when the drive for corporate achievement in the innumerable non-material areas of human endeavour has been exhausted.

Mr. Wilson's Resignation

And while the core-concept of Fabianism was found through three decades of experience to have escalated social discontent, the intolerable cost of the welfare state was being acknowledged even in the top echelons of the Labour Party. A White Paper which was published in February, 1976 conceded that welfare programmes were breaking Britain, and announced sensational cuts in public spending amounting to some £3,000 million. The economic implications of Fabianism could no longer be rationalized away. In the previous three years the nation's gross output had risen less than 2 per cent while public expenditure had jumped by close on ten times that figure. Average tax was now 41 per cent of income: and in comment on the White Paper, Chancellor of the Exchequer Denis Healey explicitly exploded the hallowed notion that milching the rich is the way to a general human happiness. In an historic reversal of Fabian priorities, he declared that without cuts in public spending and incentives to private industry, taxes would have to be increased to the point where they would corrode the will to work throughout the country. Britain could not go on consuming wealth until her industries produced it first: "if we want to regenerate manufacturing industry we must leave enough resources free from public expenditure."

The White Paper was attacked from all quarters. Representatives of industry described Mr. Healey's proposals–sweeping though they were–as too little too late. The Conservative Shadow Chancellor called them "a devastating admission of the Government's huge mistakes in the past." For a spokesman of the Liberal Party it was "the price of years of debauchery conducted on tick." For the Labour Party's ideological left-wingers the White Paper was a betrayal of socialism, "a document of shame." In the Commons when the proposals came up for discussion, they rebelled: the Government was defeated; and within days Mr. Wilson announced his decision to retire.

Mr. Wilson had been a member of that Parliament which 30 years before had begun the quiet Fabian revolution. Still in his late twenties he was handsome, brilliant, ambitious. At the age of ten he had told friends that one day he would be Prime Minister: at the age of 24 he was a lecturer in economics at Oxford. In politics he was soon to prove himself a cutting orator, a superb parliamentarian and a peerless tactician. His admirers looked to him to consolidate and perfect the welfare state.

Kingsley Martin, editor of the Fabian journal, the *New Statesman,* wrote of Mr. Wilson when first he became Prime Minister: "He seemed to speak for England. Nobody dared contradict him. He had enormous prestige, enormous power. He invented a new image of technocratic socialism."

But what was the verdict of events? In the 12 years prior ·to his resignation–during eight of which he headed the Government–Britain fell from any semblance of greatness, her reputation in the world was battered, the economy stagnated (with the value of the pound falling to an all-time low), her sense of national purpose was lost, and political power moved progressively from Parliament to the communist-infiltrated trade unions. That was the culminating yield, under Mr. Wilson's leadership, of 30 yeras of Fabianism . . . and yet it would appear to have caused him little concern. In his farewell remarks from 10 Downing Street he said that on looking back on his eight years as Prime Minister he had only two causes for regret–his inability to resolve the conflicts in Rhodesia and Ulster. It was a remarkable statement because serious though the Rhodesia and Ulster situations were, the scene of his overwhelming failure–of his "huge mistakes"–was Britain herself. If his predecessors presided over the liquidation of the British Empire, it was Mr. Wilson who presided over the disintegration of the British economy and political system; but this supreme fact of his performance as Prime Minister he appeared not to recognise.

As Mr. Callaghan assumed his reponsibilities, the burning question was whether this blind spot would be removed from the eye of the new leadership of the Labour Party: whether, if it was not, the Labour Party would be resolved: whether Britain would understand that the alternative to free enterprise in Western society is not Fabian socialism but only totalitarian communism. If there were such understanding, then the recovery of Britain as a member of the European Community could begin . . .

Stop that utilitarian bandwagon, that trackless tram, to utopia: we want to get off! The Western world must: will Britain? With her place in the world now settled, with the end of the disastrous post-war chapter in her domestic politics signalled by Mr. Wilson's departure, she may well do so. She has often in the past led the West. Can she now, forgetting Bentham and Marx, strike a balance between the capitalist exploitation and labour blackmail? She has the genius–and as much experience of each as any other.

The Third World

This part of the picture so far: The United Nations, designed in 1945 as the custodian of world peace, was based on the principle of non-interference in the internal affairs of member states. By tolerating through some three decades the violation of this principle in respect to Pretoria, the Western countries opened the way to the attack on themselves by the Third World. Whatever the subject at issue—even the environment, population control or food—it was exploited for their own purposes by the Third World–communist coalition and used to lash the West. By the end of 1974 Peking was saying that "the new majority" had written a brilliant chapter and was "sweeping ahead with full sail" . . . Now read on:

It was in 1968 that George Ball wrote that the developing nations should not be treated as though their political and economic idiosyncrasies had a large impact on the balance of world power. In the event they continued to be so treated; and by 1975 their idiosyncrasies had degenerated into ugly farce. "Theatre of the Absurd" was how Patrick Moynihan described the General Assembly: and while US Ambassador at Turtle Bay in 1975 he, as no man before him, cut away the illusions that surrounded the world body, diagnosed the condition of the Third World, and fearlessly advocated corrective measures. His Third World diagnosis centred on what he termed the British Revolution: on the spreading to all quarters of the globe of the principles of Fabian socialism by those countless young students from the British colonies who had streamed to the Motherland in the period between the two world wars. Non-British colonies were also influenced by Fabianism; and it was this that shaped the collective attitude of the less-developed countries (the LDCs) as they came to dominate the General Assembly. The precepts of a social doctrine developed for the conditions of Britain were converted directly by the Third World to its own purposes. The idea of independence from autocratic and aristocratic rule, the Third World converted in the post-war years to a demand for independence from colonial masters: they converted the socialist opposition to discrimination based on class, to opposition to discrimination based on race; and as the socialists claimed that the workers had been exploited by the capitalist class in Britain, so the Third World claimed they had been exploited by the capitalist nations of the West. And with the socialists they came to demand as a right a share in the wealth of others.

There were those among them (wrote Moynihan) who saw the future

245

not just in terms of redistribution but of something ominously close to looting: the past was by no means to be judged over and done with: there were scores to be settled, nationally and internationally . . . And what had America's reaction been? "We go about dazed that the world has changed. We toy with the idea of stopping it and getting off. We rebound with the thought that if only we are more reasonable perhaps 'they' will be. But 'they' do not grow reasonable." In Washington three decades of habit had created patterns of appeasement so profound as to seem wholly normal. It was time that the LDCs were informed (Moynihan maintained) that growth was not governed by Western or American conspiracies but by its own laws, and that it was not an egalitarian process. "Those nations which have put liberty ahead of equality have ended up doing better by equality than those with the reverse priority", he wrote. "It is something to be shouted to the heavens in the years now upon us. *This is our case. We are of the liberty party,* and it might surprise us what energies might be released were we to unfurl those banners."

What an explosion of ideas! And whatever Moynihan may do in future, he added in 1975 a new and permanent dimension to an understanding of this confrontation between the Third World and the First Worlds. It explains why capitalist America (exploitation) and apartheid Pretoria (discrimination) are main targets of the Third World–communist coalition. It explains not only the loud-mouthed self-righteousness of the LDCs, but also the guilt complex of the First World and its pandering to them. That is the nub of the whole problem–the West's guilt complex: but what justification is there for it?

The West's Guilt Complex

I have dealt earlier with Pretoria's rejection of imperialism and colonialism. However, it remains a matter of fact that the benefits which the colonial powers won from their colonies were well-matched by the benefits they bestowed on them. It is true that they could have done much more to develop their dependencies economically–but without their coming there would have been no development at all. Socially, the colonies were provided with education and medical and other services which they would not otherwise have known. Politically they were given modern administrations and the idea of an independent judiciary and democratic government (whether or not–*not* it proved to be–they chose to adopt them). It is, of course, a fact that there would have been no population problem in the LDCs today had it not been for the coming of the white man and his technology: frequent death in infancy, short life,

246

disease, pests, drought, flood, famine and internecine strife would have maintained the balance as in countless ages past.

Moreover, the justification of the joint Third World–communist attack on the First World is belied by conditions within their own ranks. Among them are nations with thrusting economies (such as Brazil and Singapore); others, notably those with oil, as rich as any. Discrepancies are enormous. Saudi Arabia, with a population of 5.7-million, had reserves in 1974 of 29-billion dollars and a *per capita* income above 5,000 dollars: India, with 100 times the population, had reserves of 1.3-billion dollars and a *per capita* income of less than 200 dollars. Within individual LDCs there is gross imbalance of wealth, with most of it in most cases in the pockets of cliques who by hook or crook gain control of the levers of power. The communists pretend to be the champions of the LDCs and often lead the attack on the Western nations: yet in 1973 the Western world gave 12-billion dollars of foreign aid to the LDCs, compared with the communists' 1.4-billion dollars. The Arab states pretend to be friends of the LDCs: yet the increase they have made in the price of oil has added to their burden 10-billion dollars a year–wiping out virtually all the foreign aid they receive.

There is no good cause for the West's guilt complex: and the first step in correcting the present absurd situation is that it should be shed, and that the West should re-examine its relationship with the LDCs in objective terms. Whatever the position elsewhere may be, in the area of technology the West is incomparably superior to them: and it is technology–the means for converting raw materials and other resources into wealth–that is the real heart of this issue. The West has established its technology through its own ingenuity and effort, and this certainly is no cause for shame either. In the key and crucial area the West is indispensable, and it should act accordingly. A cringing posture, as though it were an offence to be ingenious, progressive and prosperous, invites a crooked deal. It is time for the West to stand upright for its own rights and achievements, and from that stance to devise a square deal for others.

So much for the general psychology of the matter. Among the specifics that need to be driven home are these: that there is *not* a limitless amount of wealth to be redistributed, and that the prosperity of the Third World, no less than of the First, depends on its ability to *produce* its own: that whatever its other virtues, British socialism has failed as a producer of wealth–even in the country of its origin: and that development rests in the final resort, not on aid given by others, but on own-exertion–in ingenuity, organisation, conservation and *work*. These are the things that Moynihan was saying in 1975–but there is a question-mark behind his final conclusion: namely, that America's contribution to righting the world situation is to "unfurl its banners as the liberty party"; and that,

247

whereas in the United Nations it is possible to deal with the Soviet Union and the Chinese only as separate political communities, it is possible to participate with the LDCs as in a single political community. This postulates a similarity of ideas concerning liberty in the First and Third Worlds which does not exist–and should not exist. Liberty is a highly subjective commodity. Its espousal in recent times in the West has led to license, anarchy and degradation; and the ideas of liberty of others may be a good bit more healthy for them than ours are. Moynihan's ideas of liberty are no more indigenous in Zaire than are the Fabians' of socialism. Let us forget all ideological prescriptions; allow all people to live according to their own lights, and co-operate with them on the basis of objective and demonstrable common interest–with all of them, not only the Russians and the Chinese, as separate political communities.

A Non-Democratic World

The United Nations is at the centre of this consideration: even more than the Westminster model, it is an example of the prime illusion of the post-war years that others are able to co-operate effectively in institutions which do not correspond in origin, tradition, nature or design with their own. The United Nations was designed upon Western concepts of liberty and Western concepts of decision-making–more particularly, decision-making by majority vote. It is the ultimate paradox that, whereas the LDCs in their own communities reject (except as a means for unseating white 'governments) the principle of one-man-one-vote, they demand (and distort because they have not the faintest comprehension of democracy's ground rules) the principle of one-state-one-vote in the General Assembly.

This is not a democratic world: it is not a world of Western civil liberties: attempts by America in particular to make it one have been a hopeless failure: it is not likely to be one in the foreseeable future, or perhaps ever. It is these illusions, embodied in the United Nations, that have precipitated the present farcical world situation. There is no possibility of ordering international affairs through majority vote in global organisations. Let us forget it. The unit of order must relate inter-state relations to real considerations. That unit is the regional grouping where ties are those of common resources, common problems, common technological requirements and common economic advantage. Here is the theatre of co-operation, whatever the ideological costume of the players: and here, where real interest cuts across ideology, the basic building brick for a workable world system of consultation and collaboration. A world order of this kind will not come into being through conferences or resolutions or declarations. It will be an organic process. The regions, as their co-operation consolidates (in the EEC in the northern hemisphere, in Southern Africa in the southern, and in many other parts of the globe) will begin talking to one another, again in their mutual interest; and the United Nations will be outflanked, isolated and become redundant.

Having regained its self-respect *vis-a-vis* the rest of the world and acted accordingly, the course of Western statesmanship should be to anticipate and assist this indicated movement of History.

CHAPTER FIFTEEN / NOW
Ethnicity *

The Spirit of Community

This part of the picture so far: "Ethnicity" was a word seldom heard in the quarter-century that followed the War: and when it was heard it evoked a hostile response. It was rejected as archaic, as harking back to primitive bonds between people which had been out-dated by the conditions of the modern world. Within states it was regarded as a hindrance to national unity and in the world at large as a threat to a universal brotherhood. Opposing foursquare the idea of the common, undifferentiated man it, of all things, called forth the scorn of the pseudo-liberals . . . Now read on:

A characteristic of the condition of the Western world in recent times has been inattention and often active antagonism to an environment suited to the expression of the spirit of community. Post-war, the State was denigrated–and, in any case, the modern, centralised State is too complex and impersonal to constitute such an environment: the concept of a world society that was propagated was too diffuse to provide one; and the cult of the individual that took hold of Western countries was its mortal enemy. The net result has been a loss of fellowship, a fragmentation of society and the kind of cultural confusion we have been looking at in the last few pages in the United States and Britain. It is in this context that "ethnicity" had all at once become a term of moment in the world's political vocabulary. It features today in articles in prestige publications, in sociological expositions, at international seminars, and in editorial comment and radio debate in many lands. There is this sudden appreciation abroad today of the importance of ethnicity: a recogntiion of the significance of those very factors in human relations and social

---

* A new world concept, a new chapter heading and a key-piece for our puzzle.

organisation that were engaging Pretoria's attention when it stood at the cross-roads 30 years ago.

Paradoxically, it was that great champion of One World and cosmopolitanism–the United Nations–which organised the first international conference on the subject: that is, the subject of protecting the rights, culture and characteristics of communities large and small against submergence by states or any other agency. It was a remarkable occasion in many respects, and these are some of them: The conference was held, upon the recommendation of the UN Economic and Social Council and Commission on Human Rights, in Ljubljana, Yugoslavia, during June, 1965. Invitations were sent to member states with first-hand experience of multi-national and multi-ethnic populations, and they numbered 28. The purpose of the conference was to recommend measures which should be taken by all states "to ensure the realisation by ethnic, religious, linguistic or national groups of the special rights necessary to enable them to preserve their tradition, characteristics or national consciousness." And the measures that were recommended were: the right to use the language of the group in everyday life, in courts of law, and in public or assembly; the right to association; the right to establish autonomous educational institutions; the right to develop their own characteristics and traditions autonomously; and the right to equal economic treatment. At the conclusion of the conference, the consensus reached was formulated in the following terms: "There was general agreement that all Governments should promote and protect the rights of ethnic, religious, linguistic or national groups, not only through the adoption of constitutional and legislative provisions, but also through the promotion of all forms of activity consistent with the political, economic and social conditions of the State or country concerned."

There it was: nothing could have been more clearly stated: though it would seem that the United Nations subsequently lost sight of these unambiguous recommendations in its consideration of South West Africa and a variety of other ethnically-centred disputes. Lujbljana was something of a freak flash in the pan: these were, in any case, early days in the emergence to world prominence of ethnicity. Indeed, it was in the year of the Ljubljana conference that historian Arnold Toynbee was castigating the existence of groups of people based on kith and kin as immoral and odious. But by the end of the decade there was a widening realisation that the expression of ethnicity was not some localised, atavistic oddity but a worldwide force undoing basic current concepts about the organisation of modern society. In 1969 Philip Mason, head of the British Institute of Race Relations, discussed the subject in the Institute's journal *Race Today*. He pointed to the resurgence of the ethnic sentiment in Europe, Africa and America. In Europe, he wrote, "there begins to assert itself a regional separatism that seemed a thing of the past. Today, Welsh,

Bretons and Basques alike insist on an identity of their own, and they talk of autonomy." Of Africa, he declared that when independence came the concept of the nation had in most of the colonies "only recently been imposed on congeries of tribes." And the idea that tribalism was old-fashioned and something to be ashamed of had only just caught hold among the educated. Today in Africa tribalism no longer seemed outdated, and it was the nation that survived precariously. Writing of America, Mr. Mason observed that the black men there sought to rise in the world without giving up what was essentially black. They wanted a self-sufficient and autonomous society divided from the white–what this expert on race relations called a regional society.

All the relevant pieces in our jig-saw that we have been moving about and trying to find a place for were suddenly coming together in a new world outlook on human relations. Historian M. K. Sorrenson wrote in the same year–1969–that the Maoris in New Zealand were searching for a sense of identity which they called Maoritanga, and which was expressed in their Ratana religion and through a variety of Maori organisations. New Zealand, like Canada, would remain a nation with two peoples and would be none the worse for the experience. Various authorities were at this time putting forward explanations for the ethnicity phenomenon, and there was wide agreement that it was primarily a reaction to the stifling uniformity of the technological age. Dr. Desmond Morris discussed the matter in his book, *The Human Zoo.* He argued that man was biologically ill-equipped to cope with the social hazards of the vast, impersonal complex community–of the city which caged him in, the human zoo; and that many of man's cultural enterprises could best be interpreted as attempts to re-create a pseudo-tribal condition which provided those who belonged to it with a sense of assurance and security. Marshall McLuhan declared bluntly: "We are re-tribalising"; and Peter Evans predicted in *The Times,* London, that the 1970s would be the decade of what he called "international tribal man."

In the event, in the 1970s, attention to the demands of community rapidly expanded. In Britain there were already the claims of the historic national groups such as the Welsh: but what of the new immigrant communities? In his book, *The Unmelting Pot,* Mr. John Brown–warden of the Cranfield Institute of Technology–dealt exhaustively with the subject, based on a survey of the condition of Bedford's multi-ethnic population. Bedford, an industrial town some 50 miles north of London, had attracted in recent years a variety of immigrants–including Italians, Indians, West Indians, Pakistanis and Poles. The author expressed the view that these communities of people–whatever their colour–had the same underlying motivation: the guiding aspiration of each was the preservation of their culture and identity. Towards this end, they established their own organisations, clubs and schools; they made their own communities with only limited reference to local society, and they had virtually no contact with other immigrant groups. It was the black man, in Mr. Brown's judgment, who faced the deepest dilemma: having lost contact on the colonial plantations with his own customs, he lacked "the sense of being" of the Indian; and his lack was much more hurtful to him than overt discrimination. He was condemned to aspire where he was rarely allowed to belong: to remain dependent on the British way of life and yet to be not fully part of it. Mr. Brown concluded that these immigrant communities wanted to fit into the structure of British society but not into its modes of consciousness. They wanted to belong in terms of organisation though not in terms of being. To belong in the full human sense would mean in effect to forfeit themselves. For this reason, the concept of integration was rarely found on immigrants' lips: most of them left the notion, with a certain smile, to community-relations officials.

In 1975 the quarterly journal of the United States Information Service, *Dialogue,* published an article entitled *The Quest for Community* by Professor Nisbet (author of *The Twilight of Authority,* already quoted). Discussing the current disillusionment with political utopias, he wrote that as recently as the 1930s there were few if any discernible impulses which could have been categorised as being consciously related to community–or to negative preoccupation with alienation, self-estrangement and the social void. Overwhelmingly then the perceived problems were economic and political, and so were the solutions. Disillusionment with the political community, with what was then called "planned economy", or with socialism on the national and international scale, had not yet set in. Only a few foresaw that the very accomplishment of then-cherished political and economic goals would bring in its wake problems of bureaucratisation of mind as well as function, of collective power wielded despotically, and of an unravelling of the social fabric. But since the 1930s a variety of forces, including widespread affluence in the Western world, had had the effect of individualising and atomising the community. However kinship, religion and neighbourhood continued to be, after countless thousands of years, evocative themes for human beings everywhere in the world. Not even the most powerful impacts of technology and industry had altered the roots of these ancient loyalties– nor had democracy, nationalism, socialism or any of the other great political forces of the modern world. In all these circumstances the ideal political state today was one which, without abandoning its responsibilities of power, allowed a pluralism of functions and loyalties in the lives of its people. "It is a state that seeks to diversify and decentralise its own administrative operations, encouraging forms of spontaneous association which are the outgrowth of human needs and desires. Such a state seeks cultural diversity, not uniformity. It recognises that the claims of freedom and cultural autonomy will require that its citizens have a sense

253

of membership in the meaningful relationships of kinship, religion, occupation and locality. Only this kind of state will be diverse enough to include the multiplicity of values of civilisation, and durable enough to withstand passing winds of ideology and doctrine."

In his *The Twilight of Authority* (1975) Professor Nisbet points to the threat of the egalitarian ideal to the spirit of community, and to its contribution thus to despotism: by enhancing the centralised power's levelling effect on the natural hierarchies of all social institutions, it makes the new despotism possible. Chief engineers of the despotism are the philosophers and men of letters without whom the idea of equality could never have gained its prominence nor the state its power. The great error was to subordinate the diverse interests of the individual, of groups, estates and classes to the interests of the whole. The inexorable growth in these conditions of the sovereignty of the state in turn "manufactured" individualism–and both the state and individualism are equally destructive of the social bond which is created by such intermediary institutions as property, family, local community, religion and voluntary association. The modern state, instead of attending to its two great historical functions–the maintenance of order and the defence of the nation–has usurped the power of all these institutions. Accordingly, the restoration of authority and the renewal of the social bond can come only through a revival of social and economic pluralism, a renaissance of kinship and a rebirth of localism. And since inequality is the essence of the social bond, social hierarchy together with tradition urgently needs reinstating.

Professor Nisbet's is one of many similar voices in America today. Commenting on *The Twilight of Authority,* Gerturde Lenzer of Brooklyn College wrote in the *New York Times Book Review:* "The notion of equality has lost its exalted position and has suffered what amounts to a loss of status as a value. Nisbet is only one among a large chorus of intellectuals who characterise the idea of equality as a dangerous social egalitarianism." It is a remarkable development: until yesteryear the notion of equality dominated the political thinking of the West: Americans in particular saw it as a main pillar of their own democratic society and as a prerequisite for just societies around the world.

Also in 1975, in February, the prestigious British journal, *Encounter,* published a section devoted to *The Ethnic Revolution* and including an article by Professor Nathan Glazer of Harvard, *The Universalisation of Ethnicity.* The author described ethnicity as referring to a vertical division of society, as opposed to class which referred to a horizontal division (the very distinction that was being advanced by Pretoria in 1948 in explanation of separatism). The individual could move from one class to another, but characteristic of the ethnic stock was that it remained immutable: and around the world the terminal loyalty of people had shifted from the state to the ethnic group. Economic forces were

254

contributing to the heterogeneity of populations and thus to the ethnic revolution. West Germany, Switzerland and France employed millions of foreign workers, and more and more they brought their wives and families with them. England had seen a substantial migration from the West Indies, Pakistan and India; and "as England struggles with its own colour problem, France wonders about the 'integration' of Algerians, and Germany considers how to educate the children of Turks and Yugoslavs." Increasingly, states were becoming multi-ethnic: because of the heavy international movements of labour; because of the universal commitment in the emancipated states against the altering of artificial colonial boundaries, and because of the re-emergence of old ethnic sentiments in old states and the creation of new ones in new states. Professor Glazer maintained that neither the drive of the past towards assimilation, nor the subordination of certain groups called "inferior," could survive long in the contemporary world. He suggested as the answer to multi-ethnicity the guaranteeing in each country of group rights; and concluded: "In a world in which the arrant nonsense of Marxism competed with the tepid confusions of liberalism, the problems of ethnicity, as a source of conflict with nations and between nations, have generally appeared as simply a left-over, an embarrassment from the past. It is my conviction that they must now be placed at the very centre of our concern for the human condition."

Soon after its publication, Professor Glazer's article was the subject of a BBC discussion in which Dr. Philip Burnham, of University College, London, and Dr. A. H. Halsey, of Nuffield College, Oxford, took part. Both rejected the supposition that ethnic differences could be submerged in shared loyalty to political states. Dr. Burnham observed that in the United States the "melting pot" theory was now seen as "utopian in the extreme", and that even small groups were able to assert their desire for "an equal possibility of having their own ways as opposed to some other group's ways." As for Africa, he said: "In the first flush of independence there was quite a long shelf of books written on the subject of building nations, of unifying political philosophies and playing down the notion of tribalism or ethnicity. Later they realised that these ethnic differences were permanent facts on the scene—not something that was going to be able to be swept under the table—and that politics was going to be rephrased in their terms for many years to come." Dr. Halsey spoke of the emergence of ethnicity out of political organisations—states—that were previously separate. "If you think of the Welsh in relation to the English, then that's the kind of thing that often makes appeals to separatism—to different languages and heritages that have been somewhat submerged by the nationalisms of the past." And he defined the contemporary problem as the need to reconcile with democracy the idea that some people, in order to be equal, must be treated differently.

And whereas a generation ago the differentiated treatment of its communities by a state was regarded as contrary to all enlightenment, it is now regarded–in the United States–as a major, a "transcendental", goal of government policy. This is explicit in an article (also published in *Dialogue*) dealing with the American Indian, entitled *Assimilation versus Separatism*, and written by Carl N. Degler, Professor of American History at Stanford University and winner in 1972 of the Pulitzer Prize for History. He wrote that whenever the Indians had been able to express their preference, they had made it clear that they did not want to be integrated into American society. It was time for other Americans to give up, once and for all, the expectation that somehow the Indians in general would be absorbed. On the contrary, starting from what they were now, they ought to be helped to work out a way of life for themselves as separate communities within the larger American society. To accept Indianness as a social fact and as part of American pluralism was but to acknowledge the debt that was incurred when one culture encountered another and pushed it aside. In short, in recognising what the past revealed about Indians and their culture, "we are in a position to transcend our own history, and to understand that most Indians want to remain Indians and not to become white men with red skins. If that policy can be carried out, the United States will have embarked on an experiment in pluralism rare in the history of European expansion. Few modern governments have undertaken to protect and nurture a technologically weaker culture for the indefinite future." . . . In fact, I know of only one–Pretoria. It has staked its very existence on this policy, and in carrying it through has had to deal not only with the immense problems which are involved at home, but with hostility and abuse from all parts of the world, including the United States.

Pretoria, 1968: The age which led to the centralisation of power within European nations and its extension to the furthest reaches of the earth is ending. Decolonisation is an aspect of it; but even more significant in the remainder of this century will be the wider dispersal of authority within the developed regions of the world. Centralisation of power was a concomitant of the new organisation of the industrial age. It contributed to the common purpose, efficiency and disposition of effort that were essential to the technological achievements of modern times. But communities were regimentalised and personality repressed. Now personality, fearing extinction, is in revolt. Science and machines have spread modern culture amorphously across nations and around the globe, and suffocation is setting in. People are demanding air of their own to breathe, and the decades ahead will be marked by localising and regionalising processes. In practice this is going to mean the creation of more and smaller units of political autonomy and of fewer but greater areas of economic co-operation. Unity is about to be replaced by association as the desirable relationship between different peoples in the modern age. (27)

Power-Sharing

Closely related to ethnicity is "power-sharing": that is, the prescriptive division of political power and the allotting of a part of it to each community in a mixed population, as a means of bringing justice to each and harmony to the whole. The crises in Ulster and Cyprus in the 1970s directed world attention to the issue: but the classic case is India.

Following the War, in 1946, Westminster drew up a plan for an all-India Government including six representatives of the Hindu Congress and five of the Muslim League: but with the scent of sovereignty in the air, Hindu and Muslim vied furiously not for a part but for all of it. The Congress Party called for democracy, one-man-one-vote and majority rule because, having the numerical preponderance, they knew that the whole prize would then be theirs. The League called for Pakistan, because they knew that without that they would have none of the prize. The inter-communal central Government became the focus of dissension which degenerated into violence, bloodshed and massacre. The power-sharing administration broke down, anarchy took over, and Britain conceded that partition was the only solution. But it had been too long delayed: terrible hatreds had developed; and when it finally came, it was followed by cataclysmic deprivation and slaughter involving millions. Moreover it was to be discovered that power-sharing failed not only between Hindus and Muslims but between different communities on either side of the great divide. In the Indian states, further partitioning was necessary in an endeavour to provide areas of security for various cultural and linguistic groups–Tamil, Gujarat, Nada, and so on. In West Pakistan there was rivalry between Pathans, Punjabis and Sindhis; and between the western and eastern parts of the state, the critical divergence of interests which culminated in war and the secession of Bangladesh.

The tragic saga of Ulster goes back centuries: and here, too, at the centre of the trouble are religious, cultural and ethnic differences. The eruption which came after World War I reached terrifying proportions, and partition was resorted to: the 26 southern counties became independent as Eire; the six northern counties remained under the British Crown as Ulster. But in Ulster (as in Pakistan) partition did not solve the problem, because a large minority of Catholics (1:2) remained within its borders. For half a century the superior power–Britain–managed to keep an uneasy peace, but there was no fusing of the two communities. Each guarded its own culture with granite steadfastness; and as Britain's power

257

and determination to go on carrying the Irish burden diminished, the peace was shattered. In November, 1973 the British Government made a bid to end the horror that ensued by power-sharing. A Ministry of 11, consisting of six Protestants, four Catholics and a non-aligned member, was installed. The members of the Government themselves appear to have made a valiant and successful attempt to work together. But the mass of the Protestant community wanted nothing of power-sharing: like the Hindu Congress they called for majority rule, because this hallowed democratic principle would enable them (as it had done in the past) to run the country their own way without minority interference. When their demand was rejected, a devastating strike was instituted; the power-sharing Government was disbanded, and direct rule by Westminster was reimposed.

As in Ulster, so in Cyprus, the decline of the superior authority–Britain–precipitated the trouble. Following a campaign of violence and terrorism in the 1950s, an independence constitution was agreed upon in 1959 in a document signed by the Prime Ministers of Britain, Greece and Turkey "setting out the agreed foundation for the final settlement of the Cyprus problem." It was squarely based on power-sharing between the two communities. The President was to be a Greek Cypriot, the Vice President a Turkish Cypriot. The armed forces and the police were to be controlled by the common consent of these two men. The Legislature was to be divided 70-30 between representatives of the Greek and Turkish communities. There was to be a supreme constitutional court under a neutral judge; and, at a lower level, separate chambers to deal with the social and religious affairs of each community. In theory there could have been no more delicate system of checks and balances than the constitution provided: but no sooner was it in operation than the structure began to collapse. The Vice President vetoed a proposal for the integration of the armed forces: the Turkish legislators withheld approval of taxation measures: and these and other conflicts, the neutral court was not able to resolve. Already by 1964 a United Nations peace-keeping force had to be introduced: and ten years later Turkey invaded to ensure power of their own for its countrymen on the island. Indescribable bitterness was generated: and the failure of power-sharing reached out far beyond the borders of Cyprus. It brought two members of the Western alliance–Greece and Turkey–into confrontation; led to Greece's withdrawal from military participation in NATO, and tore a gaping breach in the Organisation's southern flank.

What are the lessons to be learnt from such experience? It would appear that a power-sharing formula can work only when there is a superior authority to ensure that its terms are respected and that competition for power in a single, multi-ethnic state is an invitation to communal strife. The issue was summed up by the British author and journalist H. V. Hodson, writing in *The Times* in July, 1974. He said that Britain's power-sharing formula for India failed because "fundamentally it could not solve the conundrum of transferring democratic power without putting the minority group, in the last resort, permanently under the rule of the majority group." In Ulster, as in India in 1945–47, "tension grows, community animosity intensifies, political forces polarise, government authority is flouted and the army has to be called to the aid of the civil power." But for Mr. Hodson, "Cyprus provides the outstanding example of mandatory power-sharing between two communities–attempted, tried in the fire and found wanting." And he asked: "Should we not recognise now that mandatory power-sharing and democratic majority rule are incompatible aims?"

Mandatory power-sharing has been proved to be a certain formula for conflict: the experience of Afrikaner and Anglosan in South Africa indicates the one condition in which voluntary power-sharing–or, more correctly, power-pooling–can work. It is a practical proposition only when it is based on the free and constitutionally unfettered consent of each of the communities concerned, *and where there is a general, absolute and unqualified recognition of the right of each to its own way of life.* In the Republic's constitution there is no stipulation as to how power should be shared between Afrikaner and Anglosan. Constitutionally the entire Executive could be (and has been) composed of members belonging to one community–and the same applies to the Legislature and the Judiciary. The two communities pool their power voluntarily because it is their mutual interest to do so, and because the indispensable principle italicised above is enshrined in the country's political philosophy.

The Anglo-Afrikaner experience is most eloquent testimony to the overriding political significance of community, culture and identity. In the constitution of 1910 the Afrikaner was given political power, but he was dissatisfied and rejected the dispensation because it did not provide security for his community: its objective was a fused South Africanism. For the past three decades the Anglosans have had no political power worth speaking of, but they are reasonably contented and accept the dispensation because the security of their community and culture is in no way threatened. Allow a man to be himself and he will co-operate with others: try to make him over in the image of someone else and he will resist. This is the truth that Professor Glazer would put today at the very centre of our concern for the human condition.

When, in the early 1960s, Dr. Verwoerd was approached for more funds to expand the country's public relations effort, he observed: "Be patient: we have on our side the most powerful of all PROs–History." And could any PRO have been more persuasive? It has led to the conclusion today in the world at large "that politics must be rephrased in times of ethnicity"; and that power-sharing, without any authority to enforce its terms, is a prescription for communal strife. Pretoria's choice of separatism in 1948 has been totally vindicated by the flow of world events: developments in a variety of countries have proved that there was no possible alternative course to harmony and progress. And it goes further than that: by giving the community the star role in its scenario, Pretoria is providing the world with a working model for bridging the chasm–for striking a balance–between the remote, impersonal State and the atomised individual.

SUMMATION

There are some positive forces working toward a return to equilibrium in leading Western nations, though they are by no means firmly established. More hopeful is the diminishing effect and attraction of the negative ones: of the forces that have caused the disequilibrium in Western society. Surfacing with the industrial revolution and carrying all before them in the post-war era as the means for achieving fulfilment and harmony, they were characterised by the confidence reposed in the machine, in material well-being, in "social justice", in individual liberty, in the franchise and in equalitarianism. The measure of merit in each of these is apparent. However the confidence they enlisted was unlimited: all of Western civilisation's eggs were placed in such baskets: they were given a priority overriding all others: they were apotheosised–and that was the cause of the disequilibrium.

With the aid of the machine the material environment was transformed and creature comforts proliferated. The United States in particular experienced an affluence undreamed of. But today Americans are tiring of affluence. Observers note among many of them a changed attitude towards wealth, prosperity and the ambition to achieve them. Others seek a sense of community in the sharing of austerity; and whatever the causes of the student revolt of the 1960s, a feature of behaviour of the privileged young people involved was a rejection of the symbols of success cherished by their parents.

In Europe it is West Germany that has surpassed all others as a producer of goods and material wealth: but a series of studies completed by the Allensbach Institute for Opinion Research in 1975 revealed that in recent years the German's traditional respect for property has steadily eroded. The Director of the Institute, Professor Elisabeth Noelle-Neumann, commented that there are clear indications that the German people are discovering that money is not happiness: they are demanding instead *ein sinnvolles Leben* (a meaningful life). Meanwhile, the inflation sweeping the entire Western world in the mid-1970s mocks money: the moth and the rust move in with a vengeance.

It was Britain who, through Fabian socialism, endeavoured to devise a formula for making out of affluence the greatest happiness for the greatest number. But her guidestar was reason and her touchstone, material security; and her social justice brought selfishness, envy and despair. A psychiatrist at a Coventry hospital reported in 1975 that the increasing suicide rate was attributable to affluence. Young women in particular who found that marriage and motherhood denied them the "good life" they had known as teenagers with money to burn, believed that life was no longer worth living. But the psychiatrist was not altogether pessimistic: he was hopeful that recession and economic hardship would cause the suicide rate to fall. So much for the issue of security from the cradle to the grave: and today Fabian socialism is being rejected. In 1974 fewer people voted for the Labour Party in Britain than in 1945, although during that period some millions of voters had been added to the electorate. In December, 1975 the socialists were overwhelmed in Australia and New Zealand.

In Britain and the United States democracy is in disrepute: in both countries serious observers consider the possibility of the institution of some kind of totalitarian regime. They see universal suffrage as being manipulated to work inequity and inefficiency and, subjecting the executive authority to a bewildering variety of pressures and curbs, as having disqualified itself in its present form as the basis for just and competent government. There is an awareness that governments must be freed from dependence on self-interest groups organised from among an amorphous mass of voters, and must be inspired by the coherently expressed will of the people: that élites must re-emerge as the custodians and interpreters of that will, and that this can be expected to happen when the sense of community and the accompanying urge to express itself are restored. The social bond must (as Professor Nisbet insists) be re-created by such intermediary institutions as the family and local community. Ethnicity, embracing the organic and traditional community, must (as Professor Glazer insists) be placed today at the very centre of our concern for the human condition.

The forces that have made for imbalance in modern Western society are waning. But so powerful have they been in recent centuries that their retreat has brought confusion and crisis. However in crisis there is promise: the Chinese symbol for crisis is a dual symbol representing both danger and opportunity. There is now the opportunity, the challenge and the necessity, if his culture is to be saved, for Western man to strike a new balance:

As against dependence on reason and science–due acknowledgement of faith and intuition;

As against the dictatorship of material requirements–the primacy of the satisfaction of the needs of the Person;

261

As between the impersonal state and the fragmented individual–the community;

As against the imperative of defending state and territory–the imperative of defending community, and thus personality;

As between totalitarianism and universal suffrage–the re-institution (in Lord Beveridge's term) of "an aristocratic tradition without the aristocrats";

As between (on the one hand) the boundless confidence in his capacity and destiny which lordship over the world gave to Western man and (on the other) the frustration and sense of guilt that accompanied the drastic narrowing of his territorial hegemony–as between these two, a new faith born of the understanding that, despite its aberrations, Western culture has made incomparably the largest contribution to the progress of man, and that it is obliged to continue to do so;

As between (on the one hand) the domination of the Third World by the First in the colonial era and (on the other) the present blackmailing of the First World by the Third–as between these two, a pattern of international intercourse founded in mutual advantage;

As against Western man's extravagant use of natural resources in virgin and dependent lands–the working with care and thrift with those that remain to him and the world at large;

As against the concept of an undifferentiated brotherhood of man–a universal co-operation inspired by recognition of the rich diversity of the manifold households of men.

The expansion which directed the development of Western culture through half a millennium has ended. The agent for the transformation of mankind's lot is no longer the global empire but the local community: the theatre for this is not the world but the region.

Despite the darkness of the present prospect, it is not unreasonable to suppose that a balance will be struck between the extremes that were encompassed, respectively, by the euphoria and then the despair of the post-war Western world. And in the long perspective of history there is another cause for confidence. During the first centuries of the Christian era, Western men eschewed the earth and looked to heaven for happiness. Whether, upon their departure, they found it we do not know. Increasingly, in the latter centuries, Western men eschewed heaven and looked for happiness on earth: but as the 20th century comes to an end we know and they know they have not found it here. A supreme synthesis is now suggested: will not more and more men come to the conclusion of the *Time* essayist that the essential balance now is between a creative awe of the worlds men can only contemplate and a creative concern for the one they live in?

The ultimate prescription for orderliness and harmony I have set aside to be fitted as the last piece into our puzzle. Meantime, South Africa comes in two ways into this part of the picture. First, a social order based on the community–as advocated now by men like Professors Glazer and Nisbet–was legislated for and put into operation in South Africa a generation ago and is now approaching full working order: second, a handy guide to the progress which the Western world may make in the years ahead towards equilibrium will be its attitude to Pretoria: its prejudice towards this country up to now has been as clear a symptom as any of its post-war imbalance and neurosis.

Part three / Section two
NOW

The Pretoria Theme: Co-existence

"A man is more than an individual. He is also a member of a community; and in South Africa we have to find a way of doing justice not only to individuals but also to communities. It may be that political and social thinkers and planners in South Africa have in the past been too rigidly divided between those who thought of individual rights and those who thought of the rights of our different communities and races. Those who find themselves to the Left in 'our political life have often, by directing their minds exclusively to individual rights and duties, virtually abandoned the field of race relations as such to their political opponents on the Right. This was surely a mistake, because racial problems are not likely to be solved simply by urging that we should all behave as though they did not exist. Now, however, it seems to me that we may at last in South Africa be moving towards a new synthesis"–Mr. H. F. Oppenheimer, Chairman of the Anglo American Corporation and staunch supporter throughout of the Progressive Party, October, 1973.

CHAPTER SIXTEEN / NOW
New Vistas

INTERNAL RELATIONS

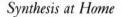

Synthesis at Home

This part of the picture so far: In 1948 the Anglosans (or those who claimed to speak for them) inseparably associated and confused apartheid with the electoral victory in that year of the National Party, with the consolidation of Afrikaner political power, with the move towards a Republic, and with the stereotype of the Afrikaner as intolerant and reactionary. Because of this–in contesting the National Party, Afrikaner power and the Republican ideal–the Anglosan opposition also contested apartheid. They went further: they disowned it. By denying any part in the policy or responsibility for it and by ascribing it to Afrikaner prejudice, they believed they were loading the Government with a burden that would break it. Moreover, in 1948 and for many years afterwards, the weight of international opinion (and particularly British opinion, so close to the heart of Opposition spokesmen) was overwhelmingly in favour of extending undifferentiated democracy to all states wherever they might be and whatever their population composition; and Opposition politicians calculated that by resisting separatism and championing the continuance of a unitary state in South Africa, they would thus enlist outside support . . . Now read on:

The Opposition held to this attitude and hope although it was beaten time and again at the polls. Then, in the 1960s, the flow of events began to bring about a re-evaluation. There was the disenchantment with Britain. The faith of the Anglosans in the good intentions of Britain towards their country died slow–but it died. It began to die when Mr. Macmillan set black Africa against white Africa in his Cape Town speech in 1960: it died more the following year when South Africa, a foundation member and inspiration of the Commonwealth, was forced out: it went on dying with the British Government's refusal to supply Pretoria with the arms needed for the defence of the Cape route. And it was on its back, its legs kicking, when in 1970 the Wilson Government instructed the Cricket Council to withdraw its invitation to the Springbok team. If there was no goodwill or honesty of purpose in the field of sport, where was it to be found? Major Piet van der Bijl, elder statesman of the United Party, had for a generation epitomised admiration in South Africa for British ways: in a national broadcast after the cancellation of the cricket tour he said: "I was a friend of Britain because I thought it was in the interest of my country to stand by an old and staunch friend in dangerous times. Now I am disenchanted." Where the rule of the game was supposed to be sacrosanct, the Anglosan's faith in Britain had been mortally wounded: other ties of convenience would survive, but Britain had finally forfeited her position as mentor and good companion.

In broader international events there was the collapse of democracy in the emergent states: at the same time the determination of all kinds of people to protect their own forms of social organisation and identity revealed itself as a basic and worldwide force. Separatism began to be seen by many previous opponents as moving not against but with-in anticipation of-the flow of contemporary history. At home the Republican goal was reached in May, 1961: with that, the main issue between the two sections of the Anglo-Afrikaner nation was removed, and Anglosans were able to regard separatism freed from its associations with other concerns. The barriers to a return to the traditional consensus on the ideal of a life of their own for the country's different peoples were slowly breaking down during the 1960s. Then came the smashing of the Afrikaner stereotype in the 1970 election.

The way to the synthesis was opening. Each of the Opposition parties-the United Party and the Progressive Party-began adapting its role to the historic separatist scenario (but simultaneously endeavoured to make it appear different from the other's and different also from the governing National Party's). In 1972 the United Party announced what the Johannesburg *Star* called "a radical race plan." Separatism was central to it, its core proposal being the establishment of 15 *community* assemblies-four for the white people (based on the existing four Provinces), eight for the black people (based on the National Party's homelands), two for the coloured people and one for the Indian people. The following year the leader of the United Party, Sir de Villiers Graaff, stated in Parliament that in a unitary system a sharing of authority could well lead to black-white conflict. "What is needed," he said, "is a federal arrangement which will allow the various peoples of the country to participate in the management of their own affairs, to consult with one another about

268

common problems and to ensure to all the universal right to security."
And for the Progressive Party, Dr. Zac de Beer, chairman of its planning
committee, stated in 1972: "Where there is an area of South Africa
which has a certain unique predominant nature which makes it a coherent
whole, then we will move towards establishing that area as a separate and
autonomous (by that I mean something less than independent) province."
The meaning of "a certain unique predominant nature" was amplified by
Dr. de Beer's observation that: "We have to accept, alongside our belief
in the importance of the human being, a realisation that the diversity of
the South African population, that the existence within our population of
groups, is a stubborn fact which cannot be reasoned away ... that the
groups will tend to be exclusive, that they will tend to operate in terms of
their own well-being and in the protection of their own things." This is
the classic argument for separatism as against integration; and Dr. de Beer
himself declared: "It is true that there is a good deal that is positive and
worthwhile in the doctrine of separate development and separate
freedoms . . . there is virtue in engineering the greatest possible decentralisation of forces and bringing about the greatest measure of local
self-government as far as is practically possible." However the Progressive Party held with the United Party that there should be a central
federal legislature for the country as a whole.

But the decisive fact is that both Opposition parties were in retreat
from the concept of a single, unitary South African state; and so were
men such as Mr. Laurence Gandar who through the years as editor of the
Rand Daily Mail had vehemently criticised separatism. In May, 1974 he
wrote: ". . . The net result is that we are all that much closer to finding
one another than we have ever been, and the point of division has been
narrowed down to the specific question of whether a single federal system
or a looser confederal grouping of sovereign independent states best
meets the realities of the South African situation. This is a relatively
refined and intellectually respectable argument." The Johannesburg *Star*
is the largest of the country's English-language dailies, moderate in tone
but no less persistent in its criticism since 1948 of the National Party and
separatism. In November, 1973 it wrote: "Everyone favours a form of
federation or confederation or commonwealth."

Federation, Confederation or Commonwealth?

Both these statements (representing substantial progress by their
authors in their acceptance of the realities of South Africa) are true. It is
no less true that there is a crucial distinction between federation on the
one hand and confederation or commonwealth on the other, which the
lumping together of them as by the *Star* obscures. According to the

269

dictionary: a federation is a union of states *each subject to a central government* but retaining control over its internal affairs; a confederation is a group of states allied for common purposes; a commonwealth is a group of sovereign states associated by their own choice and linked by common objectives and interests. The crucial distinction, thus, is whether or not the constituent states relinquish a part of their sovereignty to a central government. A federation (which postulates such a government) is especially opposed to separatism: a confederation or commonwealth which safeguards the respective sovereignties is in conformity with it.

The assumption of the federalists that their system would protect the identity of members and that the central government would not intervene in their affairs is not supported by experience. Attempts at federation in Central, West and East Africa have disproved the assumption and have consequently failed. Evidence from advanced countries in the Western world is for South Africa more appropriate and more impressive. Washington, despite its federal constitution, intrudes more and more into the domestic concerns of the member states of the United States. It decrees even the ethnic composition of their schools—but its best endeavours notwithstanding, the federal dispensation has been unable to offer the country's black citizens the opportunity of self-expression and self-fulfilment. Federation in Canada has been no better able to satisfy the aspirations of its French community. In the mid-1960s a Royal Commission reported that tension between English- and French-speaking citizens was acute and that Canada was threatened with disintegration. Australia is one of the loosest of federations: but had the State of New South Wales invited a Springbok rugby team to play there, the invitation would have been voted by Mr. Whitlam's government in Canberra—and the Australian system has done nothing to inspire a sense of community among its aboriginal people.

If federations in such countries are unable to allow freedom and self-realisation to their component parts, what hope could there be for the system in South Africa, with its uniquely diverse population? A central legislature and government, whether in a union or a federation, would inevitably in this country set the scene for a struggle for political power. How would representation among the communities be apportioned?—surely not by mandatory power-sharing that has failed so disastrously elsewhere. Which of our some dozen languages would be used? And what about the formulation of foreign policy, the distribution of taxation, the declaration of war, the control of the armed forces? Those who believe that such functions could be harmoniously performed by a central, multi-ethnic authority in South Africa are making of federalism a fool's paradise. And if such functions were excluded from the ambit of a central legislative authority, there might just as well not be one.

But there is a third scenario that is also canvassed and was advanced by

270

Professor S. P. Cilliers, Professor of Sociology at the University of Stellenbosch, in 1971. The contention here is that South Africa's future is not to be found either in constitutional separatism or integration but in a combination of the two. It recommends the separate development of the black homelands "at all levels and with the utmost vigour" into full-fledged nation-states; and, at the same time, the integration of whites, blacks, coloureds and Indians permanently resident in the rest of the Republic–the Republic Proper–into a single political society. The whites, the coloureds and the Indians (so runs this scenario) already have enough in common, socially and economically, to provide the basis for a shared culture: and "in this they are further strengthened by a growing proportion of the Bantu who have been living with them for some time–especially the permanently-urbanised Bantu. In fact it should be quite clear that those among these population groups who share what is commonly called Western civilisation would form such a comfortable majority that a political system accommodating all these elements could be developed that would have a reasonable chance of survival and stability."

But if the whites, Indians, coloured and permanently-urbanised blacks share the same Western values, they certainly share them in a less degree than, say, the Walloons and the Felmings, the Scots and the Welsh, the English- and the French-Canadians, the Basques and the Spaniards, the white Americans and the black: yet in these common societies ethnic frustration is rife. It is a fallacy, as our discussion of ethnicity has indicated, that the characteristics, preferences and prejudices of groups of people, generated through the generations, are eliminated or equalised by industrialisation, urbanisation or the sharing of the same patch of the earth's surface. The West African carried the borders of his ethnic and cultural consciousness across an ocean and through three centuries: can it be supposed that the Zulu does not carry his to Durban, the Xhosa his to Cape Town, the Tswana his to Johannesburg? Experience in emergent Africa confirms the tenacity of ethnic ties in conditions of urbanisation. Professor Walter Goldschmidt, of the University of California in Los Angeles, wrote in 1963 that the cities of black Africa "tend to be mosaics of small communities made up of people of common tribal background; the newcomer seems impelled by some unseen force to gravitate to the area where his friends and kinsmen are": the cultural background survived even the most severe detribalisation.

Professor Cilliers's argument on this score is not sound: adoption by the black man in the city areas of superficial white ways does not elimi-nate adherence to innate black ways. But a second reason is put foward in support of political integration in the Republic proper: it is that the non-Bantu elements would have roughly the same numerical strength as the Bantu elements there. However population proportions are in no way a determining factor. The proportion of non-whites in Britain is about 4 per cent; of Negroes in America about 12 per cent; of French in Canada, about 30 per cent; of Walloons in Belgium, about 40 per cent. And what is the proportion of Basques in Spain or of Ibos in Nigeria? I do not know off-hand, and I am not going to bother to find out because it is manifestly irrelevant. The simple proposition, supported by experience from all quarters of the globe, is that communities with an identity of their own, whatever their relative numerical strength, resist assimilation into a single and undifferentiated society.

> *Pretoria, 1971:* The workable scenario for South Africa is this: The black homelands–an integral and inseparable part of the plan for a *modus vivendi* for all people throughout South Africa–will move steadily towards independence, and having achieved it will not yield it. They will be the spring and the reservoir for nourishing the sentiment of nationality of all their people, wherever they may live. This sentiment cannot be expressed through the institutions of a common or mixed society. Accordingly, the inspiration of the over-all political architecture will be to design an association of separate national societies–a group of neighbours each with accommodation styled to its own particular way of life and girded with the bonds of kith and kin. The black people in the Republic Proper will express their sentiment of nationality through participation in the political life and destiny of their own nation. In more mundane concerns (the bread-and-butter ones), they will be given a voice in the political institutions of the part of the country where they live; and in the co-ordinating councils of the confederation, representatives of their own government will watch over their interests. The coloured people and the Indians will be autonomous, self-fulfilling communities. They will have their own political institutions, linked with those of the white people; and they will be represented together with the sovereign national communities at the confederal level. Details will change according to evolving circumstances: but whatever the nature of the links between the communities, the goal will remain constant: not a single household of disparate and discordant inmates, but an association of stable neighbour households. (28)

In designing the shape of the confederal machinery there will be a variety of models to draw from. There is the British Commonwealth which, until the confusion of the post-war years, was an admirable example of co-operation without interference among independent states. There are the special agencies of the United Nations which co-ordinate and conduct programmes in a variety of fields, ranging from civil aviation to agriculture, in sovereign member states spread about the globe. There are the institutions of the European Community–and here two prerequisites listed for its success by President Pompidou are illuminating: the upholding of the personality of the nations composing it, and the development and control of new institutions for co-operation exclusively through mutual consent of the sovereign governments concerned. In rejecting federation, the President said: "It would seem to me that the aim of confederation is ambitious enough for countries with histories as long as ours, even if we do have in common a tradition of civilisation both Christian and rationalistic" (which South Africa's nations do not have). There are models such as these from which to learn when the times come, but that will not be until the black nations can negotiate as full and free partners. *But the broad guideline for the future should be autonomy for each community at the legislative level to design and manage its own affairs; and institutionalised co-operation among all communities at the executive level to deal with matters of common concern.*

Meanwhile the area of consultation and co-operation steadily expands. After the victory of the National Party at the election in 1974, the Minister of Bantu Administration and Development, Mr. M. C. Botha, said that the Republic was making way for an association of states–"a constellation of states each in its own orbit." Pretoria's relations with the homeland governments would be extended to include arrangements concerning labour, customs and excise, trade, communications, water and electricity supply, diplomatic relations, the security of individual states and the defence of the country as a whole. Subsequently, the summit conference between the Pretoria and homeland leaders was instituted: a black man, a Coloured and an Indian were included in South Africa's delegation to the United Nations; and Prime Minister Vorster announced his proposal for a Joint Cabinet Council in which the coloured and Indian authorities would be represented together with the Pretoria government.

A next natural step in this development would be a Joint Commission overseeing a network of co-operation embracing Mr. Botha's constellation of states. The idea of a Joint Commission between states in Southern Africa is not new. One was set up in 1971 by Pretoria and Tananarive, and the plan was that it should meet alternately in one or other of the two capitals each six months to deal with common interests. It collapsed because of the fall of President Tsiranana: but it had set a precedent for a kind of negotiating machinery in respect to a government which has incomparably less in common with Pretoria than do those of the homelands. The time to give thought to this development is now–before independent black nations in South Africa move perhaps into orbits of their own in other constellations.

A permanent Joint Commission, of which the Anglo-Afrikaner and black governments were members, would have several specific advantages. It would be the focal point–the orbital centre–of the South African

273

community of states, giving visible expression to it: it would delineate the position of the Anglo-Afrikaner nation as one of several nations in South Africa: it would enable the kind of arrangement mentioned by Mr. Botha to be negotiated and executed on an effective multilateral basis: it would provide the black leaders with experience in multi-national negotiation, and facilitate their transition from self-government to independence: it would open wider the way to dialogue, contact and co-operation with other states of black Africa by serving as an intermediary between them and Pretoria (in negotiating with the Commission, these states would be negotiating with an international body and not Pretoria *per se*): it would facilitate the organising of activities, including sporting activities, on a South African (that is, an international as opposed to a national) basis: it would be the precursor of confederal or commonwealth machinery, demonstrating in practice the alternative to the central legislature advocated by the federalists.

And it could help to solve a major problem in the present set-up—namely, the geographical fragmentation of the homelands. Great effort and large sums of money have been devoted in recent times to their consolidation, but the fact is that they remain divided by larger or smaller blocs of territory which have belonged through the generations to Anglo-Afrikaners. KwaZulu, for instance, will remain divided in seven parts even when the current consolidation programme is completed. Such fragmentation is rightly objected to by the black Governments as a serious hindrance to the administration of their states. Might a remedy not be to have the interspersed blocs of Anglo-Afrikaner land included within their borders as Community (or Confederal or Commonwealth) Territory–that is, territory in which the rights of the occupants would be guaranteed by the community of states? The idea of Community Territory could be extended to land occupied by ports, roads, railways, telephone-lines, power-lines and pipe-lines in which the associated states have a vital shared interest, as also to the black townships in the Republic Proper. And the concept could likewise embrace a confederal or commonwealth—a *South African*–citizenship for each and every member of the associated nations.

There will be great challenges of this kind in the years ahead to be dealt with: and the best interest of South Africa and all its people requires of the Opposition parties the substitution in such areas of critical co-operation for obstructionism.

After the general election in 1974 the *Rand Daily Mail* wrote: "If separate development (confederalism) is indeed the solution to our race problem, it must be rapidly implemented. If it is not the solution, then the sooner this becomes clear to everyone so that they can start facing up to the alternative–the sharing of power on a federal basis–the better . . . So let separate development be implemented as swiftly as possible. Then

274

perhaps South Africa can settle down to solving its race problem." That is a fair proposition. A deeply entrenched Government is irrevocably committed to confederalism. If, with the critical co-operation of the Opposition, it can be established and meets the needs of South Africa–well then, well and good for everyone. If it proves in practice inadequate, the option of federalism will still remain. What the country cannot afford is negative and destructive Opposition tactics in the decisive years ahead: the new consensus within the Anglo-Afrikaner nation makes the employment of them, in any case, politically inexpedient.

EXTERNAL RELATIONS

Outwards to Africa

This part of the picture so far: In the years immediately following World War II there was co-existence inasmuch as there was peace among the countries of Africa, and there was co-operation inasmuch as the colonial powers then responsible for them set up various organisations for common action, such as the Commission for Technical Co-operation South of the Sahara. However the Commission and like bodies did not represent a spontaneous effort originating from within Africa. At that time the black states, with the exception of Ethiopia and Liberia, were dependencies, while Pretoria was a junior member of a worldwide association of nations, the British Common-wealth. The centres of political gravity were situated far outside Africa; and the inclination was for the countries of the continent to turn towards them and away from one another. Co-existence and co-operation in those days were the result of the inspiration and planning of others. A dozen or so years after the War, the situation began to alter radically. The colonies were emancipated, and at the same time (1961) the Union of South Africa cut away from the Commonwealth to become the Republic of South Africa. The whole pattern of co-operation previously dictated from abroad collapsed. The first reason for this was clear enough: foreign rule over most of Africa had been liquidated. The second reason was more complicated: many an emancipated state tended to regard programmes for regional co-operation as a reflection on its ability to stand on its own feet and as a device designed by others to diminish its independence. The third reason was the most disruptive. The black states saw the Republic as a projection into the continent of the Western authority from which they had just freed themselves: they saw its policy of separatism as an affront to their dignity; and, expediently, they saw hostility to the Republic as a means for closing their ranks and for asserting their new status in the world. Year by year relations between black and white in Africa deteriorated–and so, as a direct consequence, did relations between the Western world and white Africa. As the 1960s closed and the 1970s opened, black guerrilla forces were making incursions across the Zambesi River, with the physical backing of the communists and with the financial and moral backing of governments, political parties, churches and private organisations in the Western world . . . Now read on:

From the time of its participation in the Commission for Technical Co-operation South of the Sahara and through the bitter years of decolonisation, Pretoria maintained its belief in the possibility of co-operation with its black neighbours. It based its confidence in the first place in the interdependence, prescribed by geography and history, of the natural and human resources of the subcontinent. Landlocked countries like Rhodesia, Zambia, Malawi, Botswana and Lesotho must rely on other states for essential outlets to the sea: waterways like the Zambesi and the Kunene link the destiny of half a dozen countries. There are advantages of regional co-operation which no kind of foreign aid could possibly replace: no arrangement with Peking or Paris could provide Mocambique with a customer for her hydro-electric power, or Lesotho with a customer for her water. It is the Republic's labour market which offers a livelihood to hundreds of thousands of people across her borders who would otherwise be destitute: and the Republic must look to them to keep her mines and industries running. The Republic has a sophisticated technology designed to meet the special requirements and problems of African conditions–whether mining, agricultural or medical: while neighbour states have natural resources which supplement hers. The potential rewards of co-operation are immense. For instance, discussing a Southern Africa–wide hydro-electric grid, Henry Olivier (an executive of a leading South African construction corporation) told a symposium in Cape Town in 1974: "Such a grid can be in existence within a decade. By linking the resources of the wet north with those of the dry south, I visualise that we could first make the entire region self-sufficient in food and basic items and then proceed to become one of the biggest granaries or food banks for the rest of the world."

There is this natural interdependence: but for both white and black Africa, following the severing of old ties with distant countries, the 1960s were a tentative, uncertain and inward-looking period. The Republic had much work of consolidation to do at home. New dispensations had to be devised for her economic development and for military and internal security. It had to be demonstrated that the Republic was good for the Anglo-Afrikaner nation: at the same time the 1960s were a crucial phase in the evolution of separatism. As for the emancipated black states, they were confronted with the immense internal problems of an independence too hastily granted. They were unsure of themselves, and this affected their attitude towards others: they turned in upon themselves, and when they looked across their borders it was often with suspicion and enmity.

276

Slowly that changed: in the early 1960s there was freedom from external political control: in the early 1970s there was freedom, for some, from internal ideological preoccupation–and for the first time in history, states of Africa were beginning to regard one another squarely.

Gradually black states, or some of them, began to see the Republic as one of themselves–an African state: and, ironically, it was Western hostility toward Pretoria that helped to open their eyes. Their initial objection to the Republic as representing an extension of Western colonialism in Africa–a Trojan Horse–was being removed: but had close bonds with Britain and Europe been maintained, that would not have happened. It was the ostracism which the Republic suffered from these very quarters that disclosed the true position (for which Anglo-Afrikaners are indebted to the radicals, the ideologues, the egalitarians, the do-gooders, the protesters, the demonstrators, the sportsbusters, the anarchists and those others in the West mentioned in my acknowledgments).

Pari passu, the exaggerated sense of independence of the black states, some of them, was diminishing. Disappointed at the progress they were making on their own and frustrated by badly-conceived aid programmes from abroad, they were conceding the need for co-ordinated action within Africa. They began, some of them, to understand the contribution the Republic could make to their advancement: consequently enmity to Pretoria was losing its effectiveness as camouflage for splits in the unity of black Africa: it was tending rather to expose them. "While other black states are criticising me for trading with the Republic openly," said President Banda of Malawi in 1967, "they are trading with the Republic secretly. While they are decrying the Republic they are doing so on full stomachs of the Republic's mutton, beef and pork. They are doing so while their shops are full of consumer and capital goods from the Republic, while employing white miners from the Republic to mine their minerals and allowing financiers from the Republic to finance their industrial and agricultural undertakings."

Though general condemnation of apartheid remained, here too black attitudes were being modified. Experience was showing that Pretoria's internal policies need not be a bar to cordial and mutually-advantageous relations. The Prime Minister of Lesotho advocated dialogue: the President of Malawi exchanged diplomats: the Prime Minister of Swaziland, after a visit to Cape Town where he was warmly welcomed, spoke of "the astonishing things I was told there." These were close neighbours: they knew the Republic: they had the advantage of a personal acquaintance and exchange of views: and their experience made its impact on others on the continent.

Then there was the growing awareness among certain of the black states of the need for common action against communism. As the 1970s opened President Houphouet Boigny of the Ivory Coast was saying: "The real menace is communist expansion. If by guilty negligence or blind fanaticism we let ourselves be drawn into a war with South Africa about apartheid we would be offering a new opportunity to communism which is always wanting to intervene, with the dire consequences one knows."

Finally, there was the dawning realisation in Pretoria of the positive implications of separatism for its inter-state relations. In terms of separatism, the incorporation of the Protectorates had been abandoned: self-determination had become the declared aim in South West Africa: the black nations within the Republic's borders were being led to independence: Malawi, having broken with the Central African Federation, had sought the Republic's friendship. It was coming to be understood in Pretoria that political independence might make a stronger cement between different kinds of people than formal union: that common recognition of the right of each to its own sovereignty and ways might well bind them faster than a common constitution–and that this was relevant to relations between nations throughout the sub-continent. It was the beginning of the concept of the Unity of Community.

Black Africa Comes In

Here were some of the reasons for Pretoria's continuing optimism concerning the prospect of co-operative sub-continental co-existence. In 1967 the prospect was put to its first practical test when Prime Minister Jonathan of Lesotho and then a three-man ministerial delegation from Malawi officially visited the Republic. The leaders of these two black states and the Republic's leaders negotiated easily together, and the result was reinforced confidence in the practicability of co-existence. In the same year–1967–Dr. Robert Gardiner visited Swaziland and Lesotho. At the time Dr. Gardiner, a Ghanaian, was Executive Secretary of the United Nations Economic Commission for Africa, and he had been mentioned as a possible successor to the Secretary General of the United Nations, U Thant. Back at his headquarters in Addis Ababa he said: "I returned from Southern Africa a week ago with the conviction that the rest of Africa must approach the problems of that part of the world with some knowledge of the facts and an understanding of the current situation." He counseled all Africans to observe the attitude of Lesotho, Botswana, Swaziland and Malawi towards the Republic with patience and sympathy: said he had noted no fear among their people of interference from the Republic: pointed out that it had to be recognized that the

278

Republic was in Africa; and made a plan for the Republic's participation in his Economic Commission.

In 1970 the lead given by President Houphouet Boigny towards a normalisation of relations with Pretoria was endorsed by Dr. Kofi Busia, Prime Minister of Ghana. At a press conference in Bonn he expressed the view that the time had come for a new approach: "I think," he said, "we can get somewhere with a dialogue." In the same month the Republic's Foreign Minister, Dr. Hilgard Muller, led a mission including several top businessmen to Madagascar; and subsequently the Joint Commission already referred to was established. Substantial progress was being made, and it was noted with appreciation in the capitals of the West. Then, in 1971, President Banda of Malawi came on a state visit to the Republic:

Pretoria, 1971: This was not only a State visit but the first visit ever by a foreign Head of State to the Republic of South Africa, and it was made by a black man. From a protocol and ceremonial point of view–at every stage between the 21-gun salutes rolling over Pretoria City which greeted and bade farewell to the visitor–no distinguished guest to any country could have been more graciously honoured. The official side of the programme was expertly devised and executed; but what gave the occasion its peculiar vitality and significance was the response of the people. No-one quite knew beforehand what the reaction would be, but after the event there was no doubt: it was spontaneous pleasure and enthusiasm. People of all races and stations in life–the most elevated in the land and the humblest–Afrikaans students, black and white school-children were glad that President Banda had come to the country, and they showed it.

The following report of the Johannesburg *Sunday Times* is typical of what occurred time and again during the five days: "With his entourage and South African officials led by Foreign Minister Hilgard Muller following in his wake, Dr. Banda headed the crowds. It created a scene which had not been witnessed in South Africa since the British Royal Family came in the early post-war years. The little man in his baggy raincoat, battered homburg hat and dark glasses, skirted along their ranks flaunting his fly-whisk, beaming at the deafening roar of approval. Police, shoulder-to-shoulder with arms linked, struggled to hold the lines."

What can be the explanation? In 1961 Dr. Verwoerd had said in London that harmony among the peoples of the sub-continent depended basically on security for each of them–security not only for today but also for the future: the very purpose of apartheid, he said, was to remove prejudice and create harmony. President Banda's visit ten years later had its origin precisely in apartheid, and it is because of apartheid that the two countries are today good neighbours. Also, the enthusiastic welcome which

279

white South Africans gave their visitor had its origins precisely in apartheid: they were pleased to have in their midst the head of a friendly state and a black man who had reached the top, and because of the sense of security which apartheid is restoring to the country's various communities they were not inhibited from showing it. (29)

Dr. Banda's greatest service to Africa may well be judged the personal courage with which he pioneered co-operation with Pretoria. However he was not regarded as a representative black leader; and meantime Pretoria's opponents had been mustering their forces. They succeeded at the OAU in smothering the first detente initiative; and both Prime Minister Busia of Ghana and President Tsiranana of Madagascar were ousted by regimes unfriendly to the Republic.

At home public interest in detente flagged: but under Prime Minister Vorster's direction, diplomats and other officials persisted behind the scenes with their bridge-building operations. Soon after becoming Prime Minister in 1966 Mr. Vorster had said that one of his long-term priorities was "a full role for this country on the world stage." But first, relations with immediate neighbours had to be properly organised; and on the home front the issue between the outward- and inward-looking elements in the National Party had to be settled. That was done in the general election of April, 1970. In June Mr. Vorster was in Europe–Portugal, Spain, France and Switzerland. The previous visit by a South African Prime Minister to Europe (to Britain) had been made by Dr. Verwoerd in 1961.

However Pretoria's primary concern was with Africa; and the next major development there was precipitated by the overthrow of the Caetano Government in Portugal in April, 1974. The consequences for Southern Africa were profound. The last of the European colonial powers gave notice to its intention to withdraw; and for the first time in half a millennium the peoples of the sub-continent were free to handle their affairs themselves. That was a momentous happening. Also, the Frelimo movement which had fought for ten years against the Portuguese in Mocambique was faced with a critical choice: should it now press its attack against the Republic or seek a *modus vivendi?* And for Pretoria, its oft-proclaimed policy of non-interference was put to the acid test. It came through the test unscathed and unperturbed. When a counter-coup led by whites was attempted in Lourenco Marques and appeals for support were made, both Pretoria and public opinion in the country refused to be enveigled: a neutral attitude was meticulously maintained. And Mr. Vorster stated that he was prepared to co-operate with any government that might be established in Lourenco Marques, no matter what its ideology, colour or composition, and provided only that it was stable and non-aggressive. In the event, when a Frelimo Government was installed,

280

Pretoria made technical and other aid available–including assistance in the improvement of railroad and harbour facilities.

It was a remarkable change in relationship. For several years Frelimo had been the spearhead of black militancy against the white South. There seemed to be no possibility of reconciliation. Frelimo was Marxist, the Republic was capitalist: Frelimo favoured confrontation, Pretoria co-operation. There was something which graphically illustrated the divide that then existed between them: it was Cabora Bassa, the great hydro-electric-cum-irrigation project on the Zambesi in Mocambique, in the financing and construction of which the Republic had a major part. When building began in the early 1970s, Frelimo vowed to destroy Cabora Bassa, and directed much military effort towards that end. It failed: and when the revolution was staged and Frelimo assumed responsibility for governing Mocambique, the project was nearing completion. Today Frelimo treasures Cabora Bassa: and the indications are that the Republic will be a regular customer for its power–to the sweet tune of R25-million a year. A symbol of ideological division had been converted into one of economic co-operation. It was altogether too early (and still is) to conclude that a satisfactory and stable relationship had been established between Pretoria and Lourenco Marques (now Maputo), but the potential of common economic interest for bridging ideological difference had been convincingly demonstrated.

Mocambique was one of a series of notable moves in Mr. Vorster's outward policy: and in early 1975 the political editor of the Johannesburg *Sunday Times* summed it up when he wrote that either personally or through his officials the Prime Minister had established a working arrangement with the Ivory Coast, Senegal, Liberia, Zambia, Botswana, Mocambique "and who knows what other countries." Referring to the secret visits he had meantime made to the Ivory Coast and Liberia, the editor commented: "Mr. Vorster has become a kind of super politician who, when darkness falls, dons his Batman suit and zooms into the African interior to accomplish most remarkable missions."

The Bridge

Then in August, 1975 Mr. Vorster made an all-out bid to end the Rhodesian dispute. Prime Minister Ian Smith of Rhodesia visited him, and after their meeting what came to be known as the Pretoria Agreement was signed. It provided that members of the Rhodesian Government and African National Council should meet not later than August 25 with the object of expressing publicly their genuine desire to negotiate an acceptable settlement. The meeting place was to be a train of the South African Railways on the bridge between Rhodesia and Zambia at the Victoria Falls. And it was declared that the Pretoria Government and the Governments of Botswana, Mocambique, Tanzania and Zambia had expressed their willingness "to ensure that this agreement is implemented by the two parties involved."

The Rhodesian and ANC delegations duly met at the Bridge on August 25 . . . but meantime this had been overshadowed by an unscheduled and last-minute appearance. Mr. Vorster had arrived at the Falls and, early in the morning before the conference began, had crossed the bridge into Zambia to be welcomed by President Kaunda. It has been described as the most dramatic meeting in Africa since the one in the last century between Stanley and Livingstone. It was world news. The millions of distant televiewers might have been a bit short on detail, but about the central fact (colour television being today what it is) there could be no doubt: here were the two most influential leaders in Southern Africa meeting not in confrontation but in friendly rendezvous–and one of them was white and the other black. And surprise and spectacle apart, even the most sober observers were impressed. *The Times,* London, wrote for instance that whatever befell the Rhodesian conference, the new relationship that had been established between Mr. Vorster and Dr. Kaunda was a triumph for Mr. Vorster's detente policy, and that it would be an influence for good for a long time to come.

It represented, truly, an historic transformation. When President Tito of Yugoslavia was in Zambia as Dr. Kaunda's guest in 1970, he stated that for the enslaved South, Zambia radiated hope and encouragement and that it was situated ."exactly on the line of confrontation with the fascist regimes of Southern Africa." Meantime, Dr. Kaunda was advocating boycotts of the Republic; he led the diplomatic campaign to smash the Cabora Bassa scheme; he invited the Red Chinese to build the railroad linking Zambia with Dar es Salaam; and in Britain he appealed for a missile system for defence against attack from the Republic. Where Zambia could have become in those years the link to friendship with the North it had become the launch-pad for attack against the South. Nevertheless there were those in the Republic who knew Dr. Kaunda as a man of integrity and saw him as a potential ally in the cause of African progress. In November, 1968 I noted in my diary (30): "President Kaunda of Zambia is the sort of man who could, if he chose, make an important contribution to a co-operating Southern Africa. His is the kind of character able to set aside expedient advantages and withstand the political pressures of the moment." And on August 25, 1975, Mr. Vorster crossed Tito's line of confrontation, and in Zambia was warmly welcomed by Dr. Kaunda and his people.

The Rhodesian constitutional talks after the meeting on the bridge got bogged down, then broke down. But now that issue had been transcended (as suggested by *The Times*) by the new general prospect for Southern African affairs symbolised in the reconciliation between Mr. Vorster and Dr. Kaunda. And a main feature of that prospect was perhaps foreshadowed in the sub-continental guarantee–by the Republic, Botswana, Mocambique, Tanzania and Zambia–which the Pretoria Agreement contained:

Pretoria, July, 1975: The record of one country after another in Africa proves that progress requires not only harmony between black and white, but harmony also between black and black and black and brown. The means for achieving this is the granting to each community of the opportunity to live its own life. What Southern Africa requires is not so much a bill of individual rights as a bill of ethnic rights: a guarantee of cultural autonomy (as recommended at the United Nations conference in Yugoslavia in 1965) for each of its peoples, in whatever part of the sub-continent they may be and under whatever form of government. This should be the ground rule of the co-operative association of states which the natural and human controls of the sub-continent foreshadow. It is a truism that no rule is of any worth without the power to enforce it, but in this case it would be backed by the joint sanction of the economically associated states, each dependent on the goodwill of the others for its well-being. To break the rule would be to forfeit the co-operation essential for progress. Economic interdependence would thus underwrite cultural autonomy, while cultural autonomy would reinforce interdependence by promoting loyalty within and among the states concerned. Eminent sociologists today regard loyalty to the ethnic group as the primary loyalty: but the loyalty to the ethnic group will be extended to the state and the association of states which protect it. Recently, upon the institution of military training (by the Republic) for the Xhosas of the soon-to-be-independent Transkei, the leader of the Transkei (Chief Matanzima) declared that his warriors would fight in defense of their own country and in defence of the Republic–*because it was the Republic that was responsible for the renaissance of his nation.*

But, it may be asked, is a bill of ethnic rights for Southern Africa not merely a political theory beyond the present capacity of the black and white leaders concerned to implement? Well, Southern Africa's economic interdependence is a matter of practical fact; and the danger of racial, tribal and ethnic strife is real indeed. The alternative to peace, Prime Minister Vorster has remarked, is too ghastly to contemplate. As for the political capacity of the white people, those in the Republic have already committed their future to the achievement of cultural autonomy, and substantial progress is being made. As for the black leaders, they have displayed in the post-colonial era a remarkable capacity for political innovation, dexterity and ingenuity. It may well be in this field–as opposed to the technological

283

field–that they have their important contribution to make. The world over today, History can be seen moving against the forces of uniformity in modern society and towards the restoration of diversity. History moves inexorably towards her goal: but wise statesmanship can help determine whether the journey will be turbulent or orderly. Will white and black statesmanship in Southern Africa work together with History towards peaceful progress, or will conflict intervene before the goal is reached? The least that can be said is that the emergence of ethnicity as a primary force in the politics of the contemporary world illuminates for statesmen the nature of the landscape that lies ahead. (31)

Detente and Angola

In April, 1975 UPI correspondent John Platter reported (from the stormy OAU Foreign Ministers' conference in Dar es Salaam): "Detente entered the vocabulary of Southern African politics only six months ago but is already a worn-out word and may soon join its ailing global counterpart."

A comparison between Washington's drive for world detente and Pretoria's for Africa detente is revealing. It is apparent that Russia proposes to use detente to expand its influence without the risk of war– and there is the same danger of the exploitation of detente in Africa. There would appear to be representatives in the OAU of three kinds of strategy: those who favour the elimination of white rule by force of arms; those who seek to achieve the same objective by, in the first place, negotiation; and those who recognise the right of the Anglo-Afrikaner nation to an existence in Africa, and whose goal is an enduring peace, stability and genuine co-operation. The second group are a more insidious threat than the first. They are the practitioners of the salami strategy: cut away by negotiation, and slice by slice, the enemy's position–first Rhodesia then South West Africa; weaken his position by attrition until he loses the power to resist–or, if he resists, make him vulnerable for the final blow. South Vietnam is only too clear an example of how the communists used the conference table as the springboard for armed victory.

Global detente can succeed only if there is a global balance of power. In Africa a balance of power exists. Pretoria's military strength and other resources are sufficient to ensure that in a war with black Africa it could not be beaten: but at the same time it could not win. On the one side there is the sophisticated weaponry (and the ability to make it), the highly-trained manpower, the wealth and the industrial capacity of the Republic: on the other side, the numbers and the vastness of black

284

Africa's hinterland. Even if there were no goodwill between white and black in Southern Africa (and there is much) this would be the strongest of incentives to devise a formula for co-existence.

Global detente as envisaged by Washington was an umbrella for America's diminishing involvement in international affairs. African detente as conceived by Pretoria is an umbrella for increasing the Republic's involvement in the continent's affairs. Pretoria's detente is a commitment to co-operation, progress and prosperity, which the Republic is uniquely positioned to stimulate. While the faltering global detente had been accompanied by contraction in the growth of the American and free world economy, the Republic has the resources, the wealth, the technology and the experience to redeem the economic fortunes of her neighbours. Co-operation with her will mean the difference between progress and retrogression for them, and it could mean the difference between plenty and famine. Pragmatists, however, mixed their motives at the moment may be, will take account of this. And confidence here is reinforced by the backing for detente that is coming from private enterprise in the Republic: detente is developing from a Government to a truly national initiative. Mr. Oppenheimer, head of the Anglo American Corporation, said in the critical opening months of 1975 that he not only hoped and prayed that Mr. Vorster's detente policy would succeed: he believed it would. The contexts of global and African detente are quite different.

It was in November, 1974 that Mr. Vorster said that critics would be surprised to see, in six to 12 months' time, where the Republic stood in Africa and the world. Not only critics but friends and foes and all and sundry were astonished or dismayed at the development I have recounted. Then, precisely 12 months later, Portugal scuttled from Angola–and the Kremlin acted. The Kremlin's action was intimately related to Mr. Vorster's detente success: it was in fact a consequence of his success: the Kremlin understood that unless it intervened immediately it would be too late, since a common front between white and black against its aspirations was about to be formed. When that is realised, the subsequent scenario assumes a quality of inevitability: the dispatch of Russian arms to the pro-Soviet MPLA faction in Angola, and then of Cuban soldiers to man them; the whipping up of sentiment among the black states against Pretoria, and the attempt to brand Pretoria in the eyes of the world community as the aggressor. But waht in fact was the nature of the part Pretoria played in Angola?

From the beginning its broad purposes were clear. First: in co-operation with the Portuguese authorities when they were still responsible for the territory, the Republic helped to build a hydro-electric and irrigation project, at a cost of some R120-million, on the Kunene River– the border with Angola. The pumping station is at a place called

285

Calueque inside Angolan territory, and the scheme was designed to provide essential water to Owambo and Kavango across the border in South West Africa. When chaos broke over southern Angola, Pretoria declared that it would protect these installations and the workers there—and it sent in troops to do the job. Second: the terrorist South West African People's Organisation (it has claimed responsibility for acts of terrorism) took advantage of the chaos to step up its activities against South West Africa. These attacks the Republic would repulse, and where necessary those making them would be pursued. Third: the Republic would take such measures as might be required to defend the borders for which it was responsible against Russian-backed aggression. Fourth: it was not concerned with the defeat of the Soviet-backed MPLA *per se,* but sought to establish conditions in which the MPLA together with UNITA and the FNLA (the other two factions) could negotiate a settlement. From the beginning it advocated a political solution. Fifth: it would act with the West in resisting Russian imperialism in Africa north of its borders, but it would not act alone. Sixth: if it was to be made the scapegoat on account of its opposition to communism, "then (in the words of Mr. Vorster) so be it—we are prepared to be counted in this."

Such were the reasons for the Republic's involvement. What were the immediate consequences? Before Portugal's withdrawal in November, the MPLA had advanced far north and south into the tribal areas which owed allegiance respectively to the FNLA and UNITA. In the south they had taken Mocamedes, four-fifth of the way down Angola's seaboard and only a couple of hundred kilometres from South West Africa. In the deep south of the country the Ovimbundu people were demoralised by the success of their tribal enemies, and a flood of refugees added to the disorder and despair. The stand which the Republic took, its contribution in sorting out the chaos and the assistance it gave stiffened the resistance of the allied forces. The leader of the FNLA, Mr. Holden Roberto, was later to refer to the example which the Republic set: it had demonstrated its willingness, when its neighbour's house was on fire, to help put the fire out. Following the stabilisation of the situation in Southern Angola, and upon the urgent appeal of black leaders, a South African column struck back: advancing northwards it recaptured in quick succession Mocamedes, Benguela, Lobito, Novo Redondo and Porto Amboin.

Russia's adventure in Angola was in danger of collapse: and while pouring massive quantities of sophisticated weapons into Luanda and airlifting thousands of Cubans to man them, it conducted a vigorous propaganda campaign branding the Republic as the aggressor. At the United Nations in December a group of black Marxist states sought to have Pretoria indicted alone for intervention. Other black states insisted that Russia and Cuba should also be put in the dock: the communist tactic had misfired and had to be abandoned. Along the battlefront and the

286

diplomatic front the Kremlin was in difficulties. Pretoria's action had kept open the option for effective intervention by the West; and now what was urgently needed was the provision of arms to the allied forces to match those the MPLA was getting. On several occasions after entering the White House President Ford had rejected what he called America's resignation from the world. He had said: "Like it or not we are a world power and our only choice is to succeed or fail in a role we cannot shirk." He had said: "As long as I am in this job our policy will be a global policy of looking at our interdependence with the rest of the world"; and in recent weeks he and his Administration had said that Russian action in Angola would be countered. People in the Republic were entitled to expect that the assistance desperately needed by the allied forces would be given: but as the Senate rose at the end of the year it refused funds for the purpose.

The next decisive event was the special meeting of the Organisation of African Unity in Addis Ababa in early January. Had it not been for the backing of the allied forces by the Republic, the meeting would certainly by that time have been confronted with the *fait accompli* of an MPLA victory throughout Angola: as it was, the result of the fighting in the preceding weeks was that the territory occupied by the three warring factions corresponded with their respective tribal boundaries. This had introduced for the crucial time being a measure of stability: the action taken by the Republic had thus provided conditions favourable to an initiative by the OAU towards a negotiated settlement. The OAU could however come to no agreement: the meeting ended in deadlock with half the states supporting and half of them opposing the MPLA.

The option which the Republic had kept open for the West and the opportunity it provided the OAU were, alike, wasted. On the eve of the OAU meeting President Ford had addressed a letter to the President of Nigeria, one of the leading supporters of the MPLA. "I want you to know," he wrote, "how seriously we regard the Soviet intervention 12,800 miles from its borders. The Soviet action could have grave future implications elsewhere in the world . . . We cannot stand idly by if the Soviet and Cuban intervention persists." The intervention persisted: effective counter-action was not taken by the United States or any other Western country–and Pretoria had said it was not prepared to fight the cause of the West alone. By mid-January it was common diplomatic knowledge that the Republic originally entered Angola at the urgent request of Dr. Jonas Savimbi, leader of UNITA and of President Mobutu Sese Seko of Zaire, supported by other black states; that in December Dr. Savimbi had made an SOS mission to Pretoria; that on at least two other occasions the Republic's "informal" allies pleaded with Pretoria to plug the dyke against a communist victory; and that following the collapse of the OAU initiative, Pretoria again came under pressure to hold the line until a cease-fire could be arranged. In early January the United States Assistant Secretary for Africa, Mr. William Schaufele, had himself said–in public this time–that the withdrawal of South African troops from Angola would strengthen the position of the pro-Soviet forces, and that their continued presence could help the factions to negotiate their differences. On Jaunary 20 came Dr. Kissinger's mission to Moscow and the toying with him by the Kremlin over Angola in the manner that has been described. The following week-end Pretoria settled for a limiting of its objectives to the defence of the South West African border and the water installations.

What has been the effect of Angola on Africa detente? The consequences of the supinity of the West–of Europe no less than the United Stats–had as 1976 opened cast a heavy shadow over Mr. Vorster's 1975 achievements. However beneath the surface there were also substantial gains. For several dramatic weeks the traditional division in Africa had been superseded: the conflict then was between black men and white men who supported foreign intervention in the continent's affairs, and black men and white men who opposed it. At both the United Nations and the Organisation of African Unity black solidarity against the Republic was for the first time broken. When the attempt at the United Nations in December to have the Republic indicted alone for intervention in Angola failed, it was the first time in the post-colonial era that it had not been possible to muster a majority in the General Assembly against Pretoria–previously massive majorities had been taken for granted. When the OAU broke up in disarray in January, it was the first time that hostility to Pretoria had failed to align its members.

Moreover, the nature of detente in Africa had been clarifed. For men like President Houphouet Boigny of the Ivory Coast and Prime Minister Vorster, the building of a common front against Russian imperialism had from the beginning been a main purpose of detente. But it was obscured: at the conference of the OAU in Dar es Salaam in April, 1975, for instance, detente was seen as referring to a relationship between various black states and Pretoria. The true issue is not that at all but whether countries of Africa are prepared to work together for, among other goals, the defence of their independence. The split in the OAU in January demonstrated that half the states in Africa were alive to this–and they included countries as influential as Zambia, Zaire, Kenya, the Ivory Coast and Senegal. It had become apparent that detente does not concern bilateral arrangements between the Republic on the one hand and individual black states on the others, but multilateral co-operation for the promotion of Africa's general interests and the protection of its integrity.

A country like Zambia has begun to talk the same language (literally) as the Republic concerning the communist danger. In January the Republic's Ambassasor, Mr. Pik Botha, told the Security Council: "The

288

Russian bear has arrived to claw a festering wound in Africa's side." And he added that it was a wound that could infect the whole of Africa. Within hours of that statement President Kaunda of Zambia declared a full state of emergency "to counter any move to destroy our country." The action was necessary because of the deteriorating situation on Zambia's borders and growing proof of internal subversion. He said: "A plundering tiger with its deadly cubs is coming in through the back door." The imagery used by these two men pointed at once to the nature of the threat to Africa, and to the similarity of the assessment of it in Pretoria and Lusaka. What had happened had shown the United States and European countries to be unreliable partners in the defence of African interests: and in this very fact was the lesson that the states of Africa must rely on one another if their independence is to be maintained.

But as Russo-Cuban arms consolidated the position of the MPLA: as the MPLA was recognised by one state after another: as the Security Council in March, 1976 condemned Pretoria as the aggressor in Angola (while the Western countries sat by)–the shadow fell across Mr. Vorster's achievements. However, the truth exposed by the Angolan conflict, that black and white must pull together if Africa is to remain free, remains. As a result of Russia's action in Angola, the building of the superstructure of Africa detente was halted; much of it was broken: but the foundation for future operations is still there.

No Cross-roads Now

However, an enduring edifice will depend on Pretoria's holding to its course. At the time that Mr. Vorster made his famous "give me 12 months" statement (at the end of 1974), his Ambassador told the United Nations that the Republic was moving away from discrimination. These statements were misinterpreted at the United Nations, in the capitals of the worlds and by critics of the Government at home, where it was said that co-operation with black Africa and a moving away from discrimination implied "change" in the Republic in the form of an abandoning of its political philosophy. It was not a new tactic: in the early days of African dialogue–in 1970–the Johannesburg *Star* wrote that the Government would have to "give ground" in domestic policy if the prospect of detente were to be kept alive. From all sides then and since has come a demand for internal "change" as the price of dialogue and detente. But change–change of its own deep kind–is implicit in separatism.

The change which the world envisaged at the beginning of the era of decolonisation was *constitutional* in nature: paper arrangements for the transfer of sovereignty, the setting up of parliaments, membership of the United Nations, and so on. The change which Pretoria envisaged in 1948 was *human* in nature. It was far more radical: it recognised that true self-determination for dependent people meant the opportunity for them, not primarily to cast a vote or to be represented at Turtle Bay, but to express and nourish their own life-style: that emancipation meant the freeing of people from alien moulds. Those who contend that change requires a departure from the course chosen in 1948 speak from ignorance or dishonesty. South Africa has changed beyond recognition since that time: but it has been controlled and gradual change, with the consequence that each phase has been scarcely distinguishable from the next. The process will continue: South Africa will be as different by the end of the century from what it is now, as it is now from what it was at mid-century. Separatism is a direction: it is not a blueprint: it allows of evolutionary adaptation: it is not architectonic: it specifies only that whatever the nature of the architecture, respect for ethnicity must be the bond.

At the mid-1970s the cross-roads of 1948 lie far behind. Without the community security of separatism, prejudice would be reinstated: with community security all discriminatory measures will be removed, save those (as recommended by the United Nations Ljubljana conference) which provide for community security. There are no cross-roads now: only the one that leads straight ahead–to a new socio-political landscape within and beyond South Africa's borders, featuring economic interdependence and ethnic autonomy: to a venture into territory beyond the limits fixed by the sub-continent's previous experience, and towards harmony and prosperity. There is no possibility of a change in direction: and if there were and it were taken, the stability which the present course has maintained through all the tumult and confusion would be destroyed: the Anglo-Afrikaner nation would be a write-off as a partner in the development of Africa and as an ally in the defence of the West: at home the country's administration, financial structure and primary and secondary industry would collapse, since an integrated, majority-rule system would yield political and business managers totally incapable of running them; and the consequences for 25-million people in South Africa and for countless others across its borders would be dreadful.

We have not been through all the trial and tribulation of three decades to change direction towards disaster for ourselves and others now. With imperialist Russia today bestriding the way ahead, the greatest challenge may be yet to come: but there are no cross-roads now.

The Last Piece

The Need for God

We come now to the last and trickiest piece of our do-it-yourself job: but since it is an essential part of the jig-saw, and the over-all picture will fall apart unless we find a place for it, let's give it a go.

To put it in a nutshell, the present trouble with Western civilisation is that modern Western man has got intellectually far too big for his boots. In the past couple of centuries he has exalted reason to godlike proportions, spelling it with a capital R. The West's political thinking and social organisation during this time have been dominated by a conviction in the attainment of happiness, harmony and progress under the guidance of Reason. The unbounded faith in education and the universal franchise was based on the assumption of the essential reasonableness of man: if all of them were given learning and the vote, they would be able together to shape constructive social relations: while those other products of Reason–science and the machine–would control according to their requirements their material environment. Under such a dispensation the ancient guides to behaviour–custom, reverence, faith–were irrelevant and redundant, hangovers from an irrational past. Freedom was to be found in release from these restraints: and out they went–into the waste-paper basket (or was it not the baggage compartment of the bandwagon?). Well, we now have our universal education and universal franchise. But if the survival of democracy in Britian today is uncertain, if liberty in France can be threatened as it was a handful of years ago, and if the inalienable rights of the individual in America issue in cultural anarchy, then what hope is there Western civilisation under this dispensation? The answer is simple: there is none. For the restoration of hope, the dispensation must be seen for the fake that it is, and Reason must be dethroned and given no

291

more than its rightful role–which, let it be added immediately, is an indispensable one.

What then shall we say of reason? It is as essential to man for maintaining life as the heart or the lungs or the liver. It correlates and gives direction to the information transmitted by the senses to the mind. It is what separates man from animals and provides him with the master tool for progress. To be without reason is likewise to be mad. But while reason is the means for progress, it can measure only backwards the progress so far made: it cannot measure forwards the margin that stands between the goal. We have come far since we lived in caves, but how much farther still are we separated from our Home? Reason expands knowledge, but the expansion of knowledge moves ever further outwards the borders of the unknown to which reason has no access. Science in all its complexity has blunted reason. The reason of the ordinary man could explain to his satisfaction the light that came from wax and wick: it takes for granted, it does not endeavour to explain, the light that comes from the electric globe. It cannot explain the atom or the hydrogen bomb: reason cannot penetrate to the heart of such things, nor even think it can. Reason must now also be mechanised, transferred to computers, since its findings can no longer be contained and co-ordinated by the single mind. Reason may direct emotion and instinct but it cannot override or eliminate them. There is an innate irrationality deep-seated in the human psyche. Reason may describe good and evil but can never be their master. The most reasonable of laws cannot alone remove disorder: neither love nor lechery will yield to logic. Reason may rationalise abortion, infanticide, homosexuality, yet like all else depends on the perpetuation and continuity of life. Reason may be the servant of equity, but also the wanton handmaiden of pride and prejudice. Reason may cause men to live wisely, but it can neither determine–nor perceive even–their fate, ordained by an external and eternal chain of happenings. Reason cannot tell us why we work and suffer, and triumph sometimes, and pass away.

Yet, I repeat, reason in our time has been apotheosised: from cradle to grave reason is the criterion and the arbiter. Ours not to do or die, ours but to reason why. The inversion is complete: each man becomes his own law-giver, judge and executioner. The disciplines of society, the authority of parents and governors is brushed aside and, as we have noted, eminent theologians say that God is dead. "Where", demanded the Roman pagan Caecilius of his Christian companion in the 3rd century A.D., "is that God who is able to keep you when you come to life again, since he cannot help you when you are in this life? Do not Romans, without any help from God, govern, reign, have the enjoyment of the whole world and dominion over you?" In the same century Tertullian boasted of the increase of Rome's population and wealth. Cyprian, a generation later, asserted that Rome was dying. Soon, Rome was dead.

Society cannot live by reason alone. Over-arching the conflict of intellects, wills, passions and ideologies, there must be authority from a transcendental source if order is to prevail and our culture not to fall.

But is not the very notion of a transcendental authority contrary to reason? It would seem otherwise: that reason in its proper role, science and the space age itself open the way wider to a comprehension of it. Half a millennium ago Cortez stood on that peak in Darien surveying a newly-revealed portion–a tiny segment–of the earth's surface. In our day a man named Armstrong–a member of the same civilisation as Cortez–steps upon the moon. He surveys at a single glance the roundness of the earth in all its entirety: he beholds more clearly than the psalmist ever could "thy heavens, the work of thy fingers, the moon and the stars which thou hast established." The astronauts have testified to the new wonder their experience in space has brought to them of the unity, order and harmony of the Universe. And those of the astronauts who believed in God felt at home in space, while those who did not were distressed.

It is a great fallacy of these days that science refutes religious faith. Technological and spiritual development may often advance unevenly: one may outstrip the other as technology has in our time: but there is an inseparable relationship between them. Beethoven's music could not have been created without the technical equipment for playing it. Arnold Toynbee perceived the imminent rebirth of religion "because of the overwhelming spiritual responsibility that technological progress has thrust upon us": and it was the greatest scientist of the age, Albert Einstein, who observed that God does not play dice with the Universe.

However Dr. Harvey Cox says we must be called away from the other worlds of metaphysics and religion and concentrate on the concrete issues of this one–like the threat of nuclear war and race discrimination. But the supposition that this little planet can be sundered off from the Universe and that its "concrete" issues can be isolated from those other worlds of thought and faith is as arrogant as it is ill-founded. What are the answers to these "concrete" problems of war and discrimination, if not love and justice? And where is the source of love and justice to be found? Not between the North Pole and the South Pole but precisely in those worlds which Dr. Cox rejects: in the comprehension of the harmony of all creation. Then there is Dr. Altizer and his like: they claim that modern man is incapable of believing in God: they are saying that modern man–that man of the space and nuclear age–is so well-informed, advanced, enlightened and sophisticated that he can no longer entertain such a notion, that it affronts his intelligence. What conceit it is: these new theologians are not fit to walk in the shadow of the great minds of the past 2½ thousand years who contemplated an order of things disturbed not one whit or iota by the greatest marvels of contemporary science.

It is Reason with a capital R, not right reason, that has induced such

293

blind conceit. There is, it says, no demonstrable evidence of a transcendental authority: God cannot be seen and his existence cannot be proved scientifically. Very well, then let us apply to this problem right reason–plain common sense.

There is a knock at the door. We see a figure: head, blue eyes, large nose, arms, trunk, legs; and because of their particular arrangement, we know it is Jack. We say: "Hello, Jack, how are you feeling this morning?" We have no doubt at all about his existence, though it is plain to our common sense that we do not see Jack himself–that is, the being who lives, perceives, thinks and feels as we do. This Jack is invisible and totally beyond scientific proof: yet we have no hesitation in accepting the reality of his being, the spirit which these physical features betoken. Is it not then the commonest of sense–when we perceive the Universe, the whole of creation, the sun, the moon, the planets and the stars, its magnificent order and harmony, the oceans and the mountains, all the living creatures on this earth–to accept within and about all this a creative spirit? And while there are these overwhelming visible tokens of God (somewhat more impressive, you will agree, than the head, arms and legs that persuade us that Jack's spirit exists), we hear him continually speaking in what we choose to call our conscience.

George Berkeley wrote on the point in the 18th century: "After the same manner (as we are persuaded of the existence of Jack's spirit) we see God. All the difference is that, whereas some one finite and narrow assemblage of ideas denotes a particular human mind, whithersoever we direct our view, we do at all times and in all places perceive manifest tokens of the Divinity: everything we see, hear, feel, or anywise perceive by sense being a sign or effect of the power of God. It is therefore plain that nothing can be more evident to anyone that is capable of the least reflection than the existence of God, or a Spirit who is intimately present to our minds. That the discovery of this great truth, which lies so near and obvious to the mind, should be attained by the reason of so very few, is a sad instance of the stupidity and inattention of men who, though they are surrounded with such clear manifestations of the Deity, are yet so little affected by them that they seem, as it were, blinded with an excess of light."

Berkeley (who, incidentally, was the subject of Dr. Malan's doctoral thesis) made these observations in his *The Principles of Human Knowledge,* still today the classic essay on the examination of conscious knowledge as evidence of divine intelligence. Read it, and you will be given a compelling account of "the eternal invisible mind which produces and sustains all things"–including computers, space-ships and atomic reactors.

Here is the explanation of what Plato described as the maker and the father of the universe: of the opening passage in the Gospel of St. John–*In the beginning was the Word:* of the eternal ideas of Plotinus which he discerned as pointing to the supreme unity underlying them: of Bergson's view of the universe as a dream in the mind of God: of Hegel's Absolute Idea. The source of all creation according to these great minds is non-material and spiritual. It is primary: the images it creates–whether of the heavens or the atom–are secondary. Therefore to imagine spirit, to form an image of it, would make it secondary–which is an impossible paradox. Spirit, in the shape of an image of any kind whatever, would be circumscribed and limited, which is against its nature. God is beyond proof or imagination, since what is proven or imagined cannot be God. So let us not be discouraged by the minor scientists. God can only be known, and the exercise of right reason corroborates that knowledge. It has done through the ages, and the contention of the new theologians that God cannot be known to modern man is absurd.

One of the great orations of modern times was made by Abraham Lincoln at Gettysburg on November 19, 1863. The prepared text of its most memorable passage read: "We are resolved that this nation shall have a new birth of freedom, and that government of the people by the people for the people shall not perish from the earth." That is the passage as Lincoln prepared it. At the last moment he made a correction. As he stood addressing his people at this great moment in their history, he made a correction. After "nation," he added "under God." At the present critical moment in our history the same correction must now be made. If not, Western civilisation will perish from the earth, as will any other arrangement for the advancement of the spirit of man. Even separatism!

A picture,
in parts,
of the waves of History
that
in recent times
have swept the world
and now again
are breaking
about South Africa.

295

Diary References

29   RSA WORLD, File 7, page 81
30   RSA WORLD, File 4, page 111
31   RSA WORLD, File 11, page 56

Index

Commission for Technical Co-operation in Africa South of the Sahara, 57, 275, 276
Committee on Race (World Council of Churches), 161
Common Market, 121, 241, 249
Communism, 114, 142, 150, 151, 161, 165, 178, 207, 229, 233, 234, 238, 245, 247, 277, 284
Communist Party (Great Britain), 122
Communist Party (South Africa), 178, 188
Community of the Resurrection (monastic order), 48
Condition of Man, The (Mumford), 74
Conference on the Human Environment (United Nations), 143
Congo, see Zaire
Congo River, 51
Congress of Democrats, 178
Congress Party (India), 34, 257
Congress of Racial Equality, 215
Conservative Party (Great Britain), 32, 35, 121, 123, 125, 130, 133, 176
Constantine I, Emperor, 3
Constantine Paleologus, Emperor, 3
Constitutional Law (Chalmers and Asquith), 193
Cortez, Hernando, 293
Coubertin, Pierre de, 152
Council for Scientific and Industrial Research, 223
Cowen, D. V., 2
Cox, Dr. Harvey, 157, 293
Cox, Richard, 55, 59
Cromwell, Oliver, 22
Cry the Beloved Country (Paton), 49, 195
Cuban missile crisis, 160
Current Affairs (editorial commentary), 204
Cyprus, 257, 258, 259, 292
Czechoslovakia, Soviet invasion of, 160, 233, 235

Daily Mail (London), 123
Daily Mirror (London), 133
Daily News, The (New Zealand), 151–152
Daily Telegraph (London), 68, 87, 88, 96, 129, 131, 142, 148, 161–162, 182, 192, 197, 210, 214, 216–217, 218, 224, 225
Darwin, Charles, 214
David (son of Chief Moshesh), 76
De Beer, Dr. Zac, 269
De Blank, Archbishop, 215
De Gaulle, Charles, 21, 24, 121
De Wet Nel, 84
Declaration of Independence, 20
Degler, Carl N., 256
Delius, Anthony, 99, 184
Democratic Party (U.S.), 108, 118
Dialogue, 253, 256
Diaz, Bartholomew, 4
Dicey, 12

Dickenson, 100
Diederichs, Dr., 173
Diefenbaker, 131
Discipline of Power, The (Ball), 118
Disillusion (1960 to 1970-), 103–173
  Black Africa, 164–173
    fall of freedom, 164–165
    GM model, 166–167
    Indians in Africa, 170–173
    non-revolution, 167–170
  Pretoria Theme and, 175–227
    achievement, 208–227
    civil liberty, 191–207
    punishment, 175–190
  in the West, 105–139
    Great Britain, 119–139
    lost dreams, 105–107
    U.S., 107–119
  world movements, 140–163
    Church, 155–163
    collective measures, 145–155
    United Nations, 140–145
Douglas-Home, Sir Alec, 165
Drake, St. Clair, 27
"Driftwood" (sermon), 50
Dugdale, John, 193
Dulles, John Foster, 42
Dumont, René, 144
Dutch Association of Homosexuals, 28
Dutch East India Company, 4, 63
Dutch Reformed Church, 66

Easter Encyclical (1967), 158
Economic Rights and Duties of States (United Nations), 144–145
Economist (London), 121, 139, 239
Eden, Anthony, 39, 40, 125
Egypt, 4, 125, 223, 235
Einstein, Albert, 293
Eisenhower, Dwight D., 26, 116, 125
Election of 1948 (South Africa), 5, 12, 25, 73, 80, 260, 267
Emerson, Rupert, 56–57, 116–117
Encounter, 254–255
Encyclopaedia Britannica, 192–193
English Constitution, The (Bagehot), 121
Enlightenment, 20
Escher, Dr. Alfred, 142
Ethiopia, 141, 151
Ethnicity, concept of, 250–263
  power-sharing, 257–260
  spirit of community, 250–256
  summation of, 260–263
Evans, Peter, 252
Evatt, 39
Evening Star (New Zealand), 187, 222

Fabian Society, 31–35, 156
Fabianism, 36, 168, 243, 244, 248, 261

302

305

307